Economic Issues

and the American Past

Economic Issues

and the American Past

Roger LeRoy Miller
Clemson University

Gary M. Walton
University of California, Davis

Robert L. Sexton
*Pepperdine University and
University of California, Los Angeles*

1817

HARPER & ROW, PUBLISHERS, New York
Cambridge, Philadelphia, San Francisco, Washington,
London, Mexico City, São Paulo, Singapore, Sydney

To Our Parents

Sponsoring Editor: David Forgione
Project Editor: John Haber
Cover Design: Betty L. Sokol
Cover Illustration: The Granger Collection
Text Art: Fineline Illustration, Inc.
Production: Debra Forrest Bochner
Compositor: ComCom Division of Haddon Craftsmen, Inc.
Printer and Binder: R. R. Donnelley & Sons Company

Economic Issues and the American Past

Major portions of this work have been adapted from *Economic Issues in American History,* by Gary M. Walton and Roger LeRoy Miller, © 1978 by Gary M. Walton and Roger LeRoy Miller; and from *Economics Today and Tomorrow,* by Roger LeRoy Miller, © 1978 by Roger LeRoy Miller.

Library of Congress Cataloging in Publication Data

Miller, Roger LeRoy.
    Economic issues and the American past.

    Includes index.
    1. Economics.   2.   United States—Economic conditions.
I.   Walton, Gary M.   II.   Sexton, Robert L.   III.   Title.
HB171.5.M64188   1985   330.973   84–15724
ISBN 0–06–044509–2

    86 87 88 9 8 7 6 5 4 3 2

Contents

Preface

Economics is more pertinent today than ever before. We are all faced with continuing economic crises, problems, and proposals for solutions. We are bombarded with economic statements in the classroom and through the media; from newspapers, magazines, television, radio, and books; from economists, cabinet members, political advisors, members of congress, and labor leaders. Now more than ever, students can appreciate the importance of having at least a basic understanding of the economic world in which we live. The question then remains, how best to teach this fundamental understanding, how best to interest students and to present them with a method by which they can acquire painlessly —or at least not *too* painfully—some basic skills. We have always advocated an *issues* approach.

The best instructors desire to impart to students a sense not only of current economic issues, but also of their continuity. Comparable economic problems and their solutions are seen throughout history. This book focuses on that continuity through the study of topics and events in the history of the United States. It is meant to satisfy the need for a historical-issues development of basic economic principles.

Each chapter begins with a general introduction to an economic concept, such as supply and demand, labor, capital, market structures, or the price level. These and other important ideas are then used to enhance our historical understanding of major issues and epsiodes in the American past. We conclude each chapter with definitions of key terms. To add further to the human dimension of economics in history, every chapter is accompanied by a biography of a significant historical figure. The biographies portray such diverse figures as Benjamin Franklin, Jay Gould, John L. Lewis, and Henry Ford II; the aim is to demonstrate the roles that individuals play in economic life and that economics can play in the lives of individuals.

The historical-issues approach should be both useful and effective either as an accompaniment to a regular course in economic principles or as a main text for a one-term introduction to economic thinking from a historical point of view. A broader set of key ideas is introduced in later chapter so that students' historical understanding will deepen as they become more used to economic thinking. With appropriate additions during lectures and class discussions, and perhaps accompanying historical materials, this text is also suitable for a nonrigorous introduction to American economic history. Instructors of survey courses in the social sciences should find this book especially appealing for use in the weeks spent on economics.

This text is not intended to be all encompassing, either historically or theoretically. Not all the institutional or historical facts have been included that a more rigorous course would require. Its goal is to get students interested in economics in an applied form so that they can be better-informed citizens.

Many instructors have expressed a desire for a book that can be used without the standard graphical tools that economists have become so fond of using. Not that there are no graphics in the text, as a quick glance through it will demonstrate. Many, many figures present unemployment rates, prices, and other historical data to give the student not only a sense of continuity in the economic events discussed, but also the gain in clarity from a more graphical presentation of ideas, as well as sheer visual relief. However, familiarity with advanced graphical techniques is not necessary for effective use of this book.

We are greatly indebted to a number of key reviewers of portions of this project, including Ben Baack, William Carlisle, Albert Fishlow, Barry Poulson, Harry Scheiber, Bill Sexton, and Samuel Williamson. Above all, we want to thank our many students who have used the book in draft form and made comments and suggestions to improve it. Student response to this text has been extremely encouraging. It is our sincere hope that you will share this enthusiasm; we look forward to your comments on this book and encourage you to send them to us.

Roger LeRoy Miller
Gary M. Walton
Robert L. Sexton

chapter *1*

Introduction

ECONOMICS AND HISTORY

Archaeologists tell us that, sometime during the Ice Age, hunters of mammoths in the great Russian steppes began to trade ivory for Mediterranean shells. We have been exchanging one thing for another ever since. Of course, the methods of exchange have grown much more sophisticated. Today we use currency, checks, credit cards, and other mediums of exchange instead of shells, and the direct **barter** of earlier times has given way to a host of other activities not obviously related to exchange at all. These range from trade and commerce to such matters as labor-management relations, governmental regulations, and welfare. But dig deep enough and, at the root of the science of economics, you'll find exchange. Why, when, where, and how do people exchange things? What are the end results of all these exchanges?

This book studies the fundamentals of exchange (that is, economic theory) by examining aspects of the American economy and its evolution from colonial times to the present. Do present-day economic theories fit in with this story? What do early America's perplexities and solutions have to say about contemporary economic concepts?

WHY ECONOMICS?

Whether we recognize it or not, every one of us applies economic principles in our daily lives—whenever we shop, figure a budget, or even sign up for a college course. A great share of everyone's time is necessarily taken up with economic concerns. Will going to college pay off better than going straight to work? What kind of job is best? How do we live within a limited income? We may not be conscious of it, but each question calls for an economic answer.

In some glorious future, we may reach the stage where our only worry is how to spend an abundance of free time. Certainly this is not the case at present. And, despite some versions of the "good old days" it was even less true in the past, as we shall see.

When understood and properly applied, economic principles are keys to interpreting not only a whole array of present-day concerns, but historical events as well. To appraise governmental policies or political party platforms, or to decide how to vote in elections, we can ask how economic principles have operated in the past and how the same principles can be expected to operate under today's conditions. Once basic economic concepts have been firmly grasped, many issues, in politics as well as everyday life, will prove less complex than they once seemed.

In any area you care to mention, an understanding of economics can go a long way in explaining how and why humans behaved as they did in the past, how they behave today, and how they may be expected to behave tomorrow.

IS ECONOMICS A SCIENCE?

Two categories of science exist: the natural sciences and the social sciences. Natural sciences deal with natural order. Chemistry, physics, and even astronomy are concerned with laws embodied in nature. Social sciences, on the contrary, deal with the behavior of people and blend natural laws with social values. Since social behavior cannot be examined under a microscope or through a telescope, some argue that the social sciences are less exact than the natural sciences. But there are parallels in the way that all scientists work.

All scientists begin by looking at what happens in the real world—they make empirical observations. Then, by a process of logical deduction, they formulate theories based on those observations, making simplifying assumptions about them. Finally, in every possible way they test the validity of their theories.

At this point, a difference arises. In the natural sciences, tests can be run in a laboratory, with the interaction of materials observed in experiments under controlled conditions. Social scientists, in contrast, have no such opportunity. People cannot always be subject to controlled experimentation. Therefore, to test theories and to make predictions, social scientists must be content with examining what is happening now and what has happened in the past.

THE NEED TO SIMPLIFY

Like any other organized body of knowledge, economics and history must be selective. The human mind simply cannot absorb the complexity of an entire economic system or the entire course of history. (That is why we have chosen in this book to examine basic economic concepts by reference to the history of a specific area during a specific period—the United States from colonial times to the present.)

But simplification must go further. All scientific investigations rest on some body of assumptions. For instance, sociologists often assume certain behavioral patterns or group characteristics, and political scientists use assumptions to explain why a nation acted as it did toward an enemy or an ally.

Economic theories, too, rest on assumptions and simplifying givens: *Given* that this assumption is true, then *this* sequence of events will occur. In this book, as we study the early development of the U.S. economy, we will put to use a whole array of assumptions. Perhaps the most important of all is one that, although still debated by some, is the basis of most of today's accepted economic theory. (You, too, may initially balk at accepting it as a basic fact of human behavior.) Throughout this book we assume that *all people continually seek their own betterment:* They prefer more to less and will respond to opportunities for gain. This premise underlies most economic theorizing.

If you do not agree with this premise, or if you question it, you should still be willing, as a scientist, to put it to the test. Use it to see whether it works. If, based on the assumption, you can predict how people will react to a certain change in their environment, and if they actually do react that way, you can say the assumption has proved correct. If your prediction fails, you must then ask yourself why. Should some other assumption be put in its place?

The statement that self-betterment is a universal incentive may oversimplify the matter. But simplification of some sort is an absolute necessity in reaching any hypothesis. If the facts are so complex that they can refer only to a specific situation, no conclusion can ever be drawn about what may happen in a similar but very slightly different case. This is one reason, too, why each science tends to draw boundaries around its own concerns. Sociologists downplay the political aspects of the problems they consider. Psychologists often leave out economic factors. This doesn't mean the other considerations are irrelevant. It simply means that we must set some limits to what we view.

However, more and more researchers are engaging in what are called *interdisciplinary* approaches. They seek to cooperate with scientists in other fields in order to draw wider and more useful conclusions. In this book, we undertake an interdisciplinary approach and consider economics as related to historical facts and events. Occasionally we shall also assume the perspective of some other social scientist, but economics and history are our main tools and focus. As a student you should always feel free to add other dimensions—to ask, "What would political science say about this? Or sociology?" The further question should then be asked: Does such an addition change in any way the capability of the economic analysis presented here to predict what would happen in the situation described?

LOOKING BACK TO SEE THE FUTURE

For economists, history not only represents the material against which to test theories and hypotheses, it also gives clues to the future. Suppose the government is considering imposing price controls to reduce inflation. In the past most such attempts have failed. Have conditions changed enough to warrant the hope that price controls would have the desired effect today? Only careful economic analysis can answer this question.

A backward look also clarifies the real meaning of some of today's "antieconomic" slogans. Those who talk wistfully about the golden past and yearn for a simpler life-style feel that if we could live in that old-time environment we would be happier and more in tune with our world. They presume that in its beginnings the nation was made up of happy yeomen sharing equally and helping each other build barns and homes. They point to the unequal distribution of personal **wealth** —the scarce things people value—that is certainly evident today.

But going back to any year before the Civil War, we discover great inequities. In colonial times, more than half the working members of the population were either indentured servants or slaves. At the top of the wealth distribution were some merchants and large landholders and at the bottom laborers and seamen. Statistics show that in 1860, on the eve of the Civil War, 24 percent of the total wealth in the entire United States was held by 1 percent of the population, and 53 percent was concentrated in the hands of 5 percent of the population.

During those years great numbers of Americans were not sharing equally in the bounty of the land. Even those who had reasonably adequate **income** in some years suffered severe losses in others because they were wholly unprotected from natural calamities such as floods, hailstorms, and frosts. Today less than 5 percent of our population engages in agriculture. Thus a far smaller share of the population would now experience such uncontrollable variation in income even if governmental programs had not been set up specifically to aid farmers.

In areas other than farming, federal and state programs also offset fluctuations of income. Examples are the Social Security and unemployment insurance programs and salary continuation plans that guarantee some level of steady

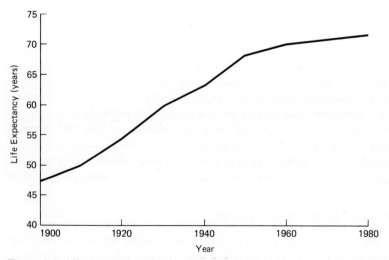

Figure 1.1 Life expectancy. (*Source*: U.S. Bureau of the Census, *Historical Statistics of the United States*, p. 25; and U.S. Department of Commerce.)

income when wage earners are injured. Relief for the needy is also available at the federal, state, and local levels.

In those "golden days" of the past, life was not only hard, it was short. A male baby born at the beginning of this century would be expected to live approximately 47 years. By the early 1980s that expectation had risen to about 74 years (see Figure 1.1).

We know, of course, that not all Americans share equally the improved health conditions reflected in these figures, any more than all Americans share income equally. Nevertheless, multitudes in other countries consider the United States the Promised Land, and it has indeed made great economic progress. But the comparatively good situation we enjoy today has not been bought cheaply. With it have come many sociological and psychological problems related to our industrialized way of life. With this in mind we ask ourselves, "How can the applied science of economics help us understand and remedy these problems confronting a perplexed world?"

DEFINITIONS OF NEW TERMS

BARTER   In a barter system, goods and services are exchanged for other goods and services without using the intermediary good called money.

WEALTH   Wealth is the stock of scarce things that people value, such as land, houses, clothes, and cars. It is also possible to include one's inherent income-earning capacities as part of wealth.

INCOME   The flow of money earnings or payments to people in a given time period (usually taken to be a year) is called income.

chapter 2

Introduction to Economic Concepts

CHOICE

We have seen that exchange lies at the root of all economic dealings. An important element of exchange is *choice*. Whenever more than one exchange is possible, the question arises, which is better? Suppose that, as a student, you have $500 that can be spent for the next quarter's tuition and books, for the down payment on a car, or for a ski trip. According to the basic assumption discussed earlier, we can predict that you will choose the alternative that by your reasoning will make you better off.

Of course, people do make mistakes, and "choice" is not always "free." In both former and modern times people have sometimes been compelled to decide against their own good. For example, the Indians who bartered away Manhattan Island for about $24 worth of beads and trinkets made the choice willingly. They viewed land as a life-giving thing that no person could own, and indeed land was abundant—so why not trade it for ornaments that would give status and enjoyment? On the other hand, the Aztecs who turned over their gold to the conquistadores did so only because their lives were at stake. For the purpose of economics, however, we recognize that normally exchanges are undertaken voluntarily because each side believes it can benefit. This is true whether the transactions occur between individuals, groups, or nations.

SCARCITY

If we all had everything we wanted in order to enjoy life, there would be no reason to exchange. All of us would already have maximized our gains. No goods would be exchanged, no transactions would take place, and economics would disappear from the scene. But such is not the case. Food is not available in endless supply and variety. Transportation costs money and uses up natural resources. The supply of many things that improve the quality of life is limited.

When confronted with this limited supply of desirable goods, people compete for scarce commodities. If two people both want a product, the one who is willing and able to give up more of some other good (money, or time spent waiting in line) will be best able to obtain it.

Scarcity, a fact of economic life, leads to questions about the way goods are to be distributed and used. Who will end up with what? At what cost? Each decision requires a choice by one or more competitors, and this necessity to choose brings us to still another economic fact of life.

THE COST OF CHOOSING

Jason really wants to buy that stereo, but he "needs" new shoes, he wants to buy tickets to a Broadway show, and he is trying as well to save money for a trip next summer. Choosing one or two of these good things means giving up the others.

When such a choice has been made, the "next best" alternative that has been forgone is known to economists as the **opportunity cost** of the choice.

All decisions entail a cost of some sort. Even a decision to work for International Business Machines (I.B.M.) is made at the cost of not going to work for another company or of giving up leisure time. From the standpoint of economics, the choice is made only after an individual has weighed the expected benefits and the expected costs of each alternative. Opportunity cost is summed up in the old proverb "You can't eat your cake and have it too." An economist translates this as "To have something, you have to give up something else." The quip that there is no such thing as a free lunch should at least remind us that even eating imposes (at the very least) time costs!

FACTORS OF PRODUCTION

We have been talking about scarcity as related to buyers of goods; but producers, too, face scarcity. Three kinds of **resources,** each in limited supply, must be used in any productive activity. These are land, labor, and capital, the "inputs" that result in "outputs" of final goods and services in the economy. (A fourth factor, entrepreneurship, is occasionally grouped with these tangible ones; it is discussed in Chapter 6.)

Land Economists stretch the term land to include all of earth's natural resources. The economic definition of land comprises such things as trees, wild berries, animals, fish, fossils, minerals, and water.

Labor The resource called labor includes the total of both physical and mental effort expended by humans in the economy.

Capital   Humanity's entire stock of created goods used in the production of goods is termed capital. Examples are such assets as office buildings, tools, machines, and factories.

Production that has a high cost in one of these resources, such as labor, let us say, is called *labor intensive.*

RESOURCE ALLOCATION

How should scarce resources be divided among members of the population? In the American economy, allocation is decided by the price system, a system that answers the three questions what, how, and for whom?

What Will Be Produced?   Society's scarce resources could be put to use in producing a selection among literally billions of different things. Someone must decide which things will be produced and which will not.

How Will It Be Produced?   Once the decision has been made to produce a certain item, the most efficient mixture of inputs with which to make the item must be determined. Is it better to use more labor and less capital, or vice versa? Should a limited amount of skilled labor be used, or a much larger amount of unskilled labor? Someone must decide on the appropriate mix of inputs and the way they should be organized.

For Whom Will It Be Produced?   Where and how will the product be distributed? In other words, what will determine the best way to distribute commodities once the production is completed?
    We find that in our price system each of these questions is answered, in turn, on the basis of "dollar voting" in **markets**, where goods and services are sold.
    First, it is predictable that those goods will be produced that are most demanded (valued most highly). Next, competition among producers (sellers) will force them to keep costs as low as possible. Producers will choose that mixture of inputs which will produce the potentially profitable goods at the lowest possible cost. Finally, the output will be distributed according to willingness to pay. The goods will go to those consumers who have demonstrated both a willingness and an ability to pay for them.

SPECIALIZATION

Most people cannot have everything they want. What they do have, in varying degree, are productive talents—muscles, skills, training, and ingenuity that can be put to work for them. Predictably, they want to use these assets in the most rewarding way possible.

In general, workers at every level seek the kind of employment that will give them the highest rewards for their working hours, including money income and personal satisfaction. Once they have found such employment, they will concentrate on it. Those who do best with their muscles and like fresh air may become construction workers or tennis pros. Skilled woodworkers may turn out cabinets or sculpture. In any case, economically speaking, each has become a specialist, putting a particular skill to work in return for income that can then be exchanged for other goods.

This basic economic principle of **specialization** applies not only to individuals but to regions and nations as well. We shall see throughout this text that the history of economic development in the United States—and in the world—is one of ever-increasing specialization. Look, for example, at the Midwest with its corn and wheat, the coastline of Massachusetts with its fishing fleets and shipbuilding, or the Northwest with its timber. Each is an example of regional specialization based on differences in natural resources and other special characteristics.

COMPARATIVE ADVANTAGE

People are different. Regions are different. So are nations. The differences extend to the capability of each to produce goods and services. Take the simplest example —a two-person society. If each of the two were exactly the same in every respect, there would be little reason to specialize. However, if one made better cloth and the other raised better vegetables, both specialization and exchange would probably take place. Economists say that one has a **comparative advantage** in cloth making and the other in agriculture.

If all nations had precisely the same resources and talents as every other, then the cost of producing any good or service would be equal. However, costs of production certainly do differ in line with a nation's labor force, skills, and natural resources (among other factors), and comparative advantage determines the direction in which a nation's economy expands. For example, what Japan lacks in fossil fuels it makes up for in technological expertise, which it applies to automobile and camera production. What Kuwait lacks in size and in supplies of fresh water is offset (in world trade) by its oil riches. These are just two examples illustrating another basic axiom: A nation will specialize in that form of production where its costs of inputs are lower and its potential profit from output is greater. In other words, a nation, like its individual workers, will make the greatest possible use of its comparative advantage.

We have now examined several of the tools and concepts used by economists: assumptions, simplification, choice, scarcity, opportunity costs, factors of production (land, labor, capital, and entrepreneurship), resource allocation, the marketplace, the price system, specialization, and comparative advantage. These terms will crop up over and over again as we analyze what has happened in America. What factors enabled a hungry little huddle of colonies (as they were at the beginning) to grow into an industrial giant? We begin at the beginning— in the early colonial era.

American History: Scarcity and Choice

Scarcity was the most pervasive fact of life for the hardy souls who first formed British outposts in the New World. In fact, what happened to the first settlement, initiated by Sir Walter Raleigh in the 1580s, remains to this day a somber mystery. The group, comprising 121 people, had been left at what is now Roanoke Island, North Carolina, in 1587 with orders to harass the Spanish treasure fleets, but when Raleigh's captain, John White, returned to the site in 1590 he found no trace of anyone, living or dead.

The fate of that "lost colony" emphasizes the hardships faced by newcomers to America. A majority of the earliest settlers in the seventeenth century died within two years of their arrival. Starvation, disease, Indian attacks, and other calamities were commonplace. In 1607 the Plymouth Company landed a group of settlers on the Maine coast. Those who survived the winter packed up and returned to England in the spring. Also in 1607, the London Company landed a group of 105 at Jamestown, Virginia. Of these, 67 died within the first year. Eight hundred new settlers joined the pitiful remnant in 1609, but by the following spring that number had been cut to 60. The disheartened few were actually heading down river to leave for England when the arrival of three ships carrying supplies and more settlers caused them to change their plans. Only this intervention enabled Jamestown to become the first permanent British settlement in North America.

During these years, scarcity—of food, of medical supplies, and of skills— was a constant problem. For lack of proper seeds and equipment, agriculture was haphazard. Some settlers, more venturesome than wise, wasted vital energy and time on futile get-rich-quick schemes. For example, in 1607 and 1608 shiploads of mica and fool's gold were sent to England, only to be termed worthless.

The human costs of settling the colonies were immeasurable. A "royal investigation" of affairs in the colonies disclosed that of 6,000 people who had sailed from England for Virginia between 1607 and 1623, 4,000 had perished. The distinguished historian Charles Andrews has written that "this was the 'Starving Time' for Virginia . . . when men suffered and died, because they had not yet learned the art of colonization, and had come to America inadequately supplied and equipped and unfamiliar with the method of wresting a living from the wilderness."[1]

Fortunately, people do learn from experience. Within a few years the colonists had assessed their situation and had learned appropriate ways to produce, to trade, and to thrive in their new environment. The period from colonization to the Revolution was one of adaptation and ever-increasing success.

Independence

By the time of the American Revolution, the white population of the colonies had reached almost 2.5 million and the blacks numbered nearly half a million. In 1776

[1]Charles M. Andrews, *The Colonial Period of American History,* Vol. 1 (New Haven: Yale University Press, 1934), pp. 110–111.

the white colonial population had an average income rivaling and often surpassing that of citizens of the wealthiest, most advanced countries in Europe. Since taxes in the colonies were well below those in the mother country, the colonists' after-tax, or **disposable,** income was particularly favorable relative to those attainable in Europe. In any case, North America was the best hope for the ambitious poor worker, for wages were highest there and land most abundant.

From Alice Hanson Jones's estimates of wealth in the American colonies, Edward Perkins has derived estimates of average annual levels of income per capita.[2] Perkins suggests average per capita income levels of £14.9 ($969 in 1980 dollars and prices) or income per free capita of £17.2 ($1,116). Today nations that comprise more than two thirds of the world's population currently have average per capita income levels below that of the free colonists of 200 years ago.

As we know, circumstances were quite different for blacks, almost all of whom were slaves. The average income of a slave as revealed in allotments of food, clothing, and housing, was probably around £7 ($455) a year. Even so, a courageous and reasonably healthy black population managed to increase steadily in numbers.

Two Centuries of Growth

Statistics on national income for the period before 1840 are few and difficult to interpret. In that year the first national income estimates were released, and for subsequent decades it is possible to calculate the nation's economic growth with some precision. Generally the growth is expressed in terms of the rate of increase of *real per capita income,* or money income adjusted for inflation (for changes in the cost of living).

In these terms, American incomes have risen approximately 1.6 percent a year, overall. Correcting for changes in the buying power of the dollar, this would mean that the income of an average worker has doubled every 43 years. This does not mean that each generation was twice as happy as its forerunner; but in terms of goods and services, there was nearly twice as much to go around for each person, and the United States is still one of the leading economies in the world.

Economic Facts at Work: Allocation

You will recall the three basic questions about the use of resources: What will be produced? How will it be produced? For whom will it be produced?

To see how these questions were asked, and answered, in early America we begin by going still farther back in time, to the earliest European settlers, the Spanish who came to the Caribbean Islands in the sixteenth century. These adventurers had two quite different goals: to find wealth, and to Christianize the natives. To maintain themselves while they carried out their objectives, they had

---

[2]See Alice Hanson Jones, *Wealth of a Nation to Be* (New York: Columbia University Press, 1980), p. 305; and Edward J. Perkins, *The Economy of Colonial America* (New York: Columbia University Press, 1980), p. 154. (We shall discuss later in this chapter the limitations inherent in per capita income as a measure of economic well-being, but it will be helpful to us in beginning our analysis.)

to determine what crops they could grow, and where and how to grow them. Should the new regions be permanently settled or merely used as a base for acquiring precious metals? How could workers be found to produce what was needed in this relatively uninhabited area?

The Spaniards began by setting up **encomiendas** ("trusts"), a system by which each populated center was put under the "protection and authority" of a Spanish overseer, or encomendero. In return for his unsought protection the encomendero was entitled to exact from the natives a tribute that was generally collected in the form of labor time. Far from the authority of the Spanish Crown and the Catholic Church, the overseers were, in effect, dictators who frequently abused the system for personal gain.

When the Spanish later came to the mainland, the evils of the encomienda system were somewhat curbed, and the practice was finally outlawed in 1549 (although it endured in some areas into the seventeenth century). Until then, it answered the questions how and by whom goods were to be produced: by forced labor. In Spanish America, harsh treatment, disease, and overwork took an enormous toll in natives. Within two decades of Cortez's conquest of Mexico in 1518–1519, the preconquest population, estimated at 25 million, had been halved. Other estimates indicate that the population of Spanish America in 1500 approximately equaled that of western Europe; by 1600 it was only one tenth that number.

In the meantime, the makeup of the population was changing. By 1650 about half a million residents were white or predominantly white, most being Spanish-born males of working age. Black slaves had been imported since 1503, although it was not until the seventeenth century that large numbers began arriving. In 1650 about a half million black slaves were working the sugar-producing islands of the Caribbean, and another half million of the population was of mixed blood. Only two million pure-blooded Indians remained in all of Mexico and the central regions of Peru and Bolivia.

What to Produce?   The Spanish colonizers wanted to make Christians of the natives and to acquire wealth in the form of precious metals, but they could not live on gold and silver. They needed foodstuffs. While the mines were being worked by forced labor, the Spaniards were turning into settlers. They were introducing new crops and importing European techniques, commodities, and animals to improve agriculture. Wheat, barley, rye, sugar, onions, cabbage, peas, apples, and peaches were imported. Horses, cattle, and oxen were brought from Europe to do the heavy plowing and for better transportation. (The native livestock population had comprised only llamas, dogs, and turkeys.) Hogs, chickens, and sheep were also brought over, leading to herding activities and to better diets. European methods for the working of metals served the settlers well, as did guns and gunpowder.

On their part, the Europeans in New Spain were introduced to tobacco, maize, beans, peanuts, white potatoes, squash, pumpkins, tomatoes, chocolate, vanilla, and avocados. By the end of the sixteenth century sugar, grown in the almost depopulated islands of the Caribbean, figured significantly in transatlantic trade. The labor to cultivate this crop now had to be imported, however. By the middle of the seventeenth century, African slaves worked the Spanish-run plantations. Agricultural capitalism had begun in Spanish America, and with it a solid commercial link was forged between the New World and the Old.

Economic Facts at Work: Scarcity

The first settlers in the British colonies lacked almost everything except courage and raw land. Without adequate tools, they could not clear new land, so they could cultivate only natural clearings and areas that had been cleared and then abandoned by the Indians. Labor was scarce, capital was almost nonexistent. As tools, horses, and other livestock began to arrive from across the seas, more land could be tilled, but hands were still in short supply, and so was capital. Since these two factors were scarce, their value was higher relative to land.

In order to increase the population of the North American colonies, the colonists (and their English backers) discovered four ways of attracting laborers to the New World.

Head Rights   Workers who would pay their own way to the colonies were promised approximately 50 acres of land apiece, and those willing to pay the way of another worker received an additional 50. The costs of transport were so high, however, that few could afford such an expense.

Land Grants   Settlers who came as groups were awarded land grants for organizing their own communities. As with the Pilgrims, such immigrants were often members of religious minorities seeking to escape oppression in Europe.

White Indenture   Many who yearned to come to the New World but could not pay their own way solved the problem by selling their labor in advance, for a specified length of time. Four years was probably the most common period, although terms ranged from two to seven years, depending on the relative skill of the worker or the desirability of the location. The indenture contract was generally signed with a shipowner or with the owner's recruiting agent. As soon as the servant was delivered alive at an American port, the contract was sold to a planter or merchant.

Servants bound by indenture worked at their employer's demand in return for room, board, and certain "freedom dues" of money or land to be received at the end of the indenture period. Indentured servants generally came from the ranks of farmers, unskilled workers, artisans, and domestic servants; occasionally, better educated and more skilled people also became indentured servants. With very few exceptions, they came voluntarily, drawn by the prospect of owning land, which in Britain and on the Continent was an impossible dream for most.

As the nineteenth century approached, higher wages and lower transportation costs reduced the average duration of service and ultimately led to the demise of indentured servitude in America. In the final analysis indentured servitude closely resembled a highly competitive labor market.

Black Slavery   Dutch traders brought the first slaves to North America in 1619, but during the seventeenth century slavery was relatively unimportant except in the islands of the Caribbean. Then, as great plantations developed in the mainland South, the demand for field hands grew. Eventually both British and American ships brought the human cargo, and by the time of the Revolution more than 450,000 slaves were at work in the colonies. Trade was booming, and the total number of incoming blacks matched that of immigrant whites. From around 4 percent of the total population in 1700, blacks made up 20 percent of the total by the 1770s. Their share of the population varied widely between colonies. In the northern colonies it was less than 5 percent, but in the South the proportion was far higher: 47 percent in Virginia, 33 percent in Maryland, and 70 percent in South Carolina. In the sugar islands of the Caribbean, about 90 percent of the population was black.

White Immigration   As word of the gains to be found in the New World spread throughout Europe, floods of migrants found some way to cross the ocean on their own initiative. As discussed earlier, most came as indentures—voluntarily—but others found the means to finance the costs of migration to America. Nearly 100,000 Germans entered the northern colonies between 1710 and 1770. From 100,000 to 125,000 Irish and Scots also arrived. Many English came, too, but their greater numbers had already settled in.

A total of between 250,000 and 300,000 whites came to the colonies between 1700 and 1775. This great tide, however, constituted only about 15–20 percent of the population increase during that period: by far the greater expansion was due to natural factors. Compared to Europe, the colonies offered inexpensive and abundant fuel, food, and housing. People typically married earlier and raised larger families. Also, the rates of mortality were lower, especially for infants. A boy who lived past infancy had an average life expectancy of 60 years. Colonial women lived only about 40 years on average because of the hazards of childbirth.

Economic Facts at Work: Comparative Advantage

There was little question how the first colonists would spend their time and effort —on survival. But as desperation gave way to security, the colonists began to look for ways to put their abilities to the best use. Historically, for regions and nations as well as for individuals, this quest has entailed finding the comparative advantage.

In most of the colonies, agriculture continued for some time to be the obvious choice. Most of the population raised crops of one sort or another, depending (again) on the comparative advantage of the region. However, the colonists *wanted* manufactured goods that could be obtained only by trade with other countries. The solution was to determine what crop could be developed for international trade, and where it could be shipped. Choice of destination was limited, partly by legal restrictions but basically because England and America shared a common language, customs, and system of prices, so that the costs of doing business (**transaction costs,** in the language of economics) were low. However, Holland also became an increasingly important customer for colonial produce.[3]

The South   By 1770 more than 1.4 million people lived in the southern colonies, in comparison to 600,000 in New England and the same number in the middle colonies. Moreover, the South grew crops that were rare and not produced in England, such as tobacco, indigo (a source of blue dye), and rice. More than half the colonial exports in 1770 consisted of these products and they found their way to England.

Tobacco had been introduced into England by traveling Spaniards. Even then not everyone approved of it: King James I termed the habit "a vile and stinking custom." But Sir Walter Raleigh and other aristocrats adopted it enthusiastically, and when it was found that better and cheaper tobacco could be imported from Virginia than from Spanish sources, even the English Crown approved its import, granting the Chesapeake Bay area a monopoly over tobacco production in the empire.

Comparative advantage explains not only why tobacco was grown in the warm southern areas, but why slavery flourished there rather than in the North. Slave labor was bought for a fixed sum of money. Since workers were not paid by the hour, there was reason to keep them working as much time as possible, which was much more practical in the South, whose climate permitted outdoor work almost every day, summer and winter. In addition, the crops that could be grown in the South required a great deal of unskilled labor that could be done under limited supervision. Everything about the plantation system favored slavery.

Tobacco production in the southern colonies illustrates other economic concepts we will be talking about: *shortages* and the *supply and demand* relationship. When the abundance of Virginia tobacco on the international market in 1639 began to reduce its price, Virginians corrected the situation by burning half of their total crop. Later (in 1733) they restricted the amount of tobacco to be grown. Both moves had the desired effect of causing the price of tobacco to rise.

In deciding to create these artificial shortages, the colonists demonstrated their awareness of the economic fact that for some products, the quantity purchased is relatively insensitive to its price. (Economists say that the demand for such goods is **price inelastic;** that is, the quantity demanded does not "stretch," or alter, significantly as prices change.) People who want tobacco will buy approximately the same quantity even with big price changes (over a significant price range). Given this type of demand, a bumper crop of tobacco would have produced no more sales unless the colonists were willing to accept a drastically lower price.

Another major crop in the South was rice, which by 1700 had become the leading export for South Carolina, whose low-lying fields and swamplands could be irrigated by controlled flooding from tidewater rivers. Like tobacco, rice required a warm climate and an abundance of unskilled labor, which made it an ideal plantation crop.

[3]For a detailed discussion of colonial trade, see Chapter 11.

Less widely produced than tobacco, rice, and indigo, but still vitally important to the southern colonies, were the forest products known collectively as naval stores. These included pitch, tar, and turpentine, which were used in the shipbuilding industry.

The Middle Colonies   Rich soil and level acres combined to give a comparative advantage in agriculture to the middle colonies of Pennsylvania, Delaware, New York, and New Jersey. Grains and livestock could be produced more cheaply there than in either the South or New England.

Since England also produced these essentials at comparatively low cost, there was little cause for direct trade with the mother country. In fact, the middle colonies typically imported more from England than they shipped there, and this created a *trade deficit.* To some degree this imbalance was offset by middle-colony trade with southern Europe, the West Indies, and their own colonial neighbors. When this was not enough to balance the trade deficit, English merchants commonly granted short-term loans to finance their trade with the colonies.

New England   The rocky hills of New England accommodated only small farms, and those grudgingly. Their produce was mostly for home consumption or for local town markets. But New England had a wealth of forests, a splendid harvest of fish and shellfish, and a coastline for shipbuilding.

Comparative advantage dictated what actually occurred: New England exported whale oil, dried codfish, and the skills of its shipwrights and seamen, who competed directly with England in carrying goods throughout the Atlantic, the Caribbean, and elsewhere.

Economic Facts at Work: Regional Specialization (1815–1860)

Some economic historians assert that the key to economic growth and development is **regional specialization**—the proper use of comparative advantage. An outstanding proponent of this view is Douglass C. North, who offers the following argument with respect to the development of the American West before the Civil War.[4] First, the South followed its comparative advantage by specializing in cotton, which it exported to New England and to foreign ports, while importing manufactured goods from New England and Europe. On the other hand, the South was deficient in foodstuffs, and as the demand for its cotton increased, so did its own demand for imported grain and other edibles. This demand motivated the settlement of parts of the West by pioneers anticipating a ready market for the grain and cattle they could raise there. As the newly opened regions shipped their foodstuffs to both the South and the Northeast, they were able to buy manufactured goods from the Northeast. Some of these goods, in turn, were made of cotton raised on southern plantations. Thus a circle of steadily growing trade

[4]See Douglass C. North, *The Economic Growth of the United States 1790–1860* (Englewood Cliffs, N.J.: Prentice-Hall, 1961).

developed among all the parts of the young nation as each became increasingly specialized and more efficient.

Some flaws can be found in this argument. What data we have indicate that even before the Civil War the South was very nearly self-sufficient in foods. The great specialized plantations raised most of their own corn and pork. It appears, in fact, that only a very weak trade linked the Cotton South to the region known today as the Midwest. Most of what the West sent to the South in 1839 was reexported, and by 1850 only about 14 percent of exports from the West were consumed in the South.

What, then, *was* the key to the boom in interregional trade that occurred during this period? It seems to have been the westward extension of transportation, first along the rivers by steamboat and later, after 1850, by railroad as well. The East, specializing within its comparative advantage, had by now become largely an industrial area, concentrating on manufacture at the expense of agriculture, and it needed food, which the West could most efficiently supply. By 1860 the West was shipping more than ten times as much produce to the East as to the South. This interdependence was one reason the West sided with the North when war broke out between the states in 1860.

By that time, almost 40 percent of the nation's population lived west of the Appalachians. The West was unrivaled in grain production, was gaining power politically and economically, and was even branching out into manufacturing. This activity, too, was based primarily on the region's comparative advantage, since it involved mainly the processing of agricultural products. The entire nation, including the West (especially along its southern reaches), was engaged in resolving the conflict between the slave-based economy of the South and the industrial organization of the northern states. We shall save this problem for later discussion, but some reasons why the Midwest allied itself with the North should now be clear.

American Economic Growth and Personal Welfare

In two centuries of nationhood, the United States has achieved a living standard envied by most of the world, but many economic and social problems (unemployment, inflation, pollution, recession, and discrimination, to mention a few) persist.

What yardstick can best measure the relative prosperity of a nation against the costs of achieving that prosperity? There is no easy answer. The assessment of per capita income is one way of quantifying prosperity, but even this method is suspect, as we shall see. Table 2.1 shows that the United States, which once had the highest per capita income of any nation, no longer holds first place. Several other countries have surpassed it. However, as is the case between nations (and even between regions of the same nation), it is difficult to estimate *living standards* on the basis of income statistics, because prices for given items vary so widely from place to place. For example, a price index for Honolulu may be 20 percent higher than the price index for, say, Phoenix. Does that mean that if you were to move to Honolulu with the same income you would be 20 percent

Table 2.1 GROSS NATIONAL PRODUCT (GNP) PER CAPITA, 1980
1980 Dollars

Countries with per capita income of $300 and less

Chad	(120)	Upper Volta	(210)	Sri Lanka	(270)
Bangladesh	(130)	Zaire	(220)	Tanzania	(280)
Ethiopia	(140)	Malawi	(230)	China	(290)
Nepal	(140)	Mozambique	(230)	Guinea	(290)
Burma	(170)	India	(240)	Pakistan	(300)
Mali	(190)	Haiti	(270)	Uganda	(300)
Rwanda	(200)				

Countries with per capita income greater than $300 and less than $1,000

Niger	(330)	Senegal	(450)	Thailand	(670)
Madagascar	(350)	Angola	(470)	Philippines	(690)
Sudan	(410)	Honduras	(560)	Nicaragua	(740)
Ghana	(420)	Zambia	(560)	Papua New	
Kenya	(420)	Bolivia	(570)	Guinea	(780)
Indonesia	(430)	Egypt	(580)	Morocco	(900)
Yemen Arab		Zimbabwe	(630)	Peru	(930)
Republic	(430)	El Salvador	(660)		

Countries with per capita income greater than $1,000 and less than $2,000

Nigeria	(1,010)	Colombia	(1,180)	Turkey	(1,470)
Jamaica	(1,040)	Ecuador	(1,270)	Korea	(1,520)
Guatemala	(1,080)	Tunisia	(1,310)	Malaysia	(1,620)
Ivory Coast	(1,150)	Syrian Arab		Panama	(1,730)
Dominican		Republic	(1,340)	Algeria	(1,870)
Republic	(1,160)	Jordan	(1,420)		

Countries with per capita GNP greater than $2,000 and less than $5,000

Brazil	(2,050)	Yugoslavia	(2,620)	Hong Kong	(4,240)
Mexico	(2,090)	Iraq	(3,020)	Greece	(4,380)
Chile	(2,150)	Venezuela	(3,630)	Singapore	(4,430)
South Africa	(2,300)	Poland	(3,900)	Israel	(4,500)
Romania	(2,340)	Bulgaria	(4,150)	Soviet Union	(4,550)
Portugal	(2,370)	Hungary	(4,180)	Ireland	(4,880)
Argentina	(2,390)				

Countries with per capita GNP greater than $5,000 and less than $10,000

Spain	(5,400)	German Democratic		Libya	(8,640)
Czechoslovakia	(5,820)	Republic	(7,180)	Finland	(9,720)
Italy	(6,480)	United		Australia	(9,820)
New Zealand	(7,090)	Kingdom	(7,920)	Japan	(9,890)

Countries with per capita GNP greater than $10,000 and less than $27,000

Canada	(10,130)	Belgium	(12,180)	Switzerland	(16,440)
Austria	(10,230)	Norway	(12,650)	Kuwait	(19,830)
Saudi Arabia	(11,260)	Denmark	(12,950)	United Arab	
United States	(11,360)	Sweden	(13,520)	Emirates	(26,850)
Netherlands	(11,470)	Federal Republic of			
France	(11,730)	Germany	(13,590)		

Source: World Bank, *World Development Report* (Washington, D.C.: 1982).

poorer? Probably not, because you would substitute cheaper items for the more expensive ones in Honolulu. You would eat less fresh meat and more frozen imports from New Zealand. You would picnic on the beach more often and dine at expensive restaurants only occasionally. The same is true when people move from country to country. Individuals react to changing relative prices by substituting more of the relatively cheaper commodities.

There is something else that official per capita income statistics seem to miss entirely. Income, properly measured, is not just money income, but includes a host of other things that yield benefits to individuals. Consider a household that owns a great many *consumer durables,* such as several cars, a boat, a stereo system, a house with a swimming pool, and a sewing machine. Throughout the year this household is receiving what is called *implicit income,* or *income in kind,* from all of these consumer durables. For the most part, the implied income stream of benefits received by this household is not counted in official government statistics on per capita income in this or in any other country. Since U.S. citizens have a dramatically higher per capita level of consumer durables, official statistics *underestimate* the true relative position of Americans on the per capita income ladder. Nonetheless, it is true that the recent rate of economic growth in this nation has been slower than at many other periods in its history. If this trend continues, U.S. living standards will continue to be surpassed by those of other nations.

Problems are solved only at a cost. America's know-how and technological advancement came at a cost of investment in research and development. The skills of American labor were learned at the cost of enormous expenditures for formal education and on-the-job training, and the solution to other problems in America today will mean even more costs.

The major issue, then, is the establishment of priorities. We want clean air, clean water, good health, a modest security for income, safeguards for our national freedom, and a host of other good things. Some way must be found to weigh the urgency of these various goals and to allocate the national budget among them all. Consider just a few of these objectives.

Clean Air and Water   Not long ago, fresh air was a free good. We could get all we wanted without depriving anyone else. In addition, every stream was a place to fish and swim in pristine conditions. Today, at times, in some cities, the air is literally not fit to breathe, and New Yorkers have been advised to limit their consumption of striped bass to one portion a month because of the polychlorinated biphenyls the fish have been found to contain.

These are not entirely new problems; the smoke-fogs of London, for example, have been legendary for centuries, and only recently has London's air been purified by the banning of soft-coal fires. We have simply become more aware of ecological dangers (as population increases) and, perhaps because our real incomes have also risen, we are willing to pay more for safeguarding our environment. How much more? Consider some examples. A Clean Water Act of 1974 passed by Congress specified that all rivers and lakes should be made safe for swimming before 1985. Soon after the passage of this act, it had to be relaxed because of the costs of the fuel crisis in 1976. Similarly, a Clean Air Act set maximum limits on how much pollution could be allowed in urban areas; the polluting emissions of cars, especially, were to be sharply reduced. Immediately, automobile manufacturers in Detroit pointed out that costly alterations in car motors would result in much higher costs to the consumer and would hurt the producers' competitive opportunities for economic survival.

Is it reasonable to expect that we can clean up *all* the lakes and waterways in the United States, or that we can enjoy mountain-pure air in every city? Or should we decide what level of pollution control is tolerable at what cost, and in what areas? Obviously, automobile emissions and belching smokestacks are doing more harm in crowded New York City than they would in the middle of the Mojave Desert.

The rule of *maximum economic efficiency* states that pollution should be reduced to that point where the additional cost of pollution abatement just equals the benefit obtained. The trick, of course, is to find out just what the long-term dangers and potential benefits really are, and how to weigh them. Obviously, some pollutants are more harmful than others. Equally obvious is that pollutants do more damage in heavily populated areas than in open empty lands.

Given the best intentions in the world, ecologists and economists may find it almost impossible to reach agreement on what is best for the American public. And this is only one of the many economic problems that the nation has faced and still faces today.

DEFINITIONS OF NEW TERMS

SCARCITY   Scarcity is the condition of being in limited supply. Almost everything that exists is scarce, or limited. The problem of scarcity exists because what people want or desire is generally not available in unlimited supply.

OPPORTUNITY COST   The highest valued alternative that must be sacrificed in order to attain something or satisfy a want is its opportunity cost.

RESOURCES   A resource is anything available for people to use. Resources can be classified as (1) those that are useful without being processed (natural resources), (2) those that can be used to produce goods (manufactured resources), and (3) those that are present in human beings (human resources). Basically, the term *resources* applies to all the things that people can use to make what they want.

MARKET   The area in which economic exchanges take place and in which goods and services that are similar tend to have similar prices is a market. Although the market may be a *geographical* area, the exchange of goods and services itself defines a market.

SPECIALIZATION   Specialization is the performance by a worker of a specific job or jobs rather than of everything required to make a product. Specialization is sometimes called division of labor.

COMPARATIVE ADVANTAGE   Individuals find their comparative advantage by seeking out the highest yielding activity that they can engage in, relative to all other activities, during any given period of time.

DISPOSABLE INCOME   Disposable income is personal income minus personal taxes (especially income taxes).

ENCOMIENDA An encomienda entitled a Spaniard (an encomendero, or overseer) in the New World to exact a tribute (due to the Spanish Crown but assigned to the overseer) from the native population. This tribute was usually collected as labor. The system was similar but not identical to slavery.

TRANSACTION COSTS All the costs associated with exchange, such as the cost of finding out the quality and price of goods, constitute transaction costs.

PRICE INELASTIC When a price rise leads to a less than proportionate decrease in quantity demanded, the good in question is said to be price inelastic.

REGIONAL SPECIALIZATION Regional specialization in production results from the opportunity to trade and from different conditions for production between areas. Each region will tend to produce and trade more of the items it can produce at lowest cost (relative to other regions).

A Man of Common Sense

BENJAMIN FRANKLIN
(1706–1790)

Statesman, Printer, Scientist, and Writer

"Remember that *time* is money. He that can earn ten shillings a day by his labour, and goes abroad, or sits idle, one half of that day, though he spends but sixpence during his diversion of idleness, ought not to reckon *that* his only expense; he has really spent, or rather thrown away, five shillings besides." Such were the words of Benjamin Franklin in his *Advice to a Young Tradesman,* published in 1748. A better example of keen understanding of the opportunity cost of one's time would be hard to find.

To be sure, his aphorisms must have been colored by his strict Calvinist upbringing. The true Calvinist was a driven man, described by British economist R. H. Tawney thus: "Tempered by self-examination, self-discipline, self-control, he is the practical ascetic, whose victories are won not in the cloister, but on the battlefield, in the counting house, and in the market." Calvin himself referred to God as the "great task maker" and looked around for tasks man should undertake. Ben Franklin claimed that he was a freethinker, but the continual exhortations from his father—for example, "Seest thou a man diligent in his business. He shall stand before kings"—must have had some effect.

Young Ben was born and raised in Boston. Family funds were insufficient for him to aim at Harvard, so he turned his hand to printing and went to Philadelphia in 1723, then decided he needed to perfect his printing knowledge in London, where he spent two years doing so and living like a bohemian. Within a few years, he began to prosper as a master printer. His simple style and great clarity in writing also started to bring in rewards. *Poor Richard's Almanac,* published annually between 1732 and 1757, was one of Franklin's most profitable enterprises, selling 10,000 copies a year. At the tender age of 23, Franklin wrote his first words on economics: *A Modest Inquiry into the Nature and Necessity of a Paper Currency* (1729). Coincidentally, Franklin was the first to print Pennsylvania's paper currency, and he stayed in this business for quite some time.

Franklin was a crusader and also a good businessman. He introduced printing and newspaper publication to many communities throughout the colonies. He also helped start the present University of Pennsylvania in 1751. Then he was named Deputy Postmaster General of the colonies.

Ben Franklin was also one of the first advertisers in America. When he started his *General Magazine,* he became disappointed that businessmen did not believe that advertising could bring better results. Franklin himself advertised his own "Pennsylvania Fire Place." The copy he wrote was persuasive: He criticized ordinary fireplaces because they caused drafts that made "women . . . get cold in the head, rheums, and defluxions," which maladies, when they "fall into their jaws and gums have destroyed early many a fine set of teeth."

During the Revolution, Franklin helped draft the Declaration of Independence, which he signed. He was also the diplomatic agent sent to France for the new republic. Then he was chosen commissioner in 1781 to negotiate peace with Great Britain. Finally, he took part in the Constitutional Convention.

To practical men, especially the officers of savings banks ("a penny saved is a penny earned"), Ben Franklin seemed the summation of good sense and morality. To others, he appeared to be a colorless and materialistic opportunist. But as John Adams once said, his "reputation was more universal than that of Leibniz, Newton, or Voltaire, and he was the first civilized American."

chapter 3

Supply and Demand Analysis

We have seen that the science of economics is rooted in exchange, an activity that usually makes each party better off. In addition, we have recognized that almost all resources and goods are in limited supply. Similarly, income, like any resource, is finite. There is a limit on what can be spent or exchanged by anyone, even a twentieth-century billionaire, for desired goods. Although the super wealthy today may buy an island, a stock-exchange seat, a railroad, or a fleet of steamships, they cannot buy everything or live forever.

From their consideration of the constraints on resources and budgets, economists draw certain conclusions. Exchanges between buyers and suppliers, they say, take place in accord with a law of supply and a law of demand.

THE LAW OF DEMAND

When people compare their wants to their incomes in trying to decide what they can buy (or consume), they are in effect asking themselves what must be given up in order to obtain what is wanted.

Thousands of years ago in a barter society 40 bushels of oats might be given up for a plough, for example. Two tangible goods would be handed back and forth. In our own society, what is usually surrendered is money—a token for a given amount of purchasing power, or command over other goods and services. The price paid for the purchase represents that much loss of purchasing power.

When the price of something goes up, those who buy it surrender a larger proportion of their buying power. Their remaining income and their ability to buy other goods are reduced by that much. You may be in the habit of taking a long drive every weekend, but if the costs of gasoline and car maintenance rise, as they did in the 1970s, you may have to cut down on driving in order to have enough money left to buy clothes and books for the rest of the year.

Economics formulates this situation in general terms:

As the price of a good rises, the quantity of it that is demanded (purchased) will fall.

The reverse is equally true:

As price falls, the quantity demanded will rise.

This is the **law of demand,** which has held true at all times and in all societies. So a great deal of economic analysis is based on the observation that people respond to changes in **relative prices.**

The word relative is important here. It means that no single price can be considered independently of all others. Let's say that the price of gasoline has risen 20 cents a gallon. The *absolute* price is higher. But meantime, suppose the price of shoes has risen by the same percentage, and so has the price of bread and jogging suits and everything else in the economy. In this case your weekend trip is not more expensive *relative* to other goods. However, if gasoline prices rise while the prices of other items remain the same or are only slightly higher, then the higher *relative* cost of driving may alter your driving habits.

For any accurate economic analysis, it is vital to make this distinction between absolute and relative prices, especially in periods when costs are changing rapidly. For example, it is meaningless to say, merely on the basis of old and new newspaper ads, that the cost of meat has shot up by 200 percent in five years. What counts is *not* the absolute price of a steak yesterday versus its absolute price today, but its price relative to other prices. Has its cost risen more or less than that of other goods?

THE LAW OF SUPPLY

The word *relative* is equally important when we consider the suppliers of goods. If one record company produces albums by a terrific new rock group, while another records the sounds of Los Angeles traffic at rush hour, it isn't hard to predict which company will sell its products and which will have trouble staying in business. Other recording studios will also have an incentive to contract with the successful band or others like it, because doing so is relatively more profitable. More resources will be devoted to rock music production, and more entertainers, technicians, and recording crews will be employed in such production than in recording freeway noise.

In short, economics predicts that, in general, the resources of an economy will flow to those areas where the rates of return are highest. Also (and here we recall one of the concepts stated in Chapter 2), workers will specialize in those areas where their skills yield the highest return. In this way, we discover a **law of supply:**

Suppliers and workers alike respond to changing relative prices. As the price of a good goes up, so too will the quantity supplied.

THE MARKET: MEETING PLACE FOR BUYERS AND SELLERS

Before anything can be exchanged (bought and sold), the buyer and the seller have to get together. In early times, deals might be carried out under a tree or in a public square. Even today we often see signs announcing garage sales or moving sales, each sign carrying the address to which prospective buyers can go to find what they may (or may not!) be looking for. From local convenience stores to large supermarkets, every store is in effect a market where buyers and sellers meet.

As used in economics, the term market has the same meaning but in a far wider sense. Economically speaking, "the market" is any setting in which transactions involving exchanges of products or services for money (or its equivalent) are carried out.

Because means of communication were so restricted in the past and goods were hardly guaranteed, transactions were almost always made face to face. During the Middle Ages, cities were just beginning to take form, and only a handful of small open-air markets had developed. Wandering merchants peddled their wares from town to town, setting up an embryonic sort of commerce as they brought produce from one area to others.

In our own day, the market has taken a quantum leap; many transactions are done by mail, by telephone (to a stock broker, for example), or by computer, often between parties who never see each other. Despite technological advances, however, these transactions still lie within the economic definition of market activity.

More important, the market itself is subject to economic analysis by the same laws and axioms we have already discovered. From the law of demand and the law of supply you can predict that (1) as the cost of making an exchange falls (2) the quantity of exchanges made will rise. That is, the easier we make it for people to take part in the market system, the more people will do so.

As we know, the difficulties and costs of making exchanges are sometimes called transaction costs. The laws of economics dictate that as transaction costs are reduced more trading will take place, more workers will specialize, more people will establish new businesses, and ultimately everyone should have more total goods. This is the bright hope of the economic marketplace.

Supply and Demand Throughout American History

We now examine how the laws of supply and demand functioned in the early nineteenth century to transform America into an industrial economy.

From early colonial times, imports of manufactured goods from Britain had satisfied a great proportion of young America's demands. In 1800, only 7 percent of the American population lived in urban areas, and domestic manufacturing was extremely limited.

Under certain conditions, business people naturally saw their highest rates of return as coming not from manufacturing, but from agriculture, exporting, reexporting, shipping, and general trading. It is true that in the 1790s a certain Samuel Slater had made heroic attempts to develop a mechanized weaving industry in Rhode Island. By 1800, a small textile industry was generally taking shape, but two thirds of its production was still based in homes, and no great interest had been shown in this kind of commercial activity.

The turning point came in 1807. Increasing tension between British and American interests led to a trade embargo, followed by a British blockade of American waters in 1812. Deprived of imports, the young nation was obliged to look to its own resources, and American industry was stimulated. Resources could now produce their highest rate of return by being channeled into industry, so that was what was done. Manufacturing became the new growth sector of the economy.

The Textile Industry and Technological Adaptation

The salutary effects of the embargo on manufacturing were quickly felt. In 1808 there were only 15 textile mills in the United States, but by 1809, there were almost 90. The rapid multiplication of mills demonstrated how little capital was needed to start one. Few of these new mills survived, however, once the Peace of Ghent in 1814 brought the War of 1812 to a close and Britain resumed massive exports to the States. The textile industry faltered, but certain large-scale concerns, such as the Waltham system of cloth weaving developed by Francis Cabot Lowell, survived and grew. His use of water-powered mills and a system that used relatively low-cost, well-supervised labor spearheaded the growth of the industry.

Britain was the front-runner in the Industrial Revolution, and American businesses borrowed English know-how in order to make certain products. However, most British technology was relatively **capital** and **labor intensive,** whereas the United States had to contend with conditions of relative labor scarcity. The great desire of American businesses for labor-saving machinery may have led to the initial U.S. emphasis on standardized parts, such as occurred with firearms. Moreover, in the early days, U.S. manufacturing development depended largely on water power, which was relatively plentiful and inexpensive compared to the more capital-intensive steam power used in Britain.

Through the forces of supply and demand we can summarize the expansion in the cotton textile industry in America during the period 1815–1860. The following factors led to an increase in demand for American cotton textiles in the antebellum period:

1. *Tariffs* imposed on British products. These increased the demand for American cloth in the short run (that is, since the price of the British good rose, the demand for the substitute, American cloth, increased).

2. *Population growth* of roughly 3 percent a year. An expanding population implies an increase in the demand for clothing.
3. *Growth in income.* Per capita income during this period was growing at least 1 percent a year. People were able to buy more clothing, especially cotton clothing produced in factories.
4. *Improvements in transportation.* Lower delivery prices resulted for those areas outside the New England states. Transportation improvements alone led to an increase in the quantity demanded of approximately 1 percent a year.
5. *Tastes.* American consumers in the antebellum period increasingly preferred cotton to woolens, increasing the demand for cotton cloth.

Recent findings suggest that demand factors alone caused cotton cloth sales to rise roughly 20 percent a year from 1815 to 1833, and thereafter around 4 percent annually until 1860.[1]

What were the factors that influenced suppliers to produce more cotton cloth?

1. *Technology.* The cost of weaving fell by 75 percent with the introduction of the power loom.
2. *Suppliers' input prices.* The price of raw cotton fell steadily until the 1840s. This drop lowered the cost and raised the quantity of production.
3. *Improvements in organization and machinery.* Better methods of production reduced costs, thus increasing profits and raising output.

The traditional view is that technical change was by far the dominant force leading to industrial development in early America. But by applying the laws of supply and demand to historical data we can see that all the foregoing factors probably worked together in the transformation of this particular industry.

Now let's see how the same laws helped to minimize a mid-nineteenth century crisis of a kind that is very much on our minds today: a shortage of energy.

Resolving the First Energy Crisis

The fuel involved in America's first energy crisis, not much more than a century ago, was whale oil. It was used for lighting, both in the United States and abroad. Because the supply of whale oil could not keep pace with increasing demand, the price rose from 23 cents a gallon in 1832 to $1.45 a gallon in 1865. But the quantity demanded fell only slightly, despite the large increase in price, because no good substitute was available; the demand was price inelastic (that is, the quantity demanded was not very responsive to price changes over a significant range).

[1]For a detailed explanation, see R. Zevin, "The Growth of Cotton Textile Production After 1815," in *The Reinterpretation of American Economic History,* Robert W. Fogel and Stanley L. Engerman, eds. (New York: Harper & Row, 1971).

The growth in the demand for whale oil was stimulated by increases in population and in income between 1830 and 1860. During this time the number of easily accessible whales diminished. In the early 1800s New England whalers had to travel only short distances to make a catch, but as supplies dwindled whalers had to go farther and farther from the Nantucket area, out into the Pacific and the Bering Sea. These extended voyages raised the costs of whaling. Other forces, however, acted simultaneously to counter this trend; new and improved technology increased the productivity of the whaling industry, thus tending to lower costs and increase supply.

With these two factors offsetting each other, it is hard to know which dominated. Because the price rise remained, however, higher costs clearly prevailed. Moreover, we do know that an increase in demand had occurred.

The discovery of petroleum in 1859 coupled with the high whale oil prices prompted producers to develop a refining process for crude petroleum. The end product of this research and development was a substitute fuel—kerosene. By the mid-1860s consumers were substituting away from the higher priced whale oil to the lower priced kerosene. Hence, prices provided the appropriate signal to the market and forestalled a long-term energy crisis.

King Cotton

Some economists have argued that the market for cotton largely determined the growth and development of the antebellum South. The historical scenario and its theoretical implications based on supply and demand analysis follow.

Cotton was an insignificant feature of the southern landscape at the time of the adoption of the Constitution in 1789. In fact, since the importance of all southern exports faded after the Revolution, there was little reaction from the South when the new Constitution stipulated that slave imports would be stopped after 20 years.

This was all to change, partly because in 1793 Eli Whitney invented the cotton gin. Before that time, a worker had to extract the seeds from cotton by hand. With Whitney's machine, the same worker could produce not just one but more than 50 pounds of raw short-staple cotton in a day. The result, of course, was to lower the cost of American cotton and raise its supply.

At the same time, England's textile industry was growing rapidly, generating increased demand for raw cotton.

The South responded by increasing its production of cotton at a phenomenal rate, doubling it almost every decade until 1840, after which growth continued, but at a slower rate. We see in Figure 3.1 that by the start of the Civil War, cotton production was four million bales a year.

Cotton quickly became the major export not only for the South but for the entire United States. Figure 3.2 shows that cotton exports rose from 38 percent of total exports from 1815 to 1819 to 65 percent just before 1840. Although the volume continued to rise, in relative terms it fell to 51 percent by the start of the Civil War.

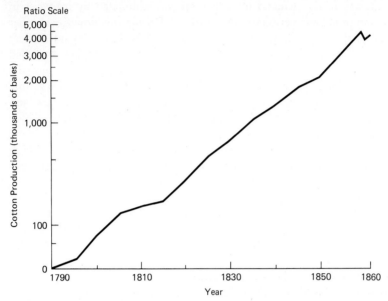

Figure 3.1   Cotton production. (*Source: Historical Statistics*, p. 302.)

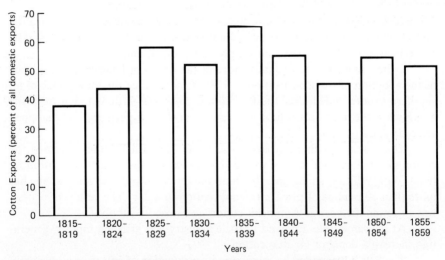

Figure 3.2   Cotton exports. (*Source: Historical Statistics*, pp. 538–547.)

There are many reasons why the South became so highly specialized in cotton production. First, the climate and terrain were particularly well suited for such a crop, especially in the New South: the cotton states of Alabama, Mississippi, Arkansas, Louisiana, and eastern Texas. The soil in these new states was very fertile and easily cultivated. Moreover, the land policy of the federal government became increasingly liberal over the period in question. Western lands were becoming easier to obtain, for small and large farmers alike, as the federal government set lower minimum land prices and as credit availability increased.

Second, southerners had the necessary know-how and entrepreneurial skills, inherited from the colonial experience with plantations. Third, the South had a large pool of unskilled labor, in bondage, to pick and carry cotton. Finally, a vast network of waterways provided an inexpensive means of transporting the cotton to ocean ports, the main one, of course, being New Orleans. Cotton farmers had only to cart their bales to a nearby river for shipment to large vessels waiting at the dock in New Orleans, Savannah, Charleston, or Mobile. Along with opportunity for both interregional and international trade, these factors enabled the South to specialize in its comparative advantage: cotton production.

Cotton and Interregional Trade

Cotton, then, was king in the South; but was its influence on the *national* economy as significant? First, we use supply and demand analysis to see how cotton affected westward growth.

In the new Southwest cotton was the reason for a migration far greater than would otherwise have occurred. We have noted cotton's need for fertile soil. Since, like most other crops, when cultivated exclusively over a long period cotton depletes the soil, it is essential for growers either to fertilize, to rest the land, or to move on to new areas.

As the price of cotton rose relative to that of other crops, growers in search of profits were induced to move to newer (and hence more fertile) fields. A great surge in westward migration lagged by only one or two years each increase in the price of cotton.

When the relative price of cotton rose in America, the sequence was generally the same.

1. The relative price of cotton went up.
2. New plantations were started, with three to four years needed to clear the land.
3. The supply of cotton rose.
4. The relative price of cotton fell.
5. Some plantations shifted to growing corn, but whenever the price of cotton went up, they went back to cotton.
6. The demand for cotton rose so much that most of the cultivated land was once more used for cotton production.
7. The relative price of cotton rose again as demand outstripped supply.
8. A new cycle started and people moved to the West.

There is little doubt that the cotton economy influenced the growth of population in the new Southwest. It also had some effect on the development of manufacturing in the North, but only to a decreasing extent, as the North branched out into industries other than textile manufacturing.

The main surges to the West occurred during the periods from 1816 to 1819, from 1833 to 1837, and, to a lesser extent, in the 1850s. These dates correlate fairly closely with the information on rising and high cotton prices presented in Figure 3.3.

That the availability of relatively inexpensive cotton was vital for the development of the New England textile industry is, of course, a well-known historical fact. Moreover, each fall in the price of cotton in the South was additional stimulus to the North, because cotton was a major input into its manufacturing sector. To some extent, then, the cotton economy encouraged the growth of industry in New England. Also, southern demand for shoes and cheap textiles with which to clothe slaves further spurred northern industry and stimulated northern shipping and commercial activities.

Agricultural Programs in the Twentieth Century

In 1933 Congress passed the Agricultural Adjustment Act, which created the Agricultural Adjustment Administration (AAA). The AAA's purpose was to keep the prices of farm products from dropping further, in order to keep the income of farmers up. The AAA attempted to raise farm prices by putting restrictions on the amount of wheat, corn, and other basic agricultural crops that could be offered for sale. This should work, according to the law of demand. The only way to sell a large amount of wheat, for example, is to offer it at a lower price. Hence, if wheat farmers offer a much smaller quantity, the price can be much higher. That is, a restriction on the supply allows farmers to charge higher prices and not have any wheat left over.

The AAA was unsuccessful, however, in keeping farmers from producing "too much" wheat and corn. Therefore, another way to keep up the price of those products was devised: **price supports,** which for many decades have been paid for such agricultural products as wheat, feed grains, tobacco, cotton, rice, peanuts, soybeans, dairy products, and sugar. Under a price-support system the government supports, or fixes, the price of an agricultural product at a particular level. This level is usually higher than the price that would prevail without government support. That is, the price support is set at a level that exceeds the market price that would be determined by the interaction of supply and demand.

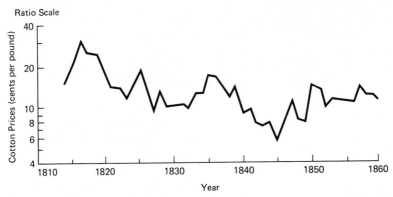

Figure 3.3   Cotton prices per pound prior to the Civil War. (*Source: Historical Statistics,* p. 124.)

Price supports have two contrary effects. On the one hand, consumers react to relatively higher prices by buying less of a product than they would buy at lower prices. On the other hand, suppliers (farmers) react in the opposite direction by producing more. As you know, at relatively higher prices, it is more profitable to produce more.

As a result of price-support levels that exceed an **equilibrium price** (the price at which the quantity supplied equals the quantity demanded), there is a difference between the quantity supplied (which is relatively larger) and the quantity demanded (which is smaller). This difference is called a *surplus*. But a surplus cannot exist very long without government support, because farmers would ultimately be forced to accept lower prices to get rid of their growing inventories.

Under a program that was in effect for many years, the federal government allowed farmers to sell surpluses to the Commodity Credit Corporation (CCC). In principle, the CCC was actually giving each farmer a kind of loan. That is, the farmer would give the CCC all of the wheat or corn on which he or she wanted to "borrow money." The CCC, in turn, would "loan" the farmer the support price times the number of bushels of wheat or corn that the farmer gave to the CCC.

Whenever a price support was set too high, farmers produced and sold their surpluses to the CCC. By the mid-1950s the CCC had begun to stockpile enormous inventories of surplus farm products, and ultimately many goods were wasted by rot. These stockpiles continued to grow throughout most of the 1960s. Meanwhile, new programs to induce farmers to produce less by reducing acreage planted had little effect, for technological developments enabled farmers to get ever-increasing yields per acre.

Finally, however, the world demand for food became so great that the equilibrium price of some products, especially wheat, was temporarily higher than the support price. In 1973 widespread crop failures obliged many countries to turn to the United States for agricultural products. This increased demand for U.S. farm goods drove the price up, and the government was thus able to get rid of all the surpluses. For a couple of years, therefore, the price-support program for many agricultural commodities was actually inoperative because the price-support levels were below the prices that prevailed in world markets.

In this chapter we have presented the concept of supply and demand and its relevance in a few important historical episodes. Supply and demand is basic to economics and can be extended into the factor market (land, labor, and capital), where its explanatory power is equally enlightening.

DEFINITIONS OF NEW TERMS

LAW OF DEMAND   The law of demand states that as the relative price of a product goes up, a smaller quantity will be demanded; as the relative price of a product goes down, a larger quantity will be demanded.

RELATIVE PRICES   Relative price is the price of an item relative to the price of something else. More generally, it is the price of an item relative to the average of all other prices.

LAW OF SUPPLY   The law of supply states that at higher relative prices, suppliers are willing to supply more of a product than they will at lower relative prices.

CAPITAL INTENSIVE   An industry in which much capital is used relative to land or labor is capital intensive.

LABOR INTENSIVE   An industry that uses much labor relative to capital or land is labor intensive.

PRICE SUPPORT   The fixing or stabilization of the price of a product by the government so that the price cannot *fall* below a certain level is a price support.

EQUILIRIUM PRICE   The price at which the quantity supplied is equal to the quantity demanded is the equilibrium price.

The Man Who Made Cotton King

ELI WHITNEY
(1765–1825)

Inventor and Manufacturer

In 1790, cotton production in the United States was about two million pounds. Ten years later, it had risen to 35 million. In the early 1790s, several northern states introduced gradual emancipation schemes, and the trend toward voluntary abolition of slavery was increasing: For example, Washington and Jefferson provided in their wills for their own slaves to be set free. This trend was soon reversed, however, and slavery in the United States grew until the Civil War.

What was responsible for the tremendous increase in the production and sale of cotton and for the newfound profitability in slaves? A simple but monumental invention —the cotton gin. And it was invented by an inveterate tinkerer, Eli Whitney.

As a boy, Eli used to putter around in his father's workshop on their family farm in Massachusetts. Eventually he started to make and repair violins in the neighborhood. When he was only 15, he was a manufacturer of nails in his father's shop, even hiring helpers to fill part of his orders. Then he turned to hat pins. But by the time he was 18 he decided he wanted more education. Working his way through Leicester Academy in Massachusetts, he finally was able to enter Yale in 1789 at the age of 23. Not able to live on the funds offered by his father, he repaired equipment and apparatus around the college. A carpenter who had lent Eli his tools remarked after watching him work, "There was one good mechanic spoiled when you went to college."

Then he decided to go into law. Having been invited as a tutor to stay with the widow of General Nathaniel Green, he overheard a conversation at one of her dinners on the Savannah plantation. The men there pointed out the deplorable state of cotton cultivation in the South. Except in certain coastal areas the only variety that could be grown was short-staple, upland cotton, which was extremely difficult to clean, requiring one whole

35

day to obtain a pound of lint. A machine was needed to remove the tenacious seed from the cotton. In ten days Whitney had invented that machine: a cylinder barely 2 feet long and 6 inches in diameter, with rows of combing teeth to separate the lint from the seeds and a brush with a fan to remove the clean cotton. This little model was 50 times as efficient as hand labor. News of the cotton gin soon spread, and the curious and interested flocked to find out what it was all about. It was soon stolen, carried off, and copied. Given the ease of duplication and weakly enforced patent laws of the time, there was little Whitney could claim for his efforts and ingenuity.

Nevertheless, his invention changed the entire history of the South, and indeed, the United States. Most southern planters went into cotton production, and land that was once considered worthless soon became valuable. Slaves were now a much sought-after part of the cotton production process, and the price of field hands doubled in 20 years.

Whitney did not stop with the cotton gin, however, and in later years he invented another process that perhaps proved to be even more important for the history of the United States. Whitney looked at the manufacture of firearms and decided he could do better. Having never built a gun before, he brashly contacted Treasury Secretary Oliver Wolcott in 1798 and took on the task of manufacturing 10,000 or 15,000 stand of arms at a price of $13.40 each. Whitney proposed to make the guns by a new method, and in so doing invented the standardization of parts. He once wrote, "One of my primary objects is to form the tools so the tools themselves shall fashion the work and give to every part its just proportion—which when once accomplished, will give expedition, uniformity, and exactness to the whole. . . . The tools which I contemplate are similar to an engraving on a copper plate."

After a slow start, Whitney perfected his method. He was able to use relatively unskilled mechanics to fashion the precise parts that when put together made a very good gun. As it was, Whitney took eight years to fulfill a contract that he promised would be done in two. During this period he had to withstand prejudice and ridicule, but in the end he won out, and his method of machine milling of parts that could be used interchangeably revolutionized the entire manufacturing process used throughout the world. As late as 1840 the British were amazed at the use of interchangeable parts, which had already begun to revolutionize industry in America.

College apparently did not spoil the mechanic in Eli Whitney.

chapter *4*

Labor Supply and Labor Demand

INTRODUCTION TO FACTOR PRICING

In Chapter 2 we briefly examined the factors of production: land, labor, and capital. As we now take a closer look at each of these essential contributors to output, we discover that each is subject to the same laws of supply and demand as the market for anything else—books, shoes, or stereos.

In fact, economists refer to a *factor market,* that is, a market for a particular factor of production. From the study of how factors are used we find that producers vary the proportion of each factor used according to the returns that each provides in the final output. In the next two chapters we shall see that precisely such considerations were influential in directing the historical development of the American economy.

The principal difference between the labor market and other markets lies in the way in which supply and demand are determined. The demand for labor depends on two important factors: (1) the productivity of workers and (2) the price at which their output can be sold.

Workers have little say about the price of what they produce because that price depends on market supply and market demand. However, they do have some control over their own productivity. One reason for going to college, for example, is that a college education increases your potential to produce goods and services and to earn income. On-the-job training and independent study are other ways in which workers can increase and improve their skills. Computers and other sophisticated machines also raise labor productivity.

The availability of such machines is the chief reason American workers are so highly paid as compared to workers in less-developed nations. Advances in technology have increased labor productivity and the value of labor, thus leading to higher wages and improved standards of living.

The supply of labor is also governed by two important considerations: (1) individual choice and (2) wages relative to other rewards (alternatives to employment such as schooling, travel, or leisure). A person's desire to work or not to work, and how many hours per week or weeks per year to work, are dependent on individual preferences, but we can examine one of the prime factors influencing that choice: wages.

Given a group of people able to work, the proportion of those in the age-eligible population who engage in the production of goods and services is called the labor force **participation rate.** When wage rates rise, some people who had not been working will choose to enter the work force. The participation rate goes up, to include such groups as homemakers, students, and formerly retired people.

In boom times producers want more workers. They must attract those people who have been voluntarily enjoying their alternatives—self-occupation, studies, or leisure. The obvious way to do so is to offer higher wages in return for working time.

The choice facing a person, in this case, can be looked at in terms of the *cost* of not working. For instance, suppose that the after-tax wage rate for a given job is $5.00 per hour; the cost of *not* working that hour was $5.00. If labor demand and wages begin to rise, the true cost of not working will go up along with the wages to $6.00 or $7.50 or $9.00. This higher opportunity cost encourages greater labor participation. It is a truism, then, that higher wages and higher participation rates are typical of boom periods.

LABOR UNIONS

Some who would like to become a doctor, a dentist, a plumber, a carpenter, or a musician may find that desire alone is not enough. Many occupations in the United States are not freely open to anyone. Certain restrictions in the labor market prevent people from casually entering professions, trades, or industries they might like to try. State or federal regulations may bar entry into a particular occupation. Some jobs and professions require specific study, practice under supervision, passing an examination, and paying a fee for a license. Other limitations are laws, such as the minimum-wage statutes, which can, in effect, reduce job opportunities for people who are young and inexperienced or who want to work temporarily or part time.

A second restriction is discrimination. Discrimination based on race or sex prevents some people from receiving wages equal to their worth or productivity. In some instances it prevents them from entering certain occupations at all.

Union membership and union regulations are a third kind of restriction on the labor market. A labor or trade *union* is an association of wage earners organized to maintain or further their interests by bargaining as a group (that is, by working out their differences) with their employer or employers. This process is called **collective bargaining.**

The constitution of the American Federation of Labor-Congress of Industrial Organizations (AFL-CIO), which represents over 75 percent of all union members in this country, sets forth the goals of the organization:

1. to improve working conditions;
2. to secure better wages and better hours; and
3. to allow employees to realize the benefits of unrestrained collective bargaining.

The services that unions provide for their members include

1. providing information about alternative job opportunities;
2. helping workers improve their skills;
3. verifying that insurance, retirement, and other fringe benefit payments are carried out according to contract;
4. reducing the cost of certain fringe benefits by buying them for all members; and
5. helping members obtain loans from union credit agencies.

Unions are strong only when they represent the majority of workers in a firm or an industry. Moreover, unions are stronger when individual workers cannot negotiate separately with an employer about wages or working conditions. In other words, for a union to remain in power, it must be the *sole* bargaining agent for most or all of the workers involved.

A union engages in collective bargaining with an employer for wages, fringe benefits, and working conditions. In a sense, the union sets a minimum wage for each classification of workers. The employer is not allowed to pay less than that minimum wage, and the worker is not allowed to accept less.

Throughout the history of the United States, personal incomes have risen fairly steadily on average, except during depressions or recessions. Wages also have risen even in industries where unions have been weak or have not existed at all. Without a union, supply and demand, as influenced by many other factors, determine wages. Then how can a union get a higher wage rate? After all, if supply and demand are working, the employer could obtain other workers at the competitive wage rate determined by supply and demand. This would be true except for one powerful tool of unions—the *strike*. Without the power to strike, unions would not function, or have the power, they do today.

Workers in the United States have not always had the right to strike. In some nations today, including the Soviet Union and Cuba, strikes are still illegal.

When employees strike, they stop working for their employer. More important, they use activities such as *picketing,* a restrictive aspect of union behavior, to prevent all actual or potential workers from crossing the line to work for the employer.

When unions successfully raise wage rates above those that would result from a competitive market, they face a difficult task. At the higher union wage rate, more workers are willing to work than employers are willing to hire. Thus, unions find a surplus of workers available for a limited supply of jobs, so the union must ration jobs among applicants.

One very effective way to ration jobs is to restrict entry into a particular labor market. (Entry is restricted for merchant seamen, electricians, teamsters, butchers, barbers, and other occupations.) Entry may be restricted by requiring a long and costly apprenticeship. (During apprenticeship, the worker is not paid the normal union wage.) In some cases, a person must be nominated by three union members in order to become an apprentice. When such a requirement exists, members generally nominate only relatives of those already in the union.

It is sometimes argued that the activities of organized workers benefit all workers and hurt employers. If this claim were true, then the share of all income going to workers in the United States would have to grow at the expense of employers. However, available evidence does not lend support to this claim. The share of all income going to workers has remained constant (between 70 and 75 percent) during the last 50 years. The remainder goes to people in the form of profit, interest, dividends, and rent.

Who gains and who loses as a result of union activities? Analysis reveals that as union workers obtain wages, fringe benefits, and working conditions greater than those that would otherwise exist, the quantity of labor demanded from the union declines. As a result, some members are unable to get union employment. Herein lies the rationing problem previously discussed. Eventually, some of the unemployed union members find that they must accept work in the unorganized sector of the economy, often at lower wages. Some economists, therefore, contend that union workers benefit at the expense of those who are working in the nonunion sectors of the economy.

A HISTORY OF UNIONS

The concept of unions dates to the craft guilds of the Middle Ages. These first occupational associations were formed by artisans in a particular field. Although the guilds were unable to obtain a monopoly over trade (each city had many crafts), they did restrict membership by requiring a long training period.

Training began with the apprenticeship of a boy to a guild master. After a successful training period, the apprentice became a journeyman—a free worker paid by the day. The journeyman was expected to save money with which to open his own shop. He was also required to work many years to provide proof of his technical competence before becoming a master craftsman.

The labor movement in the United States, like that in Europe, started with local associations, called **craft unions,** of workers skilled in a specific trade, such as baking, shoemaking, or printing. The organizing efforts of many early craft unions were defeated by unfavorable court judgments. Table 4.1 shows the growth of union membership from the 1830s to the present.

With the rise of industry after the Civil War, the movement to organize labor on a national basis began to grow. In fact, the first permanent union on a national scale was formed in 1852. It still exists as the International Typographical Union.

Table 4.1 UNION MEMBERSHIP IN THE UNITED STATES

Until 1900, union membership never exceeded 3 percent of the U.S. labor force. Union membership as a percentage of the labor force reached its peak in 1960 and has since slowly declined.

	Union Membership (thousands)	Labor Force (thousands)	Percentage Organized
1830	26	4,200	0.6
1860	5	11,110	0.1
1870	300	12,930	2.3
1880	50	17,390	0.3
1883	210	—	—
1886	1,010	—	—
1890	325	23,320	1.4
1900	791	29,070	2.7
1910	2,116	37,480	5.6
1920	5,034	41,610	12.1
1930	3,632	48,830	7.4
1940	8,944	56,290	16.6
1945	14,796	65,600	22.6
1950	15,000	65,470	22.9
1960	18,117	74,060	24.5
1965	18,519	77,177	23.9
1970	20,589	85,903	24.1
1975	20,468	94,793	21.2
1980	22,829	104,719	21.8

Source: L. Davis et al., *American Economic Growth* (New York: Harper & Row, 1972), p. 220; and U.S. Department of Labor, Bureau of Labor Statistics.

The Knights of Labor   The first important national labor organization was the Knights of Labor, formed in 1869 under the leadership of Uriah Stevens, a Philadelphia garment worker. By the late 1880s its membership of both skilled and unskilled workers had grown to nearly 800,000. Although many of its demands, such as the eight-hour work day, were eventually accepted, the Knights of Labor rapidly lost popularity when it engaged in a number of violent, unsuccessful strikes. Its decline and ultimate demise were also hastened by the rise of the American Federation of Labor.

The American Federation of Labor   The American Federation of Labor (AFL) was formed in 1886 under the leadership of Samuel Gompers. Unlike the Knights of Labor, the AFL was a decentralized federation of independent national trade unions. Its membership was limited to skilled workers.

Through the strong leadership of Gompers, membership in the AFL grew steadily. In 1900 it had more than 500,000 members, and on the eve of World War I, it had more than two million. A major reason for its growth was its acceptance of the capitalist system and its concentration on practical economic objectives—higher wages, shorter hours, and improved working conditions. Under Gompers's leadership, the AFL did not militate for social reforms or engage directly in politics. Although the AFL could claim that it spoke for the vast majority of organized labor, union membership began to decline in the 1920s. One reason for the decline was the antilabor attitude of many businesses that refused to recognize unions as the bargaining agents for workers. This attitude carried over to the courts, which ruled against such labor activities as picketing and boycotting. Still another reason was that no national organization represented the hundreds of thousands of unskilled workers employed in industry.

The Congress of Industrial Organizations   It was not until the depths of the Great Depression that unskilled workers acquired union representation. A group of dissident AFL leaders, headed by John Mitchell, recognized the need to organize labor on other than a craft basis. In 1935 they formed the Congress of Industrial Organizations (CIO). Unlike the AFL, the CIO organized all workers in an industry, skilled and unskilled.

With the emergence of **industrial unions**, union membership grew rapidly. By 1955, when the AFL and CIO merged into one national labor organization, it represented over 17.5 million members. One of the underlying causes of this growth was government support of labor, which began with a series of laws passed by Congress during the Great Depression.

LABOR LEGISLATION AND THE MINIMUM WAGE

The passage of New Deal legislation in the 1930s granted the legal right to strike and fostered the growth of American union activity. After World War II, however, considerable antilabor sentiment developed because of what many saw as excessive striking. In particular, John L. Lewis's United Mine Workers defied a court order to return to work after a long and violent strike. The union and its leaders were fined for contempt of court, and the miners did finally go back to work. Nonetheless, legislation to curtail union power was already in the making, and the Labor-Management Relations Act of 1947 was passed. Sometimes called the Taft-Hartley Act (and, by union people, the Slave Labor Act), it allowed individual states to pass their own right-to-work laws. A **right-to-work law** makes it illegal for union membership to be a prerequisite for employment in any individual establishment. In general, the Taft-Hartley Act outlawed such union practices as "make-work" rules and the forcing of unwilling workers to join a particular union before being hired. But the most famous aspect of this act is its provision that the president can obtain a court injunction that could last for 80 days against any strike that is believed to imperil the nation's safety or health. President Nixon applied this feature of the act to the longshoremen's strike in 1971. President Eisenhower had done the same to striking steel workers in 1959. Other labor legislation passed during this postwar period involved union-supported increases in the minimum wage.

Minimum-Wage Legislation   Minimum-wage legislation, which grew out of a general movement to help the poor and raise the pay of those toiling under bad working conditions, has been around for at least three quarters of a century. In

1912 Massachusetts passed a "a moral suasion" law to compel employers to pay standard wage rates, which were to be set by a state wage board. Any employer who did not comply would have his name published and would therefore be subject to community censure. A year later eight more states passed minimum-wage laws, seven of them making the rate compulsory. The laws, however, applied only to women and minors, which meant that most workers were unaffected.

Roosevelt's New Deal and the National Industrial Recovery Act (NIRA) in 1933 set up the first federal minimum wage. It started at a rate between 30 and 40 cents an hour. When the NIRA was declared unconstitutional, the Fair Labor Standards Act was passed in 1937, establishing a minimum wage rate of 25 cents for all industries that were involved in interstate commerce. This act has remained the basis for the current federal minimum wage. The national minimum wage went to 30 cents in 1939. By 1950 it was 75 cents; then it increased in steps to $1.60 per hour by the start of the 1970s. By 1982 it was $3.35 per hour.

Unions in favor   Why did unions support this legislation? Although union workers already make considerably more than minimum wage rates, labor services at low wages are often substitutable for union labor services at higher wages. If nonunion workers must be paid a higher wage rate than they would be paid otherwise, the demand for union workers will, in fact, be greater. In other words, the high union wage rate will no longer be *relatively* as high if other workers must be paid more than they would receive under competitive conditions.

Who gets hurt?   Some people are definitely hurt by minimum wages, and most economists recommend mandatory minimum wages not be used. Such respected economists as Nobel laureates Paul Samuelson and Milton Friedman indicate that teenagers and blacks are affected most by the minimum wage. In fact, Paul Samuelson once said, "What good does it do a black youth to know that an employer must pay him $1.60 an hour if the fact that he must be paid that amount is what keeps him from getting a job?" Milton Friedman called the minimum-wage law "the most anti-Negro law on our statute books—in its effect, not its intent." This is so because although the statute requires that employers pay workers higher wages, it does not require them to hire the same number of workers. It instead leads to *more* unemployment for certain groups, especially the young.

When the wage rate is arbitrarily increased by government edict, some workers may become unprofitable to employ. If these **marginal workers** (those whose output in terms of value barely equals what they are paid) suddenly have to be paid more, they may just be fired instead if the market value of their contribution to output is now less than the minimum-wage rate. In this case employers lose money by keeping them on. The marginal workers who lose their jobs have to find work in sectors of the economy that are not covered by minimum-wage legislation; and in those sectors of the economy, the additional supply of workers will cause wage rates to fall. By eliminating marginal job opportunities, the minimum-wage rate actually hurts many of the very people it is intended to help.

Some facts   In 1956 the minimum wage was increased from 75 cents to $1.00 an hour, a one-third jump. Three years later the secretary of labor concluded in a report that after the increase in the minimum wage in 1956, "there were significant declines in employment in most of the low-wage industries studied." From other evidence we find that teenagers are predominantly in the low-wage groups if for no other reason than that they have less experience in working and are therefore less productive than older experienced workers. Therefore, they are the most affected by the minimum wage. If we look at white teenage unemployment from 1950 to 1956, it ranged between 6.5 percent and 11 percent. When the minimum wage was raised to $1.00 in 1956, white teenage unemployment shot up from 7 percent to 14 percent. Ever since then it has remained in excess of 12 percent. Even more startling is what happened to black teenagers, whose unemployment jumped in 1956 from 13 percent to 24 percent. A 1965 study by Arthur F. Burns concluded that "the ratio of the unemployment rate of teenagers to that of male adults was invariably higher during the six months following the increase in the minimum wage than it was in the preceding half year." In 1984 President Reagan advocated cutting the minimum wage in half for workers under the age of 20. Today black teenage unemployment is typically 40 percent or more.

Labor Supply: Its Role in American History

We have seen that the supply of labor is one cog in the complex machinery of market operations. We now focus on this element as we examine how the size and growth of the American population influenced the direction of economic development.

The half century between the Civil War and World War I saw an enormous expansion in the number of people living in America. Population was growing at an average rate of 2 percent a year, which brought the total from 36 million at the end of the Civil War to more than 100 million by the beginning of World War I. (By then the growth rate of population was starting to slow down to some extent.) Floods of immigrants had come to America during that time, but natural increase added even greater numbers, because the birth rate exceeded the death rate.

According to the estimates by Stanley Lebergott, the total labor force grew at a rate of 2.67 percent per year from 1800 to 1830. Then the rate increased sharply between 1830 and 1860, climbing to 3.3 percent per year, whereas in the decades following the Civil War the rate of growth in the labor supply fell to 2.7 percent per year.[1]

[1]See Stanley Lebergott, *Manpower in Economic Growth: The American Record Since 1800* (New York: McGraw-Hill, 1964), p. 18.

Immigration

Note, in Figure 4.1, how closely the waves of immigration coincide with economic "good times" in the United States. The dark bands in the figure represent business depressions. During those periods potential immigrants looking for a better standard of living found no incentive to uproot their families, because prospects of finding employment in America were dim.

Natural Increase

It is not so obvious why the birth rate of the resident population also decreased toward the end of the half century between the Civil War and World War I. Economic analysis may provide part of the reason: This was a time of **urbanization**. All across the nation farm families were packing up and moving to the city, lured by good wages in the developing industries. Women, too, increasingly found opportunities to work outside the home. Living on a farm, children could begin at a very early age to help with the chores; but children were less useful in the cities and more costly to raise. The net result of the higher relative price for children was a lowered birth rate.

Supply and Demand for Slave Labor

On the issue of slave labor, we again find that the tools of supply and demand yield helpful insights. Certainly the price of slaves was directly related to the supply and demand for cotton. As the price of cotton increased, so too did the price of slaves, for, after all, the demand for labor is derived from demand for the product of that labor.

Some historians have argued that on the eve of the Civil War slavery was dying out, that it was proving unprofitable and so would have ended even without the conflict between North and South. But recent evidence indicates that this was not true. Slavery was never justifiable ethically or morally. Economically, how-

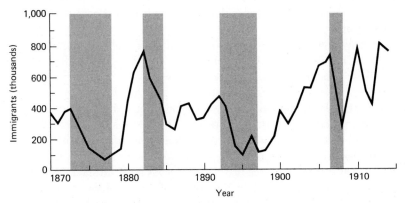

Figure 4.1 Immigration into the United States. [*Source:* Simon Kuznets and E. Rubin, *Immigration and the Foreign Born* (New York: National Bureau of Economic Research, 1954), p. 95.]

ever, it would presumably have continued because it was in line with the laws of economics—the laws of the marketplace.

The Background   For almost the full first century after the settlements in mainland North America, slavery was relatively unimportant. More than 90 percent of all blacks taken as slaves from Africa went to South America (mainly Brazil) and the Caribbean islands. Most were engaged in sugar production. In contrast, before 1730 there were fewer than 100,000 slaves in all of the 13 American colonies.

Between 1730 and the time of the Revolution, however, that number doubled and more than doubled again. The discovery that tobacco would grow well in Maryland and Virginia created a demand for large numbers of unskilled workers to cultivate many acres of land. The same held true for growing rice and indigo in South Carolina.

The Dutch were the first to develop the slave trade with the American colonies, but England soon joined in. Slave investments returned higher profits than their next best substitute, indentured servants.

The southern contribution to total exports remained high until right after the Revolution. It then fell sharply until, after 1800, cotton became king of the South. In 1788, when the Constitution was being written, the founding fathers had agreed, as part of a great compromise, to end the import of slaves. Accordingly, slave trade became illegal after 1808. The demand for slaves temporarily stagnated but it soon recovered with the demand for cotton. Slavery declined in the North but throve in the South.

Not Everyone Was a Slave Owner   Although there were many more slave owners in the South than in the North, it was far from true that most whites in the South had slaves. At the start of the Civil War there were 1.4 million free families in the southern states. Of these, some 380,000 owned slaves, which means that only about *one fourth of all southern white families were slaveholders.* Of this group, moreover, fewer than one fourth held ten or more slaves, which means that not even 4 percent of the southern white families worked ten or more slaves on their farms. This 4 percent held more than three fourths of the total number of slaves at that time.

Hence, slavery was not the pervasive institution it is often thought to have been in the pre-Civil War South. However, those who held power in the southern states were likely to be the owners of slaves, because slaves were a significant part of southern wealth. It is therefore understandable that any threats by the North to emancipate the blacks met with vigorous opposition from the South.

What about the theory that before the Civil War slaves seemed to be unprofitable and less productive than free workers, and that the institution of slavery would have died of its own accord? If we examine what was actually happening there at that time, we see that the South was far from stagnating. Table 4.2 shows that per capita income in the South, although more unequally distributed, was certainly not much lower than the national average, and it was much higher in some places, such as in the West-South-Central area. It was also

Table 4.2 PER CAPITA INCOME BEFORE THE CIVIL WAR
1860 Prices

	Total Population		Free Population	
	1840	1860	1840	1860
National average	$ 96	$128	$109	$144
North	109	141	110	142
Northeast	129	181	130	183
North Central	65	89	66	90
South	74	103	105	150
South Atlantic	66	84	96	124
East-South-Central	69	89	92	124
West-South-Central	151	184	238	274

Source: Robert W. Fogel and Stanley L. Engerman, "The Economics of Slavery," in *The Reinterpretation of American Economic History* (New York: Harper & Row, 1971), Table 8, p. 335.

higher in all cases compared with the North Central region of the United States, a region that historians customarily cite as having had a high standard of living at that time. If we consider the per capita income of only the free population in the South, we see that in 1840 and 1860 it exceeded the national average.

Moreover, the South certainly was not declining in terms of economic growth rate. Per capita income grew at an average rate of 1.7 percent a year, which exceeded the national average of 1.3 percent; it also exceeded the growth rate of the North Central states. The South was thriving, and its inhabitants anticipated that things would continue to improve. Table 4.3 shows that throughout this period, the price of slaves increased, indicating their rising economic value to southern plantation owners.

Slaves: A Profitable Investment   Until quite recently, some historians hypothesized that by the end of the 1850s slave owners were losing money on their investment in slaves. To understand how the price of slaves was determined, we have to view them as a **capital investment**.[2] That is, the potential owner would decide how much to pay for a slave by determining the current value of the slave's *future* net income.

Slaves provided owners with a stream of income. This income was the value of the product that the slave produced for the owner minus the cost of the slave's maintenance. For example, a slave could help the owner increase his annual cotton production by, say, 15 bales of cotton. Let's say that those bales could be sold in the open market for 10 cents a pound, or $10 a bale. This would mean that the total revenues of the plantation owner would go up by $150 if he employed this additional slave. We cannot accept this figure as the first year's net revenues on the slave purchase, because we have to subtract the cost of maintaining the slave, say $25 per year. The net profit to the owner from having the slave

[2]A slave, although treated as labor in this section, is like a capital investment from the decision makers' perspective. For example, if slave maintenance costs (input) fell or if demand for cotton (output) rose, demand for slaves would rise.

Table 4.3   SLAVE PRICES IN THE UPPER AND LOWER SOUTH
There was a gradual increase in the price of slaves for the period from 1830 to the Civil War. Just prior to the War prices in the lower South peaked at $1,658.

| | Price | |
Period	Upper South	Lower South
1830–1835	$ 521	$ 948
1836–1840	957	
1841–1845	529	722
1846–1850	709	926
1851–1855	935	1,240
1856–1860	1,294	1,658

Source: R. Evans, Jr., "The Economics of America Negro Slavery," in *Aspects of Labor Economics* (Princeton, N.J.: Princeton University Press, 1962), p. 216.

would then be $125 per year, and it would continue over the expected lifetime of the slave.

This stream of net earnings (properly accounting for the fact that some of it occurred in later years) was a function mainly of the price of cotton and the productivity of slaves minus maintenance costs. Putting aside the question of productivity for the moment, we look at the prices of cotton and find they were, for the most part, either stable or rising. Slave owners anticipated that these prices would continue to be high well into the future, so on the eve of the Civil War they were far from pessimistic about the profitability of slavery.

Figure 4.2, which shows the real price of raw cotton in cents per pound, corrected for general changes in the price level, clearly supports this view. The price grew from 7.4 cents in 1840 to 12.4 cents in 1850, then fell during the first few years of that decade but started to rise again in 1857. Any drop in the price of cotton was viewed as temporary by plantation owners, but the price they were willing to pay for slaves fluctuated in step with their estimates of the immediate

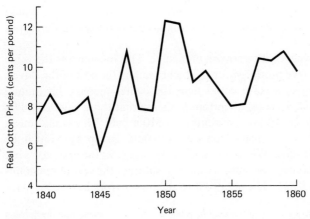

Figure 4.2   Real price of raw cotton, 1840–1860. [*Source:* Robert W. Fogel and Stanley L. Engerman, *The Reinterpretation of Economic History* (New York: Harper & Row, 1971), Table 2, p. 317.]

cotton market. The price of slaves in the upper South, for example, was only $521 during 1830–1835, but by 1856 it had risen to over $1,200. In the lower South in 1860, a prime slave might fetch $1,800. Table 4.3 shows the prices of slaves as five-year averages.

What does all this have to do with the profitability of slavery? Correctly interpreted, these data show that slaveholding compared favorably with any other capital investment available to southerners during the period from 1830 to 1860. In the lower South, for example, it yielded a 12 percent rate of return during the period 1830–1835, falling to about 10 percent on the eve of the Civil War. This was at least as high a yield as prevailed elsewhere in the economy. As long as the rate of return on investment in slavery was as good as or better than the rates of return in other capital investments, we would expect the institution of slavery to expand, which is exactly what happened.

Was Slavery on the Way Out?   We have seen, then, that on the eve of the Civil War slavery was well established in the South. But would it have remained so, indefinitely, had there been no war?

Slavery was certainly a good investment for southern plantations so long as the value of the slaves' output exceeded the costs of their reproduction and maintenance. It might have remained so, on a narrower scale, even if plantation labor had become temporarily less profitable. Some important developments during this period, however, tended to diminish the productive value of slaves. In the world markets, India and Egypt were increasingly competing with long-staple cotton exports. Moreover, voices were being raised, not only in the North, but throughout the world, against the institution of slavery itself.

Recalling these facts, we may well ponder whether slavery would not have died out of its own accord sometime late in the nineteenth century. But emancipation was certainly hastened by the Civil War, which, although not begun as a war to end slavery, did bring about its demise in North America.

Postbellum Black Migration

The Emancipation Proclamation signed by Abraham Lincoln on September 22, 1862, stated in part that

> all persons held as slaves within any State . . . the people whereof shall then be in rebellion against the United States shall be then, thenceforward, and forever free; and the executive government of the United States . . . will do no act or acts to repress such persons . . . in any efforts they may make for their actual freedom.

A large proportion of the American labor force in the final decades of the 1800s consisted of slaves who had been abruptly freed in 1862. Yet for half a century after the Civil War emancipation caused no great change in the location of the four million freed workers.

Exslaves were at liberty to move wherever they chose, but until the beginning of World War I very few migrated northward.

By 1916, however, the trickle of black migration to the North became a flood as southern blacks undertook a mass exodus unprecedented in the nation's history. In 1900 only 23 percent of blacks lived in urban areas; barely a half century later 60 percent were urban. Not surprisingly, almost all the movement was toward the war-stimulated industrial cities. The 1920 census revealed that almost three fourths of northern blacks lived in the ten industrial centers of the nation, including New York, Chicago, St. Louis, Pittsburgh, and Kansas City. By the time of the Great Depression (1929) more than 50 percent of the blacks in New York, Chicago, Philadelphia, Washington, Detroit, Memphis, St. Louis, Cleveland, and Pittsburgh had been born in some other state. Detroit, for example, had more blacks from Georgia than did Augusta or Macon. Chicago had as many Mississippi-born blacks as the entire black population in Vicksburg, Meridian, Greenville, and Natchez.

Was it mere chance that the start of World War I signaled the start of black migration? Perhaps; but there is another explanation. It involves two aspects of the war and another element unrelated to it. On the one hand, the war caused a greater demand for workers at the very time that immigration from Europe was decreasing sharply. On the other hand, cotton crops in the South were suffering an invasion by the boll weevil, which destroyed much of the yearly cotton crop. Table 4.4 shows the havoc wrought by the insidious pest.

Like the European immigrants before them, the blacks moved north primarily for one reason: to achieve higher incomes and higher material standards of living. Just before our entry into World War I, blacks had been earning 10–15 cents an hour in the South. Soon they heard that northern employers were willing to pay 30 and even 40 cents an hour. The prospect was alluring; but what about the costs of pulling up roots?

Costs of Migration   As in any other economic decision, costs must be assessed relative to potential benefits. For migration, the most obvious cost is for transportation. By the time of the war, the railroad linked almost all parts of the nation, greatly reducing costs. The fixed price of a railroad ticket was now the known cost for traveling. After that would come the matter of searching for a job on arrival in the city. The job search cost could be high if, in fact, the migrant were to remain out of work for long. At the time, however, migrants generally felt assured that they would find work immediately on arrival.

The cost of setting up a new household in a strange city and of dismantling the old home was yet another consideration. And not only economics was involved—there was the pain of leaving old friends, the effort of making new ones, the separation from relatives left behind. In the economic decision, then, the total of these anticipated migration costs had to be weighed against the anticipated stream of lifetime benefits.[3]

[3]One reason blacks did not move North for 60 years after their emancipation is that they moved *within* the South to enhance their level of satisfaction. For a formal discussion see Graves, Sexton, and Vedder, "Slavery and Factor Price Equalization: A Note on Migration and Freedom," *Explorations in Economic History* 20 (April 1983): 156–162.

Table 4.4 BOLL WEEVIL DESTRUCTION, 1911–1925

The percentage of reduction in full yield per acre of cotton due to the boll weevil rose dramatically during World War I and a few years thereafter, reducing the profitability of cotton growing for many rural blacks (and whites).

Year	Reduction in Yield/Acre of Cotton Due to Boll Weevil (%)
1911	1.3
1912	3.3
1913	6.7
1914	5.9
1915	9.9
1916	13.4
1917	9.3
1918	5.8
1919	13.2
1920	19.9
1921	31.0
1922	24.2
1923	19.5
1924	8.0
1925	4.1

Source: U.S. Department of Agriculture, Statistical Bulletin No. 99, Table 52, p. 67.

Labor Raids The blacks had good reason to believe that they could obtain instant work in the North at higher wages, for northern labor contractors were swarming through the countryside offering to pay the cost of transfer to the North. Whites in the South were annoyed by this raiding of their labor. Various state and local southern governments passed ordinances to prevent this practice: The raiders could be fined or imprisoned for "enticing" a laborer to leave his job. Other states exacted heavy license taxes from the agents. So pressing was the northern demand for labor, however, that four agents found it profitable to pay $1,000 each for licenses in order to continue operating in Birmingham, Alabama.

The Effects of Immigration Laws For decades before the First World War the industrial economy in the North had been expanding. But in those years the demand for labor had been satisfied by Europeans arriving through wide-open doors. Figure 4.1 shows that immigration under the liberal laws sometimes reached as high as 1.28 million people in a single year. More than 12 million newcomers found their way to the United States during the first 14 years of the twentieth century.

This influx stopped abruptly when America entered the war and immigrants, now suspect, were subjected to more careful scrutiny, including literacy tests. In 1915 the number of immigrants was one third that of 1914, and in 1916 only one fourth. In 1918 a mere 110,618 foreigners came to the United States, while 94,585 chose to leave that year. The flow of relatively cheap foreign labor had been effectively shut off, precisely at the time when industry's need for labor peaked. Blacks and other low-skilled laborers found unprecedented opportunities as the North knuckled down to meet the demands first of a war-ravaged Old World and then of America itself.

DEFINITIONS OF NEW TERMS

PARTICIPATION RATE   Participation rate is the percentage of the working-age population in the labor force or the percentage of a specific group employed.

COLLECTIVE BARGAINING   Negotiations between management of a company or of a group of companies and management of a union or a group of unions for the purpose of arriving at a mutually agreeable contract establishing wages, fringe benefits, and working conditions for all employees in the union(s) are known as collective bargaining.

CRAFT UNIONS   Craft unions consist of workers who, like printers, bakers, or shoemakers, have one particular skill.

INDUSTRIAL UNIONS   Organizations of workers in an entire industry irrespective of their particular job classification, such as the United Auto Workers, are industrial unions.

RIGHT-TO-WORK LAW   A right-to-work law is one that makes it illegal to require union membership as a condition of employment in an individual shop.

MARGINAL WORKERS   Marginal workers are those whose output is barely equal in value to what they are paid.

URBANIZATION   When a larger fraction of the total population lives in towns and cities (urban centers), there is said to be urbanization.

CAPITAL INVESTMENT   Capital investment is investment in a productive asset, that is, an asset that will yield a stream of income in the future. The purchase of a slave was a capital investment.

The Industrial Unionist

JOHN L. LEWIS
(1880–1969)

President, United Mine Workers, 1920–1960

"I have never faltered or failed to present the cause or plead the case of the mine workers of this country. I have pleaded your case not in the wavering tones of a mendicant seeking alms, but in the thundering voice of the captain of a mighty host, demanding the rights to which free men are entitled."

These dramatic words from John L. Lewis were a combined program, epitaph, rallying call, and challenge to business management, consumers, and presidents alike. During his 40 years as president of the United Mine Workers (UMW) and as the major spokesman for industrial unionism in an era of increasing consolidation between craft and industrial unions, Lewis ran the United Mine Workers with absolute control. He brought the union to prominence in the American Federation of Labor, formed the Congress of Industrial Organizations (CIO) and broke with the American Federation of Labor (AFL), then returned to the AFL, and eventually forced the union to stand on its own for the 20 years before his death.

Industrial unionism received its greatest push during the early 1930s. The combined effects of the Depression and the increased numbers of unskilled and semiskilled workers in most American industries presented a serious challenge to the craft union doctrine of the AFL, founded by Samuel Gompers. It became evident to men such as Lewis that it was no longer valid to base union solidarity and bargaining positions on skills, irrespective of industry; he believed strongly that it was important instead to organize unions within specific industries, drawing the membership from as wide a basis within the industry as possible.

One of the major "advantages" of the tactic is the crippling effects of a strike within the industry. And through the late 1940s and into the early 1950s, Lewis led some of the most economically dangerous and emphatically effective strikes in American history.

53

Lewis was born to Welsh immigrant parents in Iowa in 1880. His father was a miner and a strong trade unionist. Along with some of his brothers. Lewis entered the mines at the age of 15, after leaving the only formal schooling he would receive. Six years later he traveled in the western United States, working in various mines and learning about the mining industry. Lewis eventually became one of America's foremost experts on the coal mining industry, and almost all of his expertise was the result of his own reading and study. Upon returning to Iowa, he joined the UMW local and began extensive work in the union leadership.

He came to the attention of Samuel Gompers and in 1911 was named a field agent of the American Federation of Labor. While traveling widely throughout the United States, he rose in the UMW ranks, becoming president of the union in 1920.

Lewis had his first of many confrontations with the federal government during World War I, while serving on the National Defense Council; in that position, he opposed government operation of the mines, a controversial question he was to take on again 25 years later.

The AFL convention in 1935 was torn by the economic troubles of the country and the internal disagreement between the trade and craft unions. In a dramatic walkout, Lewis joined with several other trade unionists to form the Congress of Industrial Organizations, leaving the AFL to the craft unionists. The momentum behind Lewis's move resulted in several important gains for his union and for labor at large.

In 1933 he had successfully fought for the passage of Section 7a of the National Industrial Recovery Act, which provided workers with almost complete freedom to choose representatives of their own choice for collective bargaining purposes. In addition to its effect on the total strength of the labor movement, the provision weakened the ability of the present union leadership to retain control.

He eventually organized four million workers into the CIO. The early years of the organization, of which the UMW was the core, were marked by violent strikes, one of which drew sharp criticism for both sides from Franklin Roosevelt. Up to that time, FDR had received Lewis's personal and organizational backing. "It ill behooves one who has supped at labor's table and who has been sheltered in labor's house to curse with equal fervor and fine impartiality both labor and its adversaries when they become locked in deadly embrace," declaimed Lewis. After that Lewis and Roosevelt were on strained terms, culminating in Lewis's support for Wendell Wilkie for president in 1940.

Lewis resigned as president of the CIO in 1942 and pulled the UMW out of the organization. He returned to the AFL for a period of less than two years before taking the United Mine Workers down its own road. In 1955 the AFL and CIO merged without the participation of the man who had had a significant impact on the histories of both organizations.

Lewis's direction of the UMW was based on an "all the wagons in a circle" approach to confrontation with the government. "It is better to have half a million men working at good wages and high standards of living than to have a million working in poverty." (Lewis certainly knew that the law of demand applied to coal miners, too.)

His program to improve the wages and living conditions of his membership was based on his skillful ability to turn potential crises to his advantage. During the 1950s increases in automation in mining were threatening to cut his membership; but automation was needed if coal was to remain competitive with oil and natural gas. He obtained a contract agreement that placed a royalty on mined coal. The royalty was channeled into the union's pension fund, eventually boosting its value above $170 million.

Probably Lewis's most trying years were those of the Truman administration, as he attempted to lead strikes in both the soft and hard coal industries in the face of court injunctions. Truman seized the mines and had them worked by federal troops, but Lewis eventually received the settlement he wanted. He ran up more than $2.1 million in strike fines, however, and probably damaged the competitive position of the industry.

One of his major achievements was the 1952 Federal Mine Safety Act, the first of its kind in the United States. His dramatic appearance at the site of a mining disaster in 1951 provided a strong push for the act in Congress. Also during the 1950s he won extremely favorable settlements, including payment for underground travel time.

After his semiretirement in 1960, the UMW fell on hard times. Under the leadership of Tony Boyle, the union suffered through a membership slowdown, and then was subject to a series of government investigations into corruption and the murder of a candidate for Boyle's office.

Two weeks before he died, Lewis was called on by Ralph Nader and other concerned observers to rescue the union from Boyle's heavy-handed policies. But Lewis was too old, and there was a conflict of interest inherent in the situation; Boyle was a devoted disciple of Lewis and held his position partly through Lewis's influence in the union.

Lewis's tenure as a major influence in American labor was rivaled by few men in its length and probably by no man in its power. His commitment to his union's membership and its needs was single-minded. When he died, the miners closed the mines in memory of him, as they had done many times in response to his call to strike.

chapter 5

Land and Capital

In its narrowest definition, land is assuredly in fixed supply. Surface land can never be increased except in comparatively tiny increments through landfills, the draining of swamps, or the diking of tidelands. But, as we saw earlier, the economist takes a broader vision of land. In economic terms, land includes not only the surface on which we walk and live, but the whole gamut of raw materials that the earth contains in their natural state: minerals, forests and timber, prairies and grazing land, lakes and rivers. All are part of the factor land, and all are in more or less limited supply.

So policymakers must decide how best to use not only the surface area itself, but also the products it is able to supply. How can that supply be best allocated to meet demands ranging from airports to farming, from condominium sites to pineapple plantations to wilderness areas?

Once more we find the answer in the laws of supply and demand: If farming were to become more profitable tomorrow than it is today, we would expect more land to be farmed and less to be reserved for recreation. In other words, the land will be used for whatever production yields the highest income to its owners. The income received by landowners, for whatever purpose, is termed **rent.**

Like any other resource, land is subject to a price that varies according to the supply available and the profitability of the uses to which it can be put. An immense supply of land is available in the middle of a desert, but its uses are few. In contrast, a square block in the middle of New York City may command an astronomical price as the site of a high-rise office building to accommodate hundreds of businesses and thousands of workers. Its *use value* and demand are extremely high; therefore, the rent to its owners will be comparably high.

Clearly, then, the demand for land is determined by the demand for the final product that its use can provide. Like the demand for labor, it is derived from the demand for the final product. In the case of an office building, the final product will be whatever goods and services are provided by companies operating in the building. In the case of agricultural land, it will be the crops or livestock or other produce raised there. In either case, as the market prices of the relevant goods and services rise or fall, the demand for the land will rise or fall. This relationship is known as **derived demand** for the land. The same applies to labor. Labor is hired because it produces something that some consumers want to buy. Land is bought or rented because it produces goods that will sell in the market.

CAPITAL: SUPPLY AND DEMAND

You will recall that capital (like land) is broadly defined by economists. Capital refers to all the manufactured objects used in the actual production of goods and services: typewriters and carpenters' tool kits, drill presses and computers, medical supplies and books, safes, and even office furniture and the buildings that house them all. This comprehensive view of capital is often summed up in the alternative terms *capital goods* or *producer goods.*

We have just seen that land produces for its owners a return called rent. Similarly, capital produces for *its* owners a return called *interest.* The interest rate is the price paid by producers for the use of someone's capital goods. Like the rental rate of land, the interest rate for capital varies under the fluctuating pressures of supply and demand.

To keep the supply of capital constant or increasing, a producer must take into account two characteristics of most capital goods. First, these goods wear out, or **depreciate,** and must be replaced after some interval. Second, many of the large items will not be available on someone's shelf. New machines, or specially designed machines, must often be ordered well ahead of the need for them. In any case, the quantity of capital goods ordered or immediately at hand will depend on how manufacturers and producers view the economy. If business is booming and the future looks promising, more orders will be placed and the demand for capital goods will increase. The quantity supplied will then keep pace by rising as well, in response to those familiar economic laws.

Land and the Shaping of the Nation

We now examine the way land, as a factor of production, has influenced the nature of the country we live in. America after the Revolution comprised a mass of land extending from the Atlantic Coast to the Mississippi River and from the Great Lakes to, but not including, Florida. The last of the former colonies to cede its land rights to the federal government was Georgia, which in 1802 relinquished its claim to western lands. From that time, the frontier continued to push westward until the present shape of the nation was finally established, in 1959, with the annexation of Hawaii.

How have these vast acquisitions affected our national economy? What was the impact on land use when, following the Civil War, labor shifted out of southern agriculture and into northern manufacturing? Does society benefit from urbanization? What are the costs of large urban centers? These questions and more will be examined in the following pages.

Improving the Land

The early westward movement continued when the Republic of Texas joined the states in 1845; the Oregon Territory became part of the United States in 1846; and two years later the Mexican Secession gave America even more land in the West and Southwest. These additional lands amounted to 70 percent more territory.

It was, of course, this rich abundance of land that saved America from the specter that occasionally haunted European nations—the fear that increasing population would overcrowd and overwork the soil until the productivity of an additional worker would fall to zero. The United States had always had new land to ease the population pressure and lower the labor-to-land ratio.

Yet land that is idle or in isolation is useless. Only when it is *improved* can it increase the productive capacity of the nation; so improving the land was a vital task, especially for a nation of individuals striving for higher standards of living. At the end of the Civil War, this 70 percent increase in the national domain was virtually uninhabited by whites. During the next 50 years, however, the frontier disappeared.

Disposal of the Public Domain

It was the intention of the federal government to facilitate westward migration through the distribution of public lands. Many different land policies were used by the federal government, and the goal of easing access to public land was achieved by reducing the minimum-size plot of land the government sold and by lowering the per acre price. In 1862 the cash requirement for buying remote, unsettled land fell to zero with the passage of the Homestead Act.

For the most part the Homestead Act was impractical economically, because the land of the Great Plains and mountain states was suitable only for the production of livestock, and raising cattle required much more land than the 160 acres provided by the government (or a 320-acre tract for a married couple). Furthermore, land speculators, mining companies, and lumber companies wanted to expand their holdings with as little outlay as possible. At the behest of special interest groups in the West, Congress passed four more land acts:

1. *The Timber-Culture Act of 1873:* This law, passed ostensibly to encourage the growth of timber in arid regions, made available 160 acres of free land to anyone who would agree to plant trees on 40 acres of it.
2. *The Desert Land Act of 1877:* By the terms of this law, 640 acres at $1.25 an acre could be purchased by anyone who would agree to irrigate the land within three years. (The serious defect of this act was that there were no clearly defined stipulations as to what constituted irrigation.)

3. *The Timber and Stone Act of 1878:* This statute provided for the sale at $2.50 an acre of valuable timber and stone lands in Nevada, California, Oregon, and Washington.
4. *The Timber-Cutting Act of 1878:* This law authorized residents of certain specified areas to cut trees on government lands without charge, with the stipulation that the timber be used for agricultural, mining, and domestic building purposes.

After 1904 U.S. land policy became less generous, but by that time nearly all the choice agricultural land, most of the first-rate mineral land, and much of the timberland located close to market centers had been disposed of. Between 1904 and 1920 about 100 million acres of land were homesteaded in the dry and mountainous sections. During this same short period, the government reserved about 175 million acres. Of the original public domain, 200 million acres of land that were yet to be disposed of were officially vacant in 1920.[1]

The outstanding feature of American land policy was the rapidity with which valuable agricultural, mineral, and timberlands were put into private hands. During the nineteenth century, the goal of making a piece of ground available to anyone who wanted it was largely achieved. In the process, great tracts of land fell into the hands of corporations and wealthy individuals. In the case of railroad grants, the disposal of land to powerful business interests was considered public policy. Large grants to the states for educational purposes could be justified, even though the politically favored often purchased them advantageously. But much good land was obtained fraudulently by mining and lumber companies and by speculators. Aided by the lax administration of the land laws, large operators could persuade individuals to make a homesteading entry or a purchase at a minimum price and then transfer the title for a song. With the connivance of land officials, entries were made for people who did not even exist. Some cheating was inevitable, however, and although the injustice of it rankles, it is not on a basis of fairness to individuals that we can decide whether American land policy was good or bad. Rather we must focus on the direct effects of American land policy on economic efficiency.

For at least the last half century the emerging consensus among American historians has been that federal land policy was economically inefficient. Moreover, because people of all sorts and conditions settled on the land, there was a high rate of failure among the least competent, who lost their holdings and became either poor tenants or low-paid farm workers. More important, the rapid distribution of the public domain, it is alleged, laid the groundwork for modern agricultural problems by inducing too much capital and labor into agriculture. As a consequence of this excessive allocation of resources to agriculture, after the Civil War the new West began to produce commercial crops at such a rate that they could not be purchased at prices that covered their costs to most farmers. The result was a 30-year period of falling prices and languishing income per farm unit.

[1]Homestead entries were substantial in the 1920s and 1930s. Since 1949, they have decreased until they are practically nonexistent, although just over 159 million acres of the public domain remained technically vacant at the end of 1970. In Alaska, there is presently some homesteading on federal and state-owned lands.

The Rise of Cities

Far more important than land availability to the rise of cities was the rise of productivity in agriculture. Whereas in colonial times nearly 90 percent of the population was engaged in agricultural activities, by 1860 this figure had fallen to 60 percent, by 1880 to 50 percent, by 1900 to 38 percent, and almost to 3% today. In spite of this percentage decline of the agricultural labor force, there were tremendous gains in total output. Up until 1920, both acreage and the absolute numbers of people engaged in agriculture increased; productivity per worker also rose dramatically; but this early period was still one of *absolute* growth, both of workers and of output, in the farming sector.

By the end of the nineteenth century there was little frontier left. The amount of land in cultivation doubled after the Civil War. The expansion in agricultural output was not as rapid as in industry, but it grew faster than before the Civil War. Two factors accounted for this expansion, the most obvious being the physical extension of cultivated land. Also important was increased productivity, the rise of output relative to the inputs of land, labor, and capital. Although productivity change in agriculture was less rapid than in manufacturing, it accounted for perhaps 40 percent of the increase in total farm output, and agricultural productivity in the last half of the century advanced at a pace several times higher than it had in the first half. This was the age of the mechanical reaper, the horse-drawn cultivator, and the improved harrow; the age, as the fortunes of Cyrus McCormick attest, of rapid expansion in the agricultural implement industry.

Of course, many of the advances in agriculture were unquestionably linked to improved transportation, particularly to the railroads. It was only with the extension of the rail network that farming moved westward to the fertile new lands in Nebraska, Kansas, Texas, Oklahoma, the Dakotas, and the Far West.

Land Use: Farm or Factory?

The half century after the Civil War and before World War I brought to the United States not only rapid economic growth, large increases in population, and westward movement, but also unprecedented change in the structure of the entire economy. We alluded briefly to some of these changes in earlier chapters. Now we deal in more detail with the problems posed by the rise of cities, by the massive concentration of industrial power, and by the vast changes in the agricultural sector. These trends and their complex results continue into our day.

As shown in Figure 5.1, only about one fourth of the population lived in cities of 2,500 or more as the Civil War drew to a close. Fifty years later, almost half the entire population was crowded into cities, and by the end of World War I there were more city dwellers than country folks. Of course, this does not mean that all cities were large. Not until recently has the population concentrated into what we consider major cities in the nation. In 1870, for example, of the 663 total cities, almost 500 had populations of less than 10,000. Even by 1910, 1,665 cities of the total 2,262 had populations of less than 10,000. Before assessing the

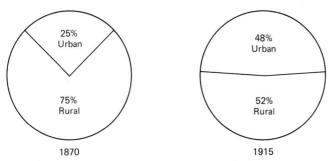

Figure 5.1   The rush to the cities. (*Source*: U.S. Bureau of the Census.)

problems that the city dweller of the past faced, let us consider some of the reasons cities exist in the first place.

The Economics of City Formation

It is not accidental that many major cities are located near areas of significant mineral deposits or natural resources, or in areas that can be easily serviced by natural transportation networks. There are many *natural* reasons why cities are located where they are. Cities serve as focal points for commerce and in some cases extractive industry (mining). Also, concentration of industry allows for decreased costs of production. This is because many more interactions between firms are possible; if the firms were spread out, they would have to engage in extensive long-distance communication and transportation in order to trade. When they concentrate in one region, they save on many of these costs. Furthermore, a concentration of production will generally lead to what are called **economies of scale.** That is, firms that can obtain sufficient levels of production will find that their average costs fall, often because of factors associated with mass production, such as assembly lines.

In addition, the concentration of people and resources in the city allows for more efficient provision of such public services as education, fire and police protection, potable water, and improved sewer systems.

A Hierarchy of Cities   Prior to the Civil War most cities had been retail trade centers. It was only after the war that many of them became oriented toward manufacturing. As manufacturing grew from barely one third of commodity output in 1860 to over one half in 1900, it was predictable that industries would congregate in certain limited areas, and indeed they did.

The hierarchy of cities that took form remains with us today. Its most basic characteristics are listed in Table 5.1. By 1890 we had indeed reached the era of big cities. New York, Chicago, Philadelphia, Boston—all had their special characteristics and their special brands of vice and social discord: tuberculosis, slums, crime, pollution, and corruption. At that time the top ten cities were also the big manufacturing centers. They accounted for more than 40 percent of all manufac-

Table 5.1

City Size	Characteristics
2,500–10,000	Mainly trading centers; the reduction in costs is enough to induce people to drive short distances in from the countryside; total demand is not high enough to warrant the provision of specialized services
10,000–50,000	Still mainly trading centers, but certain specialized services, such as stock brokerage, might be provided
50,000–250,000	Still commercial trading, plus increasing specialized services: stock brokers, insurance salesmen, more specialized doctors
250,000 and more (major urban centers)	Commercial trading; specialized services now extend to such amenities as operas, orchestras, and gourmet food

turing output and were the focal points of commerce, finance, and communications.

Businesses in the growing cities flourished to the extent that land values for inner-city properties could double almost overnight. In Chicago the value of such property rose by more than 700 percent between 1873 and 1910.

A Struggle for Life   While industry was profiting, however, and perhaps providing higher real living standards for the nation at large, the populations compressed into urban areas were paying a price. By 1860 it had become far safer to live on a farm than to reside in the city: The death rate per 1,000 in the countryside was about 20, as compared to about 30 in the large city. What did people die of in the city? Mainly communicable diseases: diphtheria, tuberculosis, and the like. They drank foul water from wells polluted by improper and unsafe sewage systems, hence they contracted typhoid and dysentery. Because they were unable to obtain as much fresh food as people who lived in rural areas, their diet was not as healthy.

These conditions changed with passing decades, as rising real incomes enabled people to demand better health conditions. They were now willing and able to pay for better diets, which lowered morbidity rates. They could also afford more spacious housing. In addition, purification of water, improved sewage disposal, regular garbage collection, and swamp draining became more common. As a result, the health of urban dwellers was considerably improved by the eve of World War I. Problems remained, as they do to this day. Nevertheless, the benefits of urban living apparently outweighed the costs, and cities continued to grow.

The most obvious benefit, of course, was the higher wages obtainable there. Uncorrected for the higher level of skill required of city workers, real wages were double those in the countryside. Urban residents enjoyed more mobility as improved intraurban trolley lines gave them access to the other advantages the city had to offer—museums, theaters, and sports events. Life in the country must have seemed dull indeed when compared to the diversified life-styles possible in New York, Chicago, New Orleans, Miami, San Francisco, and, to a lesser degree, places such as Austin, Sacramento, Gainesville, and Burlingame.

Apparently it still does, for on the whole, workers continue to throng to cities despite their crowding and attendant drawbacks, such as poverty, ghetto living, and deteriorating housing and air. These are the costs of city living, to be set against the lure of greater earning potential and the greater opportunities for enjoyment that come only with sizable demand. Few towns of 5,000 provide a symphony orchestra—or even a choice of movies.

Physical and Human Capital in the American Economy

As mentioned in Chapter 2, physical capital was limited in the colonial period, especially in the seventeenth century. Since wood was in abundant supply, much of the physical capital was produced by using this relatively inexpensive resource. Wood was used in the production of houses, barns, wagons, wheels, wharfs, ships, and shipyards. Conversely, metal products were scarce and expensive and consequently were used sparingly. For the most part, capital formation was a formidable challenge to the colonists, and the American colonies had a difficult time attracting investments in capital at home and abroad.

The nineteenth century witnessed a sharp acceleration in **capital formation,** that is, in additions to the stock of capital. The increases in capital formation were for the most part a result of increases in investment demand, and accompanying the increases in investment demand was the rise in the **capital-output ratio.** For example, if the capital-output ratio is 2:1, then two units of additional capital will yield one additional unit of output. Two sectors with high capital-output ratios in the nineteenth century were housing and railroads. In fact, the railroads accounted for at least 15–20 percent of gross capital formation in the 1870s and 1880s. There were also increases in the capital-output ratios in agriculture, "light" industries (textiles), and "heavy" industries (iron and steel). Part of the explanation for the rise in the capital-output ratio was the declining relative price of capital. The capital-to-labor ratio increased markedly between 1840 and 1910, and the amount of capital per worker was roughly seven times greater in 1840 than in 1920. In other words, the economy had become more capital intensive.

However, the growth of the labor force was the most important input leading to economic growth in the 80 years following 1840, while the growth of capital stock was the second leading factor and assumed increasing significance during the period 1880–1920. The changes in capital formation were in part a result of the structural changes that occurred in the postbellum economy. Let's examine some of those changes.

Structural Change

By the end of the Civil War it had become clear that America had shifted once and for all from an agricultural to an industrial economy. The signs had been evident for some time. The whole structure of the economy had been changing

Table 5.2 THE CHANGING COMPOSITION OF COMMODITY OUTPUT

Year	Agriculture	Manufacturing	Mining and Construction
1869	53	33	14
1874	46	39	14
1879	49	37	14
1884	41	44	15
1889	37	48	15
1894	32	53	15
1899	33	53	14

Source: R. E. Gallman, "Commodity Output, 1839–1899," in National Bureau of Economic Research, *Trends in the American Economy in the Nineteenth Century* (Princeton, N.J.: Princeton University Press, 1960), p. 26.

in step with such other developments as a rising standard of living, the thrust of the railroads, the faster pace of life attendant on high finance and improved communications, and the explosive growth of the cities.

Now, in Table 5.2, we see that from 1870 until the end of the century farm produce (while still expanding in absolute quantities) declined as a percentage of total commodity output—from 53 percent in 1870 to 33 percent in 1899—whereas manufacturing followed exactly the opposite course. During that period mining and construction held steady.

Meantime, of course, the surge of manufacturing demanded increasing quantities of capital investment as well as of labor. In 1870 more than half the working population had been engaged in farming, fishing, or mining. Barely one third made their living in those occupations in 1910, and this trend has continued to the present, when little more than 3 percent of our population is engaged in agriculture.

As the population changed occupations it was also changing location. Americans have always been highly mobile, following where economic opportunities beckon. For many, the new West was the place to go, a place of new opportunity, and with them went a corresponding shift in the regional distribution of capital investment.

The Postbellum South: Loss of Income and Capital

Following the Civil War, the southern economy recovered faster in manufacturing than in agriculture, in part because emancipation altered the whole basis of the agricultural society. Manufacturing industry had always been staffed largely by a free white labor force. Thus by 1870 southern manufacturing production had returned almost to its prewar level, and transportation and railroads were also revitalized.

In those postwar years the South was certainly burdened by tragic losses in both men and material goods. Moreover, the changed status of slaves was a cause of social upheaval. The full cost of any war can never be shown in statistics; nevertheless, Table 5.3 shows in rough terms the losses in production suffered by the South. Even after 15 years of postwar recovery, the region's per capita output

Table 5.3 REAL COMMODITY OUTPUT PER CAPITA
1879 dollars

	Outside the South	South
1860	$ 74.8	$77.7
1870	81.5	47.6
1880	105.8	61.5

Source: Stanley L. Engerman, "The Economic Impact of the Civil War," *Explorations in Entrepreneurial History* (Spring 1966), 181.

of commodities was lower than at the War's beginning. In the decade from 1860 to 1870, per capita income outside the South rose by almost 9 percent, whereas income per capita in the South stood at only about 60 percent of its 1860 level.

Of course, much of the South's productive capacity had been destroyed. Nearly 259,000 Confederate soldiers had been killed and another 261,000 wounded. These were almost all men of working age and were a direct loss to the southern labor force. Many were planters or sons of planters, and the loss in entrepreneurial and special human skills, as well as in raw labor, was very high.

How to reorganize the entire agricultural system? How to contend with the social disorganization of a large, politically free, but still economically dependent, black population? Having been freed, many blacks, especially the women and children, abandoned the fields; and males typically chose to work fewer hours. In the cotton belt the overall reduction in labor effort was about 30 percent. Output fell, and the highly efficient plantations became monuments to an extinct social structure.

The Postbellum North and the National Perspective

The North faced no such problems of economic reorganization. Nevertheless, 360,000 Union men had lost their lives and 365,000 had been wounded. The Civil War was more costly in blood and human suffering than any we have ever fought.

In long-term perspective we can view its effects this way. Nationwide, the growth rate of total commodity output from 1859 to 1869 was only 2.0 percent per year, the lowest it had been in decades. The long-term trends show that total commodity output rose at an average annual rate of 4.6 percent between 1840 and 1860, then dropped to an average annual rate of 4.4 percent between 1870 and 1900.

Industrialization, too, lost ground as a result of the War. Although the shift from agriculture to industry continued at the same rate during the two decades after the war as during the two decades preceding it, the **value added** to total output by manufacturing fell from an annual 7 percent before the War to 6 percent annually between 1870 and 1900. In the first decade after the War (1860–1870) the productivity of labor also declined markedly.

In short, that postwar decade marked a sharp departure from the generally rising trends in output, productivity, and income that had formerly prevailed.

This is not surprising, since 15 percent of the nation's labor force of 7.5 million had been involved in the fighting.

Education as Investment

You may not have thought of education as a form of investment, but in economic perspective that is precisely its purpose. When you learn useful facts, you invest in your own future. When the owner of a business trains (educates) a worker, the cost of training is an investment in the firm's productivity. And, like any other investment, education involves a trade-off. You exchange what you would otherwise buy or enjoy today *(present consumption)* for the expectation of better wages or living conditions tomorrow *(future income)*. Economists say that education is an investment in **human capital.** Keep in mind, however, that the costs of education are not only the direct ones (books, tuition, and the like), but also the indirect burden of losing current income. A person going to school is giving up potential working time. This is the opportunity cost, which must always be balanced against the benefits to be gained from investment in human capital.

Looking at the history of the United States during the nineteenth century, we discover the part played by education in developing the national labor force. We find, too, that differences in educational opportunity actually affected the direction and speed of development of the various regions.

Not surprisingly, during that century the South lagged far behind the rest of the nation in providing educational opportunities per capita. It is not certain why the free white population generally fell behind the rest of the nation in literacy. For the slaves who formed a great share of the population, the answer is obvious. Slave owners saw no point in providing formal education for slaves. Cotton was king, and its harvest required no book learning. In some states it was even illegal to educate slaves! For each southern white person, the schools available averaged almost 20 percent fewer than in the North. Based on total populations, almost 50 percent fewer students attended school in the South than in the North.

The picture was far brighter in the nation as a whole. In 1870 almost 90 percent of all adult white Americans could read and write; that figure rose to 96 percent by the beginning of World War I. Meantime, the former slaves were making phenomenal progress educationally. From a literacy rate of only 20 percent in 1870, they raised that level to 70 percent by 1910. Today literacy is expected of every American.

DEFINITIONS OF NEW TERMS

RENT   The income received for the ownership of land is called rent.
DERIVED DEMAND   Derived demand is the demand for a resource that is ultimately based on the demand for a consumer product made by that resource.
DEPRECIATION   Depreciation is the amount of value a resource loses over time (also the process of losing that value).
ECONOMIES OF SCALE   Reductions in the average per unit cost of producing something brought about by producing on a larger scale are economies of scale. Strictly

speaking, economies of scale occur when an increase in all inputs leads to a more than proportionate increase in output.

CAPITAL FORMATION   Capital formation is the addition to productive capacity in the nation. Capital is formed when businesses invest in buildings, machines, and equipment.

CAPITAL-OUTPUT RATIO   The ratio of net investment (that is, after depreciation) to the subsequent increase in output is the capital-output ratio. If the ratio is 2:1, it takes a 2 percent increase in net investment to create a 1 percent increase in final output.

VALUE ADDED   Value added is the total value of output minus the cost of raw materials and intermediate goods included in their production.

HUMAN CAPITAL   Human capital includes those past investments in schooling, on-the-job training, and health care that increase productivity.

The Man and His Reaper

CYRUS HALL MCCORMICK
(1809–1884)

Inventor, Manufacturer, Philanthropist

The year was 1851, the place was London's Crystal Palace, where the Great Industrial Exhibition was being held. The American participants were sad. Many American exhibitors had backed down at the last minute, so that numerous stalls stood unused. And besides a huge quantity of native products on exhibition—tobacco, preserved peaches, and Indian corn—there wasn't much in the way of manufactured products. But then a man on a horse-drawn contraption slowly worked his way to a wheat field at Tip-Tree Farm in Essex. What he did was unbelievable. He harvested the field in a time that no one believed possible: Grain was gathered from 74 yards in 74 seconds, which meant that McCormick's mechanical reaper would clear 20 acres a day. The *Times* (London) declared, "[McCormick's] reaping machine has carried conviction to the heart of the British agriculturist." McCormick's invention had indeed done that. It had already begun to change farming in the United States.

McCormick was born on a farm in Rockbridge County, Virginia. His formal education was limited. It wasn't until the age of 22 that his inventive spirit allowed itself to blossom. He invented and took out a patent for a hillside plow of quite original design. During this same year his father attempted for the twentieth unsuccessful time to perfect a reaping machine and finally abandoned the project; Cyrus decided to take it on. Within a very short period, starting from scratch and avoiding the mistakes his dad made, young Cyrus had a successful invention. The principles contained in his earliest reaper have proved essential to reaping machinery down to the present time. Actually, McCormick's patent, taken out in 1834, was preceded by one entered by Cincinnati's Obed Hussey. For some unknown reason, Hussey moved his plant to Baltimore while McCormick went to Chicago, where he would be closest to the grain country. It was in Chicago that McCormick built his fortune. Here he pioneered installment sales geared to the farmer's own seasons and made it a practice not to sue for overdue payment. Soon McCormick's output rose to 1,000 reapers a year, and his name became synonymous with the product.

By 1860 Cyrus McCormick was a millionaire, but the best was yet to come. During the Civil War, farm machinery sales took off like a rocket.

You'll remember that in the North up to 15 percent of the labor force was involved in the war effort. Young men were taken off the farm. Lincoln's Secretary of War, Edwin M. Stanton, was moved to say in 1861, "Without McCormick's invention, I feel the North could not win." The mechanical reaper was in part responsible for the development of the large-scale farming that we find throughout this nation.

By 1902 the McCormick farm machinery business had sales of $75 million. In that year, through the successful services of J. P. Morgan and company, the McCormick firm and three of the other top industrial firms in the farm machinery business joined forces to become the International Harvester Company, accounting for 85 percent of the machinery used by America's 10 million farmers.

By the turn of the century the reaper originally invented by McCormick permitted one man to harvest as much grain as scores of men in 1840. Food costs were consequently dramatically lowered, benefiting everybody; Cyrus McCormick got rich by performing a useful social purpose.

chapter 6

Entrepreneurship and Technology

A fourth factor that is often included among the factors of production (along with land, labor, and capital) is intangible—entrepreneurship. It cannot be banked or built, like capital; farmed, like land; or placed at the controls of a bulldozer, like labor. Yet entrepreneurship is essential for a viable economy. It is the willingness of someone (an **entrepreneur**) to venture along risky, sometimes uncharted, pathways; the willingness to provide leadership (and often capital, as well) for new businesses or for foundering older ones. Entrepreneurs may waste all their effort or lose their money (or both); so why take such a chance? The answer, of course, is that they believe they will realize substantial profits.

Some critics of capitalism assert that this system, wherein entrepreneurs have an important function, is parasitic because it exists for the sake of profits. But is this criticism justified? Ask yourself whether you would be willing to lend money to a person who wants to start a business if you could not foresee some reward in the form of interest on your money? Even if you were willing to lend the money for a short time without interest, you would be worse off financially, because you could have spent the sum on something you wanted or banked it to earn interest. And if the business failed, your money would be lost. In these circumstances you would probably feel that the risk you are taking warrants a reward—the interest on your money.

Following this line of reasoning, we see that little industry would have developed in early America if all those wanting to start new businesses had anticipated that their effort and money would go unrewarded. Profits are the reward for sound investment and useful enterprise.

The entrepreneur who starts a business, or who loans money to someone else for that purpose, does so to produce income—to maximize gains. It is not at all surprising, then, to find that the laws of supply and demand apply to entrepreneurship as well as to the other factors of production. Entrepreneurs will invest in those areas in the economy where demand for products is booming. They will withdraw their investments from areas where demand is shrinking. When Henry Ford drove his first automobile through the Michigan countryside, a few farsighted entrepreneurs undoubtedly lost interest, right then, in the horse-and-carriage trade. They were willing to invest capital in the new industry precisely because it promised high profits.

TECHNOLOGICAL PROGRESS

When technological progress takes place, more output can be had from the same amount of inputs. Hence, technological progress determines, at least in part, a nation's rate of economic growth. The ability of a country to effect and sustain **technological change** depends on (1) the scientific capabilities of the population, (2) the size and quality of the nation's educational and training system, and (3) the percentage of income that goes into basic research and development each year.

Basically, technological progress comprises new knowledge of any type that results in gains in measured output. Thus, it includes not only technological innovation but also managerial and organizational changes that improve productivity.

Our next step will be to examine the roles of entrepreneurship and technology in the shaping of the American economy.

The Role of Entrepreneurship and Technology in American Development

The better, and steadily improving, use of manpower and of resources has been a major contributor to U.S. economic growth. One way that productivity can be improved is through technological change—innovations that allow either more output to be produced with a given level of resources, or the same level of output to be produced at smaller cost of inputs. We shall see later how two technological marvels, the iron horse on land and the paddle-wheeler on water, contributed to expanded productivity in America.

During the colonial period relatively little new technology had been developed. Gains in efficiency, both in agriculture and in distributive activities such as shipping, resulted largely from the adaptation of production methods used elsewhere. In farming, the types of tools used, the care of animals, and the methods of production in general were derivations of what had always been done. Yet output did increase relative to inputs as markets grew larger, risks declined, and the organization of the economy improved. In shipping, the types of vessels used changed little over the decades. Between 1675 and 1775 freight rates had fallen almost one half, but most of this decline was due to the elimination of piracy and the more efficient handling of ships in port.

Once the British Navy had routed the pirates from the western Atlantic, near the turn of the eighteenth century, insurance rates tumbled. Moreover, vessels that once had carried men and armaments as well as cargo could now use all their space for profitable loads. For this purpose, ships similar to the Dutch flute (first produced in 1595) served very well, and so that type of ship construction became popular. This sort of adaptation from region to region is known as **technical diffusion.** Another advance due not to new technology but to adaptation was improved centralized warehousing of goods, which shortened the costly delay of ships in port. This reduced both crew costs and the waste (underutilization) of capital.

Transportation and Technology

Such fairly modest improvements in early American shipping served well enough until a new era brought new demands. That era began with the westward movement. New areas had to be linked to old so that produce and resources could be exchanged. A new transportation network was needed, and it had to be formed at sizable but affordable cost.

In colonial times a principal deterrent to interregional trade was the lack of cheap transportation except along the Atlantic coast. This had to change if the United States was to become an integrated market in which specialization would be encouraged. New roadways were a possible solution, but little help was to be expected from the federal government because it was believed that a federal road-building program would impinge on states' rights. Many private companies did undertake the job. By 1810 in New England alone 180 turnpike construction companies were at work. Three years later a tally showed about 1,400 miles of privately built roads in New York, and by 1832 Pennsylvania could boast of more than 2,000 miles of roads. Even so, new areas were opening up faster than new roads could reach out. Fortunately, the solution lay close at hand: the great natural waterways of the Mississippi River, the Ohio and the Missouri, and the Great Lakes beyond.

The Rivers   At first, all freight and passengers were carried along these arteries by flatboats and barges (keelboats). Then, in 1815, the steamboat was introduced, and it took over the upriver struggle. Since the upriver part of any round trip was the part that produced the greater revenues, the steamboat was unquestionably more efficient for upriver shipping than flatboats. However, surprisingly, the steamboat did not displace flatboating but actually helped it in one way. Once flatboats had made their downstream run, their crews could return upriver by steamboat at lower cost of time. So flatboats remained a viable part of the transportation system in the mid-nineteenth century.

The steamboat was a vital force in early westward expansion, and a stream of improvements between 1815 and 1860 greatly increased its efficiency and safety. In the beginning, steamboat boiler explosions introduced Americans to the hazards of industrialization. These became uncommon after 1850. Meantime, various changes in the hull and design greatly increased the steamboats' carrying capacity and their extent of useful service in shallow-water seasons (and areas). As a result, freight costs on the rivers tumbled between 1815 and 1860. As late as 1845 the rivers still carried more traffic than all other modes of transportation combined.

Most of the gains in efficiency in steamboating resulted from minor modifications in the design and structure of the vessel and in its handling and operating. However, the sum of these many small improvements was actually more significant in reducing the cost of river transport than was the introduction of steam power itself. In turn, such reductions in the costs of transportation in the first half of the nineteenth century were so important that most historians refer to the period as the transportation revolution.

Canals The reductions in transportation cost became a still greater impetus to trade as waterways were constructed to link the natural rivers and lakes. Canals shared with natural waterways such disadvantages as freezing in the winter, but they offered some special advantages. Mainly, they allowed for relatively cheap transportation between fixed points. The greatest canal-building activity occurred between the late 1820s and during the panic of 1837. The most famous canal was the Erie, which ran from the Hudson River near Albany, New York, to Buffalo on Lake Erie. Completed in 1825, it extended some 360 miles and could accommodate 30-ton barges. Other canals were constructed in Pennsylvania, Delaware, Maryland, Ohio, Illinois, and Michigan.

From the standpoint of some eastern cities, however, New York's Erie Canal was all too successful. By tapping the interior and bringing its resources to New York, the canal was threatening the commercial interests of other areas. For example, Baltimore could not compete efficiently in the canal-construction business because the terrain of the region presented engineering difficulties and high costs of construction, so Baltimore (and many other areas) turned to railroading to traverse the hilly areas.

Railroads Like canals, railroads created an incentive for the development of interior lands that would otherwise have stood idle. In combination with coastal shipping and natural waterways, the rail routes provided a low-cost transportation network that advanced regional specialization and interregional trade. The result was the growth of a truly national economy and a lessening of the nation's dependence on overseas markets.

The beginnings of the railroad were unimpressive. At the time of the Civil War only about 30,000 miles of track had been laid in all of the United States. But a mere 40 years later, by the start of the twentieth century, most of today's railroad bed and track had been completed; and by far the greater part of 200,000 miles of track stretching from coast to coast was of standard gauge, quite unlike the unmatched system that had been the rule prior to 1860. Railroad bridges, almost unknown before the Civil War, dotted the landscape by 1900.

In those same 40 years, locomotives had been increasing in power and in number. Freight cars multiplied 20-fold, and the capacity of each car increased 300 percent; hence, the rolling car capacity of the railroads had jumped by a multiple of 80 by the end of the century. Employment on the railroads also expanded, from 100,000 to 1,000,000 in the same two-decade period. In 1860 only 1 percent of the labor force had been engaged in railroad work; three times that percentage were railroaders by the turn of the century.

Inevitably, some mistakes had been made along the way. Baltimore tried to build its railroad over a mountain pass before steam locomotives had been properly designed to meet such a challenge. It was a classic entrepreneurial mistake. But such risks had to be taken, and the advantages of railroads were too evident to be ignored. Railroads were speedier than canal transportation, they could be used in almost all weather, and they served overland routes. These features were particularly advantageous for passengers when the railroads first were built. However, another change was taking place during those 40 years. While passenger miles were increasing 500 percent, ton-freight miles soared an astonishing 6,000 percent. Travelers were finding other means of getting about, and the railroad reached its peak year of transporting people in 1910. Thereafter, it became increasingly a carrier of freight, its role to this day.

Agriculture and Technology

In both the eastern farms and the vast, sprawling lands of the West, agriculture, too, was experiencing technological change during the nineteenth century. Clever minds were at work devising new machines to save human hands, while others sought ways to improve strains of livestock and plants and to increase the yield of the soil through scientific experimentation.

In the first category, *mechanization,* the period from about 1830 to 1880 brought a wealth of basic inventions. The first working reaper was introduced by Cyrus McCormick in 1830; three years later Obed Hussey obtained the first patent on this mechanical replacement for human effort in the harvesting of grains. That prosaic instrument, the plow, was improved in 1819 by the introduction of replaceable parts. However, the tough prairie soils were too much for the original cast-iron plows; parts gave way faster than they could be replaced. A steel plow solved the problem; by 1857 John Deere was producing 10,000 steel plows annually at his plant in Illinois. Seed drills, cultivators, mowers, rakes, and threshing machines were in common use before 1860, yet this array of machines reduced the amount of human labor by surprisingly little. In the 1850s, after reapers came into general use, only about one third less labor was required.

An overlapping second period of improvement in agricultural productivity (from roughly 1860 to 1910) was a time when literal horse power—working horses—provided the energy that moved the new machines about their tasks of planting, reaping, binding, and hauling the products of the farms and ranches. By 1900 total animal power available on farms in the United States had reached a little more than 18.5 million horsepower—roughly three times its total in 1850. An additional 3.5 million horsepower was provided by steam engines. Oddly, the horsepower *per agricultural worker* in 1900 remained at a low 2.2 compared with

1.8 in 1850, since the number of workers as well as the amount of animal power had almost tripled in the half century.

Around 1900 another stage began—the era of power-driven machinery that continues to the present. In 1905 the gasoline tractor was introduced. By the outbreak of World War I it was apparent that tractors would one day supersede the draft horse. By 1920 a quarter million of the new "workhorses" were in operation, and the number continued to climb steadily, soon to be supplemented by trucks, automobiles, and (after electrification) other motor-driven equipment.

The second category, *scientific experimentation,* was little esteemed by rank and file farmers until the late years of the nineteenth century. "Book farming" was derided except by the well-to-do gentleman farmer and by those pressed by rapidly deteriorating soils.

Some scientific improvements had been made in earlier years, however. Many modern breeds of animals had been imported before 1860, and these were rapidly improved after the Civil War. Gradually, too, it became apparent that the "fellows in the laboratories" knew what they were about in changing the characteristics of plants for the better, to resist adverse climate and diseases. Farmers began to choose their seeds carefully and to try out fungicides and insecticides. By 1890 much had been learned about the chemistry of soils, and artificial fertilizers embodying essential plant foods enabled producers in older regions to revitalize their acres. By World War I, the groundwork had been laid for the "miracles" of modern science to go to work on the farms.

Textiles and Technology

Another notable example of machinery enhancing productivity can be found in the cotton and textile mills of nineteenth-century America. Shortly before the Civil War, power-driven machines were being substituted for hand labor at a faster pace in this industry than in any other. Indeed, machines had first proved themselves in the processing of fibers. Following the war, improvements, intended mainly to make the machines more fully automatic, continued at a fast pace. Ring spinning, introduced around 1830, had made it possible to draw, twist, and wind yarn in one continuous process. For the first time, either unskilled or semiskilled labor could do a job that had once required long experience. Moreover, ring spinning produced stronger yarns, which were required when automatic looms finally entered the factories.

The automatic loom did not gain commercial acceptance until 1895. Various power looms had been experimented with for decades when the Northrup loom was finally produced. With its predecessors, operators had needed to shut down operations whenever a shuttle ran out of yarn or a warp thread broke. The Northrup loom could deal with both problems, thereby securing its place in American factories. Still further advances in the early years of the twentieth century were tying-in and drawing-in machines, which mechanically attached new warp threads to those already in place.

In the clothing industry, or "needle trades," similar changes took place when the sewing machine was introduced into factories in the 1850s. During the

Civil War, the production of uniforms led to standardized sizes; afterward, men's "ready-to-wear" could be produced to these approximate measurements. By the 1870s several thicknesses of cloth could be cut at one stroke by rotary cutting machines and reciprocating knives. Power-driven sewing machines were operating at speeds up to 2,800 stitches per minute. Pressing machines were replacing hand irons.

Women's wear presented more of a problem because of fashions. Before 1900 only coats, hosiery, and underwear were produced in factories; dresses were usually made in the home or by dressmakers. In every case, many hand operations were needed to complete factory-made garments, and as late as 1920 only half of the garment workers were machine operators or assistants.

Footwear experienced an earlier transition from hand made to machine made—at least for the "man in the street." As early as 1810 the small shoe-crafting shop was giving way to larger scale production and then to factories. However, a problem existed; the machines stubbornly ignored the difference between left foot and right foot! Until a decade or so before the Civil War, ladies and gentlemen fussy enough to care about fit had to have their shoes custom made. Gradually, to establish a broader market, machines and techniques were devised that provided the right variety of design and finish, as well as accuracy of fit.

A notable innovation in 1875 was the Goodyear welt process, which attached soles to uppers without allowing nails or stitches to penetrate the inside of the shoe. Then followed machines for eyeletting, heeling, and shaping on the last. By 1914 the shoe industry was highly mechanized.

Food Production and Technology

Flour milling can rightfully claim the earliest mechanization of any American industry. Even in colonial times some of the great mills were almost completely mechanized for continuous-process production. They operated so well that little change took place (or was needed) until after the Civil War. Then technological improvements came thick and fast, and the size of the mills increased to accommodate them. Larger mills could draw supplies from a larger range, so various types of wheat grown in widespread areas could be incorporated to blend flours of uniform quality. This had not mattered to the small individual baker, but for commercial bakeries a standardized flour was crucial.

Thus, flour became a factory product. Bread was another matter entirely. Until after the turn of this century, the fragrance of fresh-baked bread remained strictly a product of the home kitchen. In fact, the first baked products to be produced mechanically were crackers and biscuits. It was not until about 1910 that it became apparent that bread baking, too, would soon be assigned to factories. Even then, commercial bakeries were typically side-street affairs until further advances in mechanization induced larger firm size after 1920.

With regard to the market for meat, the most useful contribution of technology would be the provision of refrigeration. Western packers had long held a great cost advantage in producing meat animals, and had shipped cured pork to the

East for decades, but fresh meat was perishable, and livestock could be transported only with a prohibitive weight loss. Thus, easterners had depended for fresh meat on local packers who generally could provide it only during cold weather, and at higher cost. By 1870 western slaughterhouses were refrigerating their premises with ice. From that, it was a step to circulating air through iced boxcars and shipping the meat to the hungry east. In spite of bitter opposition from local packers, the market for cheaper fresh meat brought a bonanza for western producers, and by 1880 the rise of the great national meat packers was well under way. Meat by-products also began to be utilized, and the relatively simple process of preparing meat animals for market produced the earliest assembly lines.

Iron, Steel, and Technology

Between 1815 and 1850 three innovations transformed the production of iron. These were the processes for rolling bars and plates, for "puddling" pig iron to make merchant bar, and for reducing iron ore by the use of anthracite coal and, later, coke. The products of different methods were (1) wrought iron, a tough, malleable, and noncorrosive product, and (2) cast iron, which was hard, brittle, and nonmalleable. Both were available in ample supply to machine makers. But wrought iron was too costly for many uses and, although ideal for agricultural implements, it could not withstand the strains imposed by the greater speeds and heavier structures of emerging industrial technologies. Cast iron was ruled out for most purposes because of its brittleness.

Steel had been known for centuries but had been produced only in small, costly quantities. Made in a crucible, or pot, by melting wrought iron and then carefully adding carbon, this high-carbon product was used principally for cutlery and fine tools. The steel of the future was to be a relatively low-carbon product. Credit for the two-step, *indirect* method of its production is shared by an Englishman, Henry Bessemer, and an American ironmaster, William Kelly, who arrived independently, and almost simultaneously, at the first successful tests of this new technique.

In a cylindrical converter that could be tipped like a huge kettle, the molten pig iron was subjected to blasts of hot air; the oxygen in the air ignited and burned out carbon and silicon, the chief impurities. When some manufacturers tried out the method in 1864, however, they denounced it as a fraud. The problem was that the process's 10 to 15 minute "blow" phase was not long enough for the steel maker to test the steel for carbon content; the manufacturer could never be certain what purpose would be served by a given batch.

To remedy this defect while not infringing on Bessemer's patents, other inventors set out to find a better way of making cheap steel. The most effective results were those of William and Friedrich Siemens in England and Emile and Pierre Martin in France. By 1868 the main features of their independent efforts had been incorporated in the open-hearth method.

Several considerations made this technique more economical than the Bessemer process. Although a large open-hearth charge required about 12 hours, as against the few minutes of the Bessemer method, this long refining period permitted sampling and adjustment of the chemical mix. Also, scrap iron and even iron ore could be added to the more costly molten pig iron in the shallow, open container. And, by a highly efficient regeneration principle, hot gases to melt and refine the charge were drawn from nearby coke ovens or blast furnaces.

In view of these advantages, it seems astonishing that the less efficient Bessemer method not only survived but far outpaced the open-hearth method until around 1890. There is just one reason: Bessemer steels were entirely satisfactory for use as rails—the great new westward-reaching tracks of the iron horse. To meet this pressing demand, Bessemer furnaces continued blazing.

Bessemer furnaces and open-hearth operations developed rapidly in size and efficiency during the closing decades of the century. In 1860 a good blast furnace had produced from 7 to 10 tons daily of pig iron. Twenty-five years later, ten times that quantity was the maximum, and by 1900 a daily output of 500 tons or more of pig iron was common, with markedly less consumption of coke, which by now had entirely replaced anthracite and bituminous coal as a fuel. The mere saving of energy was a major accomplishment during this period. Coke ovens were placed close to blast furnaces, which, in turn, moved closer to the steel furnaces to speed the delivery of molten pig iron. Finally, both converters and open hearths were situated near the roughing mills to minimize the need for reheating before the first rolling.

By 1890 structural engineers were beginning to recognize the superiority of steel produced on the open hearth. In 1910 the open-hearth process accounted for 63 percent of the 26 million tons of steel produced that year, and the Siemens-Martin technique had clearly taken the lead, which it has held ever since.

A second major development in steel production during the decades before the century's end was the increasing use of alloys in steel making. Like most innovations in this industry, the idea of hardening steel by the addition of alloys originated in Europe. Chrome steel was known there by 1821, and a process for nickel steel had been patented in France in 1876. But innovation crossed the ocean when Bethlehem Steel Works purchased patent rights to the French process. By 1890, the company was making nickel-steel plates for the U.S. Navy. Tool steel, gear wheels, die castings, and other industrial products soon followed off the production line, and by 1905 the United States had become the global leader in ferroalloy production. By 1905 more than half a million tons of alloy steels, made not only with chrome and nickel, but also with tungsten, molybdenum, manganese, vanadium, titanium, and other additives, were being produced by U.S. mills each year.

A prime market for the hard new steels was found in the manufacture of metal-working machinery. This consists of two types of power-driven machines: those that shape parts by pressing, forging, and hammering; and those that cut gears, grind, and mill. (The latter are called *machine tools.*) Given alloy steels to work with, inventors could now turn drawing-board concepts into working models with unprecedented assurance that their products would stand up to the demands made on them.

The period from 1890 through the end of World War I brought enormous improvements in the power and precision of metalworking machines. Under pressure of prewar and wartime demands by the automobile, armament, and aircraft industries, America's machine industry reached maturity. Two major technical advances were made: the increased automation of machines and the use of compressed air and electricity to drive high-speed cutting tools and presses. By 1919 great electrically driven shears could cut steel slabs 12 inches thick and 44 inches wide. In the same period, the precision in machine tools had increased from one-hundredth of an inch (in Civil War days) to a tolerance of one-thousandth of an inch and even, in extreme cases, to one ten-thousandth. Meantime, the massive presses now available could stamp out parts for automobile bodies at a rate that inaugurated the age of mass production.

Sources of Power

Through the first half of the nineteenth century America's industry was driven almost totally by direct power. Men cranked huge wheels. Horses pulled loads. Wind spun the vanes of windmills. Water turned the creaking waterwheels in mills. In 1850 more than three quarters of all power was furnished by animal energy, and human energy produced more power than machines did. In addition, water running in rivers and streams was far more important as a source of energy than its derivative, steam.

Throughout the 1850s, after the coming of the steamboat and steam engine, there was much disagreement as to the relative costs of steam and direct power. By the end of the Civil War the argument was settled, for it became apparent that sites on streams large enough to power mills and factories were in short supply. Those that were available were often too remote for effective industrial concentration. Sometime during the 1870s, steam won out over direct water power. Neither the ancient waterwheel nor the more recently developed water turbine could compete with the increasing efficiency of the steam engine, given the increased safety of high-pressure boilers. Moreover, the railroads had opened up access to almost inexhaustible supplies of coal—the essential substance for the transformation of water to steam.

Thus, steam became king on the American industrial front, but its reign was short. A new contender for the crown—electricity—soon appeared on the scene. Like steam, electricity was not a new *source* of energy; it was simply a new means of using energy generated by either the flow of water or the burning of fuel; but electricity offered bonuses that steam did not. An electric plant could be a long distance from the user of its power, and that power could be divided among many users. It was instantly on tap; no need to stoke up steam boilers nor to transform the to-and-fro action of the steam engine into rotary motion by cumbersome devices.

An early landmark was the construction of Edison's central power plant in New York in 1882; until World War I, however, most electrical power was generated directly by the establishment that used it, and fewer than half the nation's electric motors were driven by power purchased from a central plant. This trend reversed itself during the war years. By then electricity was powering more than one third of the nation's industry—far more than in any other country. Electric lights burned in almost half of all urban homes (although 98 percent of farm families still read and kept their accounts by kerosene lamplight).

We now summarize the *sources* of America's industrial power: In 1890 coal provided 90 percent of the energy furnished to industry, whether in the form of steam or electricity. That dominance held firm as late as 1920, when coal was still used for at least 80 percent of industrial energy, although petroleum was rapidly gaining a place and hydropower was regaining some attention. Just over the horizon, however, lay a new age, the time when petroleum and natural gas would become the strategic fuels—workhorses to drive America's industrial machine.

Two New Ideas: Mass Production and Scientific Management

During the nineteenth century certain American industries had been stretching their muscles to the limit. Demand was steadily increasing for such goods as farm implements and bicycles, so the producers of those goods were approaching the modern concept of mass production. However, true mass production involves considerably more than mere numbers; it implies a continuous process of manufacture, the availability of interchangeable parts, highly accurate power-driven machinery, and uniform quality of all materials. By midcentury some firms were meeting most of these standards, but two functions remained to be mastered: a mechanical means of moving materials from one stage to another, and some way to minimize the time needed to assemble each unit within complex products.

Carriages and railroad cars were traditionally produced by stationary assembly; each unit remained in place from start to finish. But then came the automobile. When Henry Ford decided in 1908 to produce a low-priced car to furnish cheap transportation, he devised a semistationary system. Subassemblies were constructed at different sites, then moved together; but there was no provision for continuous movement from *A* to *B* to *C.* Ford had perhaps underestimated how many people would demand his new Model T. By 1913 the Ford plant was compelled to adopt a technique that had already been inaugurated in the manufacture of smaller, simple products; the first moving assembly line, pulled along by a windlass. One year later, a Ford chassis that would formerly have been put together only after 12 hours of labor was being turned off the assembly line in a little more than 1½ hours.

It was time now for a supplemental idea to take hold—scientific management. One of the first and most vocal proponents of this theory was Frederick W. Taylor. Even before Ford's "common-sense" acceptance of an efficient assembly line production, this scientific thinker had been arguing that worker efficiency could be improved by

1. analyzing in detail the movements required to perform a job,
2. carrying on experiments to determine the optimum size and weight of tools and the optimum heights for work, and
3. offering incentives for superior performance.

He also developed principles governing the best physical layouts for a shop or factory, the correct routing of work, and the accurate scheduling of production orders. His arguments were strongly buttressed in 1911, when, in a hearing before the Interstate Commerce Commission, the famous attorney Louis D. Brandeis asserted that instead of being allowed to raise their rates, railroads should institute the intelligent ordering of their operations in accord with scientific principles.

Under the pressure of increasing industrialization, nineteenth-century workers had already become restive. Many were concerned that these high-flown new theories would push them beyond their limits. But where the system was given a fair trial, workers found that along with their increasing productivity they were earning higher real wages. Moreover, having the materials flow faster did not necessarily force them to work faster, they did not have to move about to handle materials, their work was easier, and they were better protected against physical strain and industrial accidents.

DEFINITIONS OF NEW TERMS

ENTREPRENEUR   An entrepreneur is one who undertakes the risks of starting a new venture or expanding an old one.

TECHNOLOGICAL CHANGE   Technological change is an advance in knowledge that permits more output to be produced with an unchanged amount of inputs.

TECHNICAL DIFFUSION   Technical diffusion is the spread of new or known techniques from one firm to another or from one use to another.

A Pioneering Effort in Early Agriculture

ELIZA LUCAS
(1723–1793)

Entrepreneur

In 1737 Lieutenant-Colonel George Lucas, who was stationed in Antigua in the Caribbean, departed for South Carolina with his ailing wife and three daughters. Shortly after they settled there, diplomatic negotiations between England and Spain broke down and, with hostilities renewed, Colonel Lucas was recalled to duty in Antigua.

Since Mrs. Lucas was in poor health, responsibility for the family's affairs in South Carolina fell to the oldest daughter, Eliza, who was then 16. Not only did she admirably discharge her duties, but she also revolutionized agricultural production in South Carolina.

For her, planting was no mere weekend or holiday business. Having three plantations to oversee, she was rivaled by none in her industriousness and ingenuity.

Like other colonists she spent much time and energy trying to discover which crops were best suited for the soil and climate. Happily, in July 1739, she wrote, in a "coppy book of letters to my Papa": "I wrote my father a very long letter on his plantation affairs . . . on the pains I had taken to bring the Indigo, Ginger, Cotton, Lucern, and Casada to perfection, and had greater hopes from the Indigo." Within three years her hopes were realized and, almost singlehandedly, she successfully introduced and entrepreneured indigo production in the mainland colonies.[1] Additionally, as an active member of the local agricultural society, she helped disseminate her findings to other planters.

Indigo was used as a blue dye to color textiles, and as a complement to textile production it was deemed so valuable in England that Parliament eventually granted a subsidy for its production. By 1770 indigo ranked fifth among the major commodities exported from the 13 colonies. Three decades earlier, only Eliza had been producing it on the mainland.

In South Carolina, rice and indigo overshadowed all other forms of commercial commodity production. Part of the reason for this was that indigo also complemented rice production. Whereas rice was grown in the low-lying, swampy regions, indigo was grown in high, dry areas. Moreover, the harvesting and planting time for these two crops did not conflict. Consequently, different soil types and work seasons for each permitted plantations to more fully utilize their land and their slaves.

By the time of the Revolution, exports per capita from South Carolina were greater than those from any of the other 13 colonies. Eliza Lucas, more than any other single person, must be credited with this relative standing. In the process of enriching her family and other South Carolina planters, she hastened the settlement of early America.

Eliza Lucas was certainly one of North America's first great entrepreneurs.

[1] Many earlier experiments with indigo had been attempted in the southern colonies, but without success.

chapter 7

Market Structure

At this point we return to a concept first discussed in Chapter 1—that it is natural for people to prefer more over less for self and family. One way this motivation reveals itself is in terms of business profitability; economists then call it profit maximization.

In the world of business, the urge to maximize profit leads to attempts to create the greatest possible demand for a firm's goods and services. Business firms, which organize resources to produce and sell goods and services, can be small or large, from one-person shops to huge corporations. A firm can most effectively win customers (1) by producing a superior product or better service and (2) by offering it at an attractive price. This implies that the firm's costs must be such that the product or service can be sold at an attractive price and still return acceptable profits.

The producer who meets these criteria will begin to establish a market and will then try to expand by making still greater efforts in the same or successful new directions. Meantime, are others going to compete for a share of the market that has been established? That all depends; and the answer to this question tells us whether the producer is a monopolist, a perfect competitor, or something in between. The degree of competition or noncompetition in a given industry determines the nature of that particular *market structure*.

MONOPOLY

Almost all producers would prefer to be monopolists. A monopolist generally makes higher profits than a competitor can. When a business has a true **monopoly** in selling a good or a service, that business is, by definition, an entire industry. No one else produces that good; buyers turn to that single producer or go without.

For various reasons, however, there are few true monopolies. First, it is not easy for an individual to become a monopolist because success attracts competition. To shut out competition requires effective barriers. True, in some parts of the business world such barriers are provided in the form of governmental regulations set up to block entry. Notable examples of this practice were once found in the provision of postal and telephone services in America. When government enters in the economic picture, a capitalist economy becomes a mixed economy. A **mixed economy** comprises both private enterprise and government ownership or regulation of economic activity.

Most electric power companies are local monopolies because an agency of the government has given them the sole right to operate in their specific geographical areas. You and your friends could not pool your money, buy a small generator, and sell electricity to neighbors, because doing so would be against government regulations.

When you mail a first-class letter, you are patronizing a monopoly, and only recently have other suppliers been permitted to produce and sell telephones. Various groups are testing the legality of the laws that restrict first-class mail service to the U.S. postal department, and package delivery is not a post office monopoly. Nevertheless, at this time the first-class mail services remain a government-owned and government-controlled monopoly.

In addition to official regulations, there are other **barriers to entry**—barriers that deter competition. One is the cost of starting up. In some cases, as with electric power, the government originally entered the industry partly because it was so costly for individuals to build dams, buy generators, or string power lines that few would have chosen to compete. Similarly, the costs of starting a competitive phone system would be prohibitive.

Another barrier is lack of raw materials. A classic example here is the diamond industry: The DeBeers Company of South Africa controls the export of nearly all of the world's natural diamonds simply because it owns most of the producing mines and raw materials and limits the output. An example from the past is the Aluminum Company of America (ALCOA), which, at the turn of this century, controlled almost all of the basic sources of bauxite and refused to sell this essential ore to other potential producers. For many years, ALCOA retained a virtual monopoly in aluminum.

OLIGOPOLY

Taken from Greek, *oligopolist* means "few sellers," as contrasted with monopolist, or "single seller." An **oligopoly** consists of a small number of firms that are interdependent in their marketing structure. Examples are the automobile and steel industries. Three giants dominate the automotive industry in the United States, and in the production of steel the four largest firms account for more than 60 percent of the industry's steel ingot capacity each year.

Within an oligopoly, each firm presumably makes its own pricing policies, but always with an eye to how rival producers will react. A change in any one company's output or price influences the profits and sales of its competitors. Thus before making any changes, an oligopolist will try to anticipate their effect on the policies of its peers. Historically, when one firm in an oligopolistic industry changes its prices, others often respond similarly.

Oligopolies have been criticized for these practices, but little proof has been advanced that such an industry structure is harmful to the economy. To define an industry as oligopolistic says nothing about an *alternative* market structure or about what such a presumably "better" arrangement might cost.

MONOPOLISTIC COMPETITION

In the early decades of this century, economists began to explore other areas of market structure lying somewhere between monopoly and perfect competition. Combining the two concepts, a Harvard economics professor, Edward Chamberlin, came up with the best-received theory, which he termed **monopolistic competition.** He defined this situation as one in which a relatively large number of producers offer similar but slightly differing products in a highly competitive market. Obvious examples are such brand-name items as beer, toothpaste, cosmetics, and gasoline. Each firm within the industry has some special product identity, but even in advertisements it may be difficult to detect much difference between Brand A and Brand B. Nonetheless, Chamberlin held that each producer selling its differentiated product was a "partial" monopolist.

In this structure each producer has such a small part of the industry that it has only a very slight control over prices. With so many firms, it is very difficult for all of them to get together to collude—that is, to set a pure monopoly price (and output!). Since there are so many firms, each one acts independently of the others. That is, no firm attempts to take into account the reaction of all of its rival firms.

PERFECT COMPETITION

At the far end of the market-structure spectrum from monopoly we find **perfect competition,** although in its extreme form it is rare indeed. Let's analyze what the situation would have to be in order for perfect competition to prevail. Two conditions would be required: a very large number of sellers of the identical product, and a very large number of informed buyers for that product. In such a case, no one seller could possibly change the price of the product without losing out. The supply of the product would also be determined by the total number of sellers. In turn, the supply would interact with the demand of the knowledgeable buyers, so that an equilibrium price would be reached and each seller would accept this price. Since all potential buyers would know exactly the going price, they would never buy at a higher price. Yet the sellers would never sell at a lower price. In other words, no rivalry exists among competitors.

ANTITRUST POLICY

In the American economy, monopoly has long been under heavy fire. On the basis that monopolists generally charge prices unreasonably higher than would prevail in a competitive market, federal and state governments have acted in the public interest to govern the behavior of monopolies and of oligopolies as well. Originally, monopolies were known as *trusts*. Thus *antitrust policy* denotes the whole body of legislation and the regulatory agencies designed to prevent the formation of new monopolies and to break up those already established. In the following sections, we shall examine the early stages of the struggle in America between monopoly and competition.

Market Structures in the American Past

In earlier chapters we examined the beginnings of American business as rooted in colonial soil—the small farms, cottage industries, workshops, and smithies. Even in those earliest days, however, one type of operation was taking on the scope and even some of the production methods that we associate with modern efficiency.

Plantation Agriculture

Until the Civil War, the distinguishing feature of southern social and economic structure was the great plantation. Scattered throughout the South, these spreading domains made functional by slave labor were far more productive than small farms or larger ones cultivated by free workers. In fact, as shown in Table 7.1,

Table 7.1 COMPARISONS OF EFFICIENCY IN SOUTHERN AGRICULTURE BY FARM TYPE AND SIZE
Index of free southern farms = 100.

Number of Slaves	Indexes of Output per Unit of Total Input
0	100
1–15	101
16–50	133
51 or more	148

Source: Robert W. Fogel and Stanley L. Engerman, "Explaining the Relative Efficiency of Slave Agriculture in the Antebellum South," *American Economic Review* 67 (June 1977): 285, Table 7.

farms working 16–50 slaves were 33 percent more efficient, and those with more than 50 slaves were 48 percent more efficient, than farms without slaves.

To explain such an advantage, we must look to economies of scale and to the way in which crops were grown and harvested. The large plantation in the antebellum South more closely resembled a factory than a farm, and the organization of labor was very much like the assembly line method in use to this day. Slaves were often organized into production units called gangs, with each worker carefully selected by skill for a specific task. Moreover, the intensity of work per hour was far greater than on smaller farms. Contemporary writers described work on the great plantations in these terms:[1]

> The cotton plantation was not a farm consisting, as the farm does, in a multiplicity of duties and arrangements within a limited scope, one hand charged with half a dozen parts to act in a day or week. The cotton plantation labor was as thoroughly organized as the cotton mill labor. There were wagoners, the plowmen, the hoe hands, the ditchers, the blacksmiths, the wheelwrights, the carpenters, the men in care of the work animals, the men in care of hogs and cattle, the women who had care of the nursery . . . the cooks for all. . . . No industry in its practical operation was moved more methodically or was more exacting of a nice discrimination in the application of labor than the Canebrake Cotton plantation.

> When the period of planting arrives, the hands are divided into three classes: 1st, the best hands, embracing those of good judgment and quick motion; 2nd, those of the weakest and most inefficient class; 32rd, the second class of hoe hands. Thus classified, the first class will run ahead and open a small hole about seven to ten inches apart, into which the 2nd class [will] drop four to five cotton seeds, and the third class [will] follow and cover with a rake.

To recoup strength for such hard-driven work, the slaves on large plantations needed, and were granted, longer rest breaks and more time off on Sundays than workers on smaller holdings. Although specialization of tasks enhanced productivity, it is obvious that much of the plantations' superior efficiency resulted primarily from the extent to which labor was forced to produce. No free-labor plantations of any size emerged during the period, and after emancipation the organization and efficiency of plantation production declined sharply.

Monopoly Capitalism

While the South was learning assembly line efficiency, the industrial North was learning the uses (and sometimes the misuses) of financial management. A classic case was the building of railroads to the developing West. The 1880s saw such scramble for competitive routes that in a short time 11 different lines extended outward from New York alone.

[1]For complete citations and quotations see Jacob Metzer, "Rational Management, Modern Business Practices, and Economies of Scale in Antebellum Southern Plantations," *Explorations in Economic History* 12 (April 1975): 134–135.

The monetary debt of all the railroad systems combined began to exceed that of the entire U.S. government. In issuing much of this debt, numerous deals enriched speculators, and some schemes led to local monopolies. Cornelius Vanderbilt, for example, was busy during and after the Civil War buying small railroad lines until he controlled all the lines running from New York City to Albany. In 1865 he started buying stock in the New York Central Railroad. Not content with the rate at which he was acquiring that company, he devised a scheme to cause the price of its stock to drop. Part of this scheme involved stopping his trains short of a bridge at Albany, thus forcing the Central's passengers to make their own way across in all sorts of weather if they wished to connect with the other line. Other underhanded deals resulted in the final capitulation of the Central Railroad and its merger with Vanderbilt's Hudson line.

There were also scandals involving both congressmen and business people. The most famous had to do with an ephemeral construction company called Credit Mobilier. It was rumored that this company drained off profits of between $33 and $50 million in building the Union Pacific—stupendous sums for that day.

The railroad industry also experienced rate wars, and some price fixing took place so that other companies could not compete. Originally, some railroad systems tried to boost their profits and reduce competition by forming associations, agreeing among themselves to fix their rates. Usually such associations (**cartels**) failed promptly. Why? Because any member of a cartel could gain a fat share of business by cheating on the agreement while relying on other members to abide by it. Cheating usually took the form of secret rebates to customers. In other cases, **price discrimination** was practiced; railroads charged more for short hauls than for long, because only in the long-haul routes were there enough lines for firm competition to exist.

Finally, in 1887, an Interstate Commerce Commission (ICC) was formed by Congress. Its stated purpose was to ensure fair business practices by making rules to govern the operation of the railroads. However, the railroads themselves had a hand in the legislation to gain governmental supervision of their rate fixing and to make their cartels government backed and thus immune to cheating.

Business Organization   The organizational structure of American business was changing. During the late nineteenth century, a shift was taking place from the earlier proprietorships (single ownerships) and partnerships to a form of organization called the *corporation*. A commonplace to us today, the corporation was not really new even in the late 1880s; but in those decades it rapidly gained dominance for several reasons. There are many advantages to incorporation. First, a corporation is a legal entity owned by stockholders who customarily have only limited liability; that is, they can lose no more than the value of their stocks even if the corporation goes bankrupt. Second, the corporation does not end with the death of officers or stockholders. Third, it has a much wider base for obtaining large amounts of capital. It can sell shares in itself, and it can issue larger amounts of debt capital than could an organization where the death of one or another owner might end the company's viability. In an era of seam-bursting expansion, industries needed that kind of access to capital.

Preeminent among capital-demanding industries was "big steel." The first billion-dollar company in the world was United States Steel, the offspring of a consolidation between properties owned respectively by Andrew Carnegie and J. P. Morgan. Another giant in the industrial field was petroleum, through which such tycoons as John D. Rockefeller made their fortunes. Early in the twentieth century the automobile industry was given a tremendous boost when Henry Ford introduced interchangeable parts and assembly line techniques in mass producing his "Tin Lizzies," the Model T. By 1919 annual sales of automobiles had rocketed to the billion-dollar level.

The Industrial Revolution had been in progress for some decades in England and was spreading throughout Europe. Now came the era of America's industrial revolution, accompanied by a new recognition of the need for engineers and for scientific knowledge. The Massachusetts Institute of Technology was founded. One subject of scientific inquiry was worker efficiency. As discussed in Chapter 6, an employee of Bethlehem Steel Company, Frederick W. Taylor, discovered that the efficiency of workers could be increased by analyzing in detail the movements required to perform a job and then experimenting to determine just the right size and weight of tools. "Taylorism" became a fad, as time and motion studies were widely adopted to improve the productivity of the new industries of America.

Success Breeds Size

Even before the Civil War, around 1850, American firms had begun feeding on each other to increase their size and shares of the market. Agreements, cartels, and mergers had been undertaken to such an extent that observers already began to talk about "the rise of big business." After the war and into the new century the tendency increased. Burgeoning firms were now cited as part of a "combination," or merger, movement.

The approaches to achieving greater firm size took three general forms:

1. verbal agreement among managements to "share the market" in one way or another;
2. the more formal linking of the management and financial structures of firms; and
3. the creation of new firms by the actual union of the management, financial structure, and physical property of two or more previously separate firms.

In the early period, the first method, the so-called gentlemen's agreement, was common. As we saw in the case of the railroads, such verbal arrangements usually died quickly. Gentlemen's agreements were informal verbal agreements made chiefly for the purpose of maintaining or setting prices.

When restriction of output was desired, however, a stronger and formal contract was needed. This more formal arrangement, known as **pooling**, involved a written contract in which participants agreed to restrict output, dividing the market among themselves and assigning a portion to each seller. Does this have a familiar sound? The OPEC cartel that choked off America's oil supply in the 1970s was an unforgettable lesson in the uses of a pooling agreement. Although cartels as such have been forbidden by American law and their agreements are unenforceable in court, pooling served much the same purposes and in many cases succeeded in circumventing legal restrictions.

As early as 1880 pooling arrangements were strongly entrenched in several important industries; whiskey, meat products, explosives, steel rails, structural steel, certain tobacco products, and railroad trunk lines all came under such controls. Both gentlemen's agreements and pooling worked, at least temporarily. They were employed over many decades and, to some extent, probably are still with us today, even though they are now punishable under antitrust laws. Yet even apart from the grey area of illegality, pools and informal arrangements have distinct disadvantages. To the extent that they are successful in raising prices and achieving "monopoly" profits, they encourage competitors to enter the field. And because they hold prices up in times of general business decline, the temptation is great for individual participants to cheat on their shares when the going is rough. Nor can violators be taken to court by their fellow poolers.

The third path to growth—merger, or combination—is the most conspicuous development in today's business. As early as 1890 there were 12 important American trusts, or combinations, boasting a total worth of $1 billion. By 1903 the combinations had a capital of $3 billion, and one year later, of $7.2 billion. This represented 40 percent of the book value of all American industry.

Why would two companies, each successful in its own right, choose to join forces? One reason is to benefit from economies of scale: that is, to further increase profits when rising output leads to a fall in average costs. A second reason is to gain greater market control.

If a firm decides to expand its market power by merging with another company, what sort of partner should it look for? Basically, there are two types of merger—**vertical** and **horizontal.** The way to integrate a firm horizontally is for the company to buy up one or more competitors at the same level of production. We hear today constant reports of some small oil company merging with, or attempting to take over, another oil company. An outstanding example from the past was Rockefeller's Standard Oil, which drew many smaller companies, one by one, into the net of the Standard Oil trust. For vertical integration, on the other hand, a firm brings under its centralized control the various steps in a single type of production, from raw materials to finished product. For example, a coal mine might merge with an electric utility plant.

Going back to the beginnings of the merger movement, we can—by a little detective work—understand the two types of integration and why each was preferred in its time. In the 1880s and 1890s trade in America was just outgrowing the small, local concerns that had served primarily agricultural populations. As railroads reached farther and farther out to link growth centers into a new national market, the producers of consumer goods experienced an incredible increase in demand. Naturally they expanded and expanded again. Then came a startling revelation. Suddenly, in many areas, too much of everything was being turned out (supply was exceeding demand), and prices were dropping below production costs. What to do? Many small firms found that by joining forces with others in the same line of production and within a now-reachable geographical area they could consolidate their equipment, standardize their manufacturing processes, close down inefficient plants, and as a result cut their costs drastically. Horizontal integration became the path to economic salvation, and this type of combination dominated from 1879 to 1893. In addition to Standard Oil, other horizontally merged giants of the period were the American Sugar Refining Company and United States Rubber.

This period of horizontal domination ended in 1893, when a sharp recession almost completely curtailed all types of merger. Not until 1896 did prosperity return. With it came a surge of combinations of such dimensions that the earlier movement was quite overshadowed. This was phase two, when vertical integration took center stage and held it from 1898 until 1905.

According to U.S. Department of Commerce figures, more than 3,000 mergers were effected in those seven years, and quite possibly hundreds of others were not even recorded. But a different sort of demand was growing, and it became apparent that a different sort of integration might provide better answers for producers of the vast quantities of goods that now were needed. The burgeoning metropolitan areas were demanding water mains and sewer systems, streets and elevated railways, power lines and telephone lines, and public health provisions. Skyscrapers, making their first appearance in the late 1880s, cried out for steel to fashion their skeletons. All these pressing needs strained the muscles of existing firms. Only companies commanding enormous capital reserves were now capable of providing goods in the quantity needed. And firms of that size could operate only by highly centralized control over all the steps of production, from the mining of raw materials to the marketing of finished products. The result was vertical integration. Firms gradually took over the whole ladder of production.

One of the earliest examples, as we have seen, was United States Steel. As early as the beginning of the 1890s, Andrew Carnegie had consolidated his scattered manufacturing properties into an integrated firm that acquired vast deposits of coal and iron. A few years later J. P. Morgan and Company formed the Federal Steel Company, which proceeded to ally itself closely with the National Tube Company and the American Bridge Company, both producers of finished products. Other steel companies began following similar courses. But when Carnegie moved toward consolidation with producers of finished steel products, his strategy precipitated a merger with the Morgan interests. Two giant firms met, shook hands, and from their union emerged the first billion-dollar corporation: United States Steel, organized in March 1901, was by all odds the largest corporation in the world, and it controlled more than 60 percent of the nation's steel business.

The previous decades had been a period of virtual "hands-off business" policy by the government. Presidents and congressional leaders had accepted Thomas Jefferson's theory that the best government is that which governs least, and had abided by the dictum. But in the face of so much consolidation, public fears had been taking shape: would big business someday swallow up the nation itself?

In 1890 Congress reacted to those early fears by enacting the Sherman

Antitrust Act. The odd result of this legislation was actually to speed up consolidations, because mergers were not actually barred, even if they tended to reduce competition within an industry. Therefore, firms that formerly had been quietly colluding or pooling now saw that their best protection against charges of restraint of trade was to merge openly. In the 17 years ending in 1905, more than 300 major combinations were formed, and of these 156 were massive enough to entail some degree of monopoly control.[2] The surge toward bigness was checked to some extent after 1905, when prosecution under the Sherman Act resulted in the spectacular dissolutions of the Standard Oil Company of New Jersey (1910) and the American Tobacco Company (1911).

However, the move toward consolidation regained momentum in the next years. By the 1920s a vigorous new wave was under way, most of it in the form of horizontal mergers. By 1933 considerably more than 50 percent of all corporate wealth apart from the banking sector was concentrated in the hands of 200 firms. Moreover, producers in some fields were clustering in "institutes" or "trade associations," which subtly influenced the marketing of the products of an entire industry.

Like any other war, World War II distorted American business and changed the patterns of organization and competition. But with the postwar years came a third form of consolidation. A new and dominant movement apparent today is neither horizontal nor vertical integration, but integration into **conglomerates.** These hybrid corporations seek market dominance by combining an array of totally unrelated enterprises. A prime example is Ling-Temco-Voight, one of the pioneer successes in this type of expansion. Beginning in 1958 as a small electronics concern with annual sales of less than $7 million, Ling successively took over small producers of aircraft, sporting goods, financial services, steel, and some 24 other assorted products. By 1969 it had become the fourteenth-largest corporation in the nation.

Conglomerates have certainly not eased the burden of antitrust enforcement. Today, more than 80 percent of the assets of the top 200 manufacturing concerns are concentrated in only six states. Thanks to conglomeration, 26 firms totally disappeared from the *Fortune* list of the top 500 corporations in 1969. However, the picture is not all dark. In few cases does it appear that competition has been greatly reduced in any of the variety of fields covered by a single conglomerate. In some cases competition has actually been stimulated by the threat of takeover or by the creative energy and new capital infused into companies by changes of management.

The State of the Worker

To see how the individual worker fared during these periods of industrial pushing and shoving, let us turn back to the mid-nineteenth century. Through the last half of that century industry was on the march, with the Civil War intruding only as a costly interruption. As the Industrial Revolution took hold, ever greater num-

---

[2]See Shaw Livermore, "The Success of Industrial Mergers," *Quarterly Journal of Economics* (November 1935), 68–96.

bers of workers were attracted away from the farms by the magnetic pull of better pay and city life.

The new environment was cruel to many of those newcomers. During this era of monopoly capitalism, the little person—the factory worker and others—eked out an existence in slums that by present standards would be almost uninhabitable. In historical perspective, however, we cannot fairly compare their situation with what we enjoy today. In terms of the hopes and expectations of the time, the new working conditions were not significantly different from the hardships and long hours of their former circumstances.

Historians and economists long believed that workers suffered losses in real income during those decades. On the basis of the scattered evidence that was then available, it was felt that because of monopolistic practices, the living standards of industrial workers actually declined after passage of the Sherman Antitrust Act and until the beginning World War I. However, more complete estimates of real wages of manufacturing workers have since become available and, as shown in Figure 7.1, the data actually counter those earlier beliefs. Real wages (that is, indexed for inflation) did fall in some short spans of time, but over the entire quarter century from 1890 to 1914 real wages rose a notable 30 percent.

Suppose there had been no "monopolist" profits at all during those years? During the first ten years of this century, when monopoly is thought to have reached its greatest force in the nation's economy, total corporate profits were about $1.4 billion annually, on average. The bulk of those profits would have represented simply a normal return to capital—say 5 or 6 percent, comparable to interest on a bank account. Certainly not all corporations were monopolies; but for the sake of discussion, let us assume that all profits were monopolistic profits. If government had been able to skim off from that $1.4 billion total all profits above what would have been the "normal" return, and then had distributed that excess among the entire population (except company stockholders and officers), the increase in per capita income nationwide would have averaged a mere 1 or 2 percent.

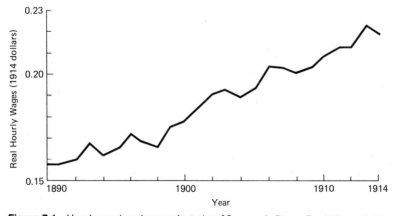

Figure 7.1 Hourly earnings in manufacturing. [*Source*: A. Rees, *Real Wages in Manufacturing, 1890–1914* (Princeton, N.J.: Princeton University Press, 1961), p. 4. © 1961 by Princeton University Press. Published for National Bureau of Economic Research. Reprinted by permission of Princeton University Press.]

Thus monopoly, though highly visible because of the enormous growth in firm size and in numbers of trusts and mergers, was no great drain on individual incomes during that period. It is doubtful even that the economy as a whole was becoming more monopolistic. In fact, new competition was entering fields where local monopoly had once held sway, because costs of transportation were falling and communications were greatly improved. In any case, we can be sure that in this era of industrialization the pay received by workers was getting higher and real incomes were on the rise.

However, not everything on the labor scene was rosy. Industrialization introduced a plentiful supply of other problems. Workers were becoming increasingly aware that living conditions around factory sites were downright dismal. Pollution, overcrowding, rundown tenements—all were the economic costs (the "external diseconomies") associated with almost any urban industrial complex. There was painfully little job security: A foreman could discharge workers without notice on a whim or if business conditions called for that action. Factory workers were also highly vulnerable to the impact of business recessions. Farm workers could weather most storms with some certainty of having enough to eat, but in the cities periods of severe recession or depression bit into workers' savings and their confidence. One of the bitterest depressions in the nation's history began in 1893. And unemployment lines lengthened during each downturn, as can be seen in Table 7.2. A rash of strikes between 1880 and 1914 and the appearance of considerable labor violence in the 1890s attest to the tensions of that time. Clearly they were directly related to the process of industrialization.

Since then, unemployment has been on a slight, but noticeable, upward path. Regrettably, it is an integral part of an industrialized capitalist society—as contrasted with a society where everyone is self-employed. But as everyone is

Table 7.2   UNEMPLOYMENT DURING RECESSIONS AND DEPRESSIONS
The unemployment rate during the recessions of the period under study was considerably higher than during the recessions and depressions in prior periods. In fact, the unemployment rate in 1894 is exceeded only by that during the Great Depression.

Year	Percentage Unemployed
1876	12–14
1885	6–8
1894	18
1908	8

Source: Stanley Lebergott, *Manpower and Economic Growth: The American Record Since 1800* (New York: McGraw-Hill, 1964), pp. 187, 512, 522.

aware, governmental programs have been established to alleviate the hardship of displaced workers, unemployment insurance being the prime example.

In short, as a highly developed industrial society the American population is—on balance—better off than would be possible if all workers returned to self-provident activities. That was true on the eve of World War I, and it remains true today. Then and now, some people have been hurt by industrialization, but even more have gained from it.

DEFINITIONS OF NEW TERMS

MONOPOLY   In its strictest sense, a monopoly is a single seller of a good or service, but more generally, monopoly denotes a seller of a good or service who has considerable control over prices and output.

MIXED ECONOMY   A situation in which there is both free enterprise and government intervention in the marketplace constitutes a mixed economy.

BARRIERS TO ENTRY   Barriers can prevent new firms from entering an existing industry. Some such barriers are government laws prohibiting entry and patents for research discoveries.

OLIGOPOLY   A market situation where there are very few sellers is an oligopoly. In it, each seller knows that the other sellers will react to its changes in prices and quantities.

MONOPOLISTIC COMPETITION   A market situation where a large number of firms produce similar but not identical products constitutes monopolistic competition. There is relatively easy entry into the industry in such a situation.

PERFECT COMPETITION   A firm that is such a small part of the total industry that it cannot affect the price of the product it sells is a perfect competitor. The competitive firm is often called a price taker.

CARTELS   A cartel is a group of firms in an industry that coordinates output and pricing decisions.

PRICE DISCRIMINATION   Charging some people higher prices than other people when these higher prices do not reflect higher costs is price discrimination. (Every time you go to a movie and pay a student price, you are the beneficiary of price discrimination.) Although often practiced, price discrimination is usually illegal.

POOLING   Pooling is a formal agreement under which participants agree to restrict output in a particular market.

VERTICAL MERGER   The joining together of businesses that engage in the various stages of producing the final product is a vertical merger. For example, the merging of a coal company with an electrical utility would be a vertical merger.

HORIZONTAL MERGER   The merging of businesses in the same activity, such as the merger of several gasoline companies or of several shoe manufacturing companies, is a horizontal merger.

CONGLOMERATES   The consolidation of firms that operate in unrelated markets into a comprehensive unit produces new corporate structures called conglomerates.

The Miracle Man of Wartime Merchant Shipbuilding

HENRY J. KAISER
(1882–1967)

An Audacious Industrialist

A World War II Liberty Ship was big, very big. Nonetheless, Henry J. Kaiser was able to produce one in eight days flat! In his seven shipyards in Oregon and California he produced over 1,500 ships during the war. How did he do it? By introducing prefabrication and assembly line techniques, along with a new and better welding process. This feat may have seemed a miracle, but should only have been expected from the man who had built up empires in paving and construction before the war. He had done that by submitting lower bids than much larger firms on all the government contracts he could apply for in the 1930s. He went on to help build the Bonneville and Grand Coulee dams. Kaiser even had the audacity to bid on providing five million barrels of cement for Shasta Dam even though he did not have a cement company! He got the bid and founded Permanente Cement Company, which had the largest plant in the entire United States, located in Permanente, California. Between 1931 and 1945 he completed 70 major construction projects.

Kaiser was not a boy to stay in school in his native Sproutbrook, New York. He quit at the age of 13 to become a cash boy, later becoming a salesman for the J. B. Wells Dry Goods Store in Utica. Then he went into the photographic supply business, and while still in his teens became a partner in the firm of Brownwell and Kaiser in Lake Placid, New York. Tiring of the photography business, he sold out in 1906 and moved to Spokane, Washington, where he went into the hardware business as a mere employee. Then the paving industry took his fancy, and he soon became a self-employed contractor, handling numerous highway and street projects in Washington, Idaho, and British Columbia. Then he moved his headquarters to Oakland, California. While still a road builder, he constructed 200 miles of highway in Cuba at a cost of over $18 million. One of the biggest innovations Kaiser introduced while in the road-building business was the substitution of diesel engines for gasoline motors in his tractors and steam shovels, thereby greatly reducing operating costs. When he went into the dam construction business, his prowess as an organizer and innovator did not abate: As head of the contractors building Boulder Dam, he got it completed two years ahead of schedule. Construction of dams led to the building of tunnels, bridges, dry docks, jetties, air bases, and troop facilities, and even to the excavation for the third locks in Panama.

Kaiser, perhaps more than any other industrialist of the time, was convinced that vertical integration was the only way to solve supply problems. For building his ships in California, Oregon, and Washington he needed steel, so he put up an integrated steel plant in Fontana, California. The ships also needed engines, so he and his associates purchased an iron works in Sunnyvale, California, where engines were built for Kaiser and other contractors. He also built a magnesium plant (magnesium was not used only for shipbuilding; in one form it was used as the incendiary material known as "goop").

The list goes on, for Kaiser got himself involved in airplane building during the war, also. He designed his plant in Bristol, Pennsylvania, where he not only built parts, subassemblies, and surfaces for flying fortresses, but also put together experimental Army and Navy planes.

After the war Kaiser saw the possibility of profit in the automobile industry. He formed the Kaiser-Fraser Corporation, which was the first major new U.S. independent auto producer after the war. The future of independent auto producers seemed bright right after the war, but by the early 1950s it was a downhill road. In an attempt to strengthen his market position Kaiser bought up the assets of the bankrupt Willys Motors in 1953. In the end, though, Kaiser Motors failed, and its over $90 million in debts were assumed by Henry J. Kaiser's more profitable enterprises.

Kaiser never stopped expanding his empire. He went into aluminum right after the war, and within five years Kaiser Aluminum and Chemical Company had sales of $150 million. By 1956, this figure had risen to $330 million, with a net profit of over $40 million. Kaiser has left his mark on American economic and social life. There are Kaiser hospitals, and Kaiser housing developments such as on Oahu, Hawaii. There are numerous other less obvious imprints of this audacious industrialist's activities, many of which are based on one man's quest for continued industrial efficiency.

chapter *8*

Money, Banking, and the Price Level

Money may be thought of as anything customarily used as a medium of exchange and measure of value, be it tobacco, wampum, or gold dust. Most Americans have a good idea of what money is in their society. They constantly use bills, coins, and checks as money.

Nevertheless, have you ever asked yourself why money exists? Why is money (currency or checks) needed as a medium in almost all economic transactions? The major reason is that income is seldom received at exactly the time and place at which a person wants to buy something, or in the correct amount. For example, many working people are paid once a week, yet they buy things every day. What do they do? They keep part of their income in the form of currency and spend only a portion of it at a time.

Consider what it would be like if people had to barter for everything— that is, exchange goods for goods. For example, suppose you had a part-time job in a grocery store. If there were no money, the grocer would have to pay you in groceries. To obtain something you wanted, you would have to exchange some of the groceries for that item. Things could get very complicated. In fact, in economies based on a barter system, people spend tremendous amounts of time and effort, thus wasting much potential output, in order to effect exchanges.

In short, money is used because

1. as a medium of exchange, it facilitates transactions;
2. as an asset, it can be stored for future use; and
3. as a measure of value, it is a convenient unit of accounting.

In regard to this third use, it is obvious that everyone needs some unit to measure the value of various items if they want to keep records: how much is owed, how much income is made, how much is being saved, and so on. Suppose those records had to be kept in terms of bushels of wheat? It could be done, but keeping up with fluctuating values and quantities would be quite difficult.

Historically, money as a medium of exchange has taken some decidedly odd forms. During World War II, for example, cigarettes were an accepted currency in some combat areas, and the silver cartwheels of the old West looked nothing like today's dollar bills. More than that, dollar bills themselves have changed, both in appearance and in what stands back of them.

Most dollar bills today carry the words "Federal Reserve Note," along with the statement "This note is legal tender for all debts, public and private" (and the motto "In God we trust"). Nowhere is there any indication that the bill can be exchanged for a certain amount of gold or silver. It is merely **legal tender** in the United States, which means that the bill must be accepted at face value in exchange for all debts owed, even though it is not backed by anything tangible. Currency of this kind is called **fiduciary,** because it is backed only by people's faith in it. They have confidence that the dollar's value, in terms of what it will buy, will not fluctuate excessively, and that others will accept it on the same basis.

Still another form of money is the check, drawn against a checking account held in a bank. The person who fills out and signs a check is authorizing the bank to withdraw from his or her account the amount of money specified. The person accepting the check either cashes it (converting it to currency) or deposits it to a savings or checking account in a bank. In the latter case, neither debtor nor creditor handles the money; the exchange is simply a paper (or recently an electronic) transaction between two banks.

HOW BANKS BEGAN

The predecessors of modern banks were goldsmiths and moneylenders. These individuals had strong vaults. Other people who had gold (and other valuables), but no way to keep it safe, asked the goldsmiths or moneylenders to store their valuables for them. The goldsmiths and moneylenders charged a fee for doing so. It turned out that only a fraction of the total amount of gold and other valuables left with these guardians was ever withdrawn by the owners in any given period. That is, only a few clients would ask for their deposits at any one time. Thus, to meet those clients' requests, the vault owners needed to keep only a relatively small fraction of the total deposits on hand at any time.

Now, if you were a vault owner and knew that only a certain percentage of the valuables in your keeping would be requested in any one period, you could lend out the remainder, charge interest for the loan, and make more income, in addition to the fee for the use of your vault. This is how banks evolved into a **fractional reserve banking system** (that is, a group of institutions accepting deposits of which only a *fraction* is held on reserve, the rest being lent out or invested). It may surprise you to learn that if you deposit $100 in your checking account, your bank is not legally obliged to keep that $100 on reserve. It can, and does, lend out a certain percentage of its deposits, or it buys bonds and other investments in order to earn income.

Bank lending makes more credit available in the economy, thus enabling people to buy now and pay later, when they have more income.

THE WATCHDOG OF BANKS

When the Federal Reserve System was established by an act of Congress in 1913, the preamble to the act stated that the purpose of the system is

> to provide for the establishment of Federal Reserve Banks, to furnish an elastic currency, to afford means of rediscounting commercial paper, to establish a more effective supervision of banking in the United States, and for other purposes.

Currently, the Federal Reserve System consists of 12 Federal Reserve Banks with 25 branches, a seven-member board of governors whose members are appointed by the president to 14-year terms, and several committees, including the very important Federal Open Market Committee.

The **reserve requirement** for the approximately 5,700 member banks is set by the board of governors, and those reserves must be kept in the Federal Reserve Banks. The reserves of the nation's banking system are made up of deposits of the member commercial banks of the Federal Reserve. Not all banks, however, are members of the Federal Reserve System. These other commercial banks are permitted to count as reserves any currency kept in their own vaults. It should be noted, however, that the bulk of total bank deposits is held in Federal Reserve member banks.

The key function of the Federal Reserve is to control the amount of money in circulation in the United States. This involves walking a tightrope: On one hand, enough money must circulate to provide for the expanding needs of business in a growing economy; on the other hand, an oversupply of money must be avoided or an inflationary cycle will ensue, as we shall see later in this chapter.

The money supply can be controlled in several ways. In explaining three of these approaches, let us assume that the present purpose is to *contract* the money supply (which would make money less available in the marketplace, to fight inflation). In each case, an opposite action by the Federal Reserve would *expand* the money supply in the same way.

The first way, which has not often been used in recent years, is for the Federal Reserve to raise its requirement for reserves to be held by member banks. Take the case of a bank that has been holding $1 million in deposits under a reserve of 20 percent. Of its total assets, it has had to hold $200,000 in reserve, but could loan out $800,000. Meantime, that $800,000 has found its way into other banks, which have, in turn, been allowed to loan out 80 percent of that total, or $640,000. So the cycle continues along a chain of banks, with the money busily changing hands. This is often called the **deposit expansion process.**

Now, to contract the money supply, let us suppose that the Federal Reserve raises its reserve requirement to 40 percent. The bank with $1 million in deposits is now obliged to hold $400,000 in reserve. Thus it will have to call in $200,000 in outstanding loans or, if the $200,000 is coming due from outstanding loans, must refuse to make further loans from that amount. Moreover, each of the other banks along the chain is similarly affected. Many who come to the banks for loans must be refused; money is tight!

A second, and more common, way in which the Federal Reserve can contract the money in circulation is to raise its **discount rate,** the interest charged by a Federal Reserve Bank when it loans money to member banks. In the Federal Reserve System, when a member bank does not have enough reserves to meet its reserve requirement, it has to borrow the difference, and it may turn to the Federal Reserve itself for the loan. When that discount rate is raised, member banks will be less ready to borrow. Money is again harder to come by in the marketplace.

The third way, which is the most powerful and often-used means by which the Federal Reserve affects the supply of money in circulation, is by changing reserves directly. It does this by buying and selling U.S. government bonds from and to the public or banks. For example, suppose the Federal Reserve buys a $1,000 bond from a member bank. To pay for the bond, it does something that individuals cannot do. It credits $1,000 to the reserve deposit account of the bank from which it purchases the bond. This means that the bank now has one less bond and $1,000 more in reserves. Therefore, the bank can loan additional money, because its reserves are now higher than before. In this manner, the Federal Reserve can increase the money supply.

When the Federal Reserve wants to decrease the money supply, it merely sells a bond to a member bank. The bank pays for the bond by having its reserve deposit account lowered by the amount of the bond. The bank then can loan less money.

To summarize, then, the Federal Reserve can curb the money supply (fight inflation) by (1) raising the reserve requirements of its member banks, (2) raising its discount rate, or (3) selling government bonds to its member banks and debiting their reserve funds. It can expand the money supply (thus encouraging employment) by (1) lowering the reserve requirements of its member banks, (2) lowering its discount rate, or (3) buying government bonds from its member banks, thus crediting their reserve accounts. These are the tools by which the economy can be controlled as the Federal Reserve deems best.

RISING AND FALLING PRICES

Do you remember how much you paid for a hamburger ten years ago? How much do you pay for it today? Quite a difference? During your lifetime you have experienced sharp increases in the cost of practically everything you bought. Watching prices rise year by year, you have been exposed to the worldwide phenomenon of inflation—a problem that has plagued society for centuries.

Later in this chapter we shall examine the course of price fluctuations in the American past. There have been many times when, as in the recent past, prices have risen sharply; but at other times the opposite trend, **deflation,** has occurred. Let us see who is helped and who is hurt in each case.

Although by definition **inflation** means a sustained period of rising prices, it certainly does not always mean a period of prosperity. Even if it did, not everyone would benefit. When prices rise unexpectedly, people who have given credit to others are repaid in dollars that cannot buy as much as they could before. Thus creditors will lose and debtors will gain. In such circumstances it might appear wise to borrow or to buy as much as possible on credit. However, when people anticipate rising prices, the cost of borrowing (the interest rate) goes up. Those who lend money demand higher interest because they will be repaid in dollars whose purchasing power has diminished. By the same reasoning, debtors will be willing to pay the higher interest rates, knowing that the car bought today would almost certainly cost quite a bit more by the time the loan is repaid. As a result, interest rates nationwide will rise in step with the awareness, and expectation, of rising prices.

Another fact of life during inflationary times is the decreased value of cash holdings. As a current example, anyone who kept an average of $10 cash in pocket all during 1980 would have found at the end of the year that the money was worth only $8.80; about 12 percent in purchasing power would have vanished over that period.

It is clear, then, that people with cash savings are hurt by inflation. So are those whose incomes are fixed (that is, those who live on the income from pension funds or from investments, so that the return remains constant no matter how much the cost of living rises). A person who retired in 1960 with a fixed pension of $200 per month can today buy less than one third the amount obtainable at the time of retirement. However, many pension plans now include an automatic adjustment clause to offset inflation.

What about the worker who is earning wages or a salary? If everything in the economy went up in price except wages, workers would be in trouble, but in inflationary cycles the wage scale goes up, too. Since 1933 disposable income (income after taxes) has been going up an average of 3.8 percent per year. In general, incomes not only rise each year, but they also often increase more than prices do. This means that most workers are actually better off at the end of each year, if they consider their real standard of living. For example, if their income has risen 8 percent and prices have increased only 6 percent in the past year, then their standard of living has gone up 2 percent in spite of inflation. Historically, most people's incomes have kept up with inflation.

ABSOLUTE VERSUS RELATIVE PRICES

The accepted yardstick for measuring inflation (or deflation) is the **Consumer Price Index** (CPI). This figure, issued monthly by the Bureau of Labor Statistics of the U.S. Department of Labor, is determined by pricing a "market basket" of specified goods and services and comparing the current price of the various items with what each would have cost at a base period in the past.

Suppose that over the last 15 years the price of televisions has fallen and the price of some other items has risen at a rate less than the Consumer Price Index. What does this tell you? It indicates that the relative price of certain goods is lower today than it was more than 15 years ago. This is an important distinction for a wise consumer to make. As you should recall, the absolute price level is not as important as the relative price of the things you buy. To illustrate, suppose that the average of all prices rises 200 percent, but the price of a washing machine goes up only 100 percent. Although the absolute price of the washing machine is higher, it is a good buy because its relative price has actually fallen.

The same consideration of relative value holds true in the case of borrowing funds. Those who lend money are going to demand higher interest rates during inflationary cycles because, as we noted earlier, they know they will be paid back in "cheaper" dollars (dollars whose purchasing power has declined). But for the borrower, the transaction may still be worthwhile. To figure out the real cost of a loan, you must subtract the anticipated rate of inflation from the interest rate. The remainder is the real cost of the loan in terms of what you are giving up in purchasing power when you choose to buy goods or services today instead of waiting.

THE CAUSE OF INFLATION

There are several theories about the cause of inflation. The debate rages on among economists, and certainly no single theory can explain why prices are rising in the United States and probably will continue to do so. Nevertheless, we can group the theories under two general headings: **demand-pull** versus **cost-push** forces in the marketplace.

Demand-Pull Inflation   One of the oldest general theories of inflation concerns the amount of money in circulation: When the money supply is excessive, there are "too many dollars chasing too few goods." The **quantity theory of money and prices** asserts that under certain conditions the average level of prices *must* vary according to the total money in circulation. (The conditions are that the volume of trade remains relatively stable and that each dollar bill will change hands about the same number of times.) According to this theory, if the money supply doubles, the price level will also double.

History shows that the quantity theory of money and prices works well for predicting the rate of inflation over a long period of time. For example, as we shall see later, Spanish importation of gold and silver from the New World caused huge price increases in Spain and throughout Europe in the 1600s. The discovery of gold in the United States, Canada, and South Africa in the middle and late 1800s brought about drastic expansions in the money supply and rapidly rising prices.

However, the theory does not work as well in predicting price levels in the short run. The chief reason is that the average number of times money changes hands varies as business activity increases or decreases.

We can categorize this theory as the demand-pull theory of inflation because it asserts that there cannot be a sustained rise in prices unless there is too much demand for the amount of goods and services existing in the economy. If too many dollars are put into circulation, individuals will spend their additional dollars outbidding each other and prices will inevitably rise.

The simplest demand-pull theory would assert that inflation can happen only when there is full employment in the economy. It is known from experience, however, that rising prices and unemployment can occur together. Economists describe that situation as one in which cost-push inflation is at work.

Cost-Push Inflation   Other theories attempt to explain why prices can rise even when the economy is not at full employment. This abnormal sort of inflation was experienced in the United States during the 1969–1970 and the 1973–1975 recessions. Analysts who hold to the cost-push theory point out three culprits: union power, big business monopoly power, and higher raw materials prices.

Those who believe that unions are responsible for inflation reason as follows: Unions often demand wage raises not necessarily warranted by the amount of output workers are producing. Since unions may be powerful, businesses often give in to union demands. When businesses have to pay higher wages, their costs increase, and to maintain normal profit, they must raise prices. This type of cost-push inflation may occur even when there is no excess demand or when the economy is operating at less than full capacity and full employment.

The second explanation for cost-push inflation suggests that inflation is caused by big business monopoly power. According to this view, powerful corporations are able to raise prices whenever they want to increase their profits. Each time this occurs, the cost of living goes up. Workers then demand higher wages to make up for the loss in their standard of living. This, in turn, gives corporations an excuse to raise prices again; and so goes the vicious cycle of price and wage increases.

Still another explanation is raw materials cost-push inflation. It often seems that the cost of raw materials will rise indefinitely. In the 1970s and early 1980s coal became more expensive; so did petroleum, natural gas, and many other basic inputs into production processes.

Short of engaging in the debate, we can only decide on the basis of historical evidence that prices will probably, overall, continue moving upward, at least periodically. Then we can attempt to guard against the effects of inflation by making wise economic decisions in our own affairs.

Price Levels in the American Past

The Wealth of the New World

We begin our look at the history of prices in America almost at the beginning. We mentioned earlier a classic case in which discoveries of new wealth caused international repercussions. That was the influx of silver and gold to Europe following the Spanish conquest in the New World. Most colonization starts money flowing in the other direction, from home base to new frontiers. It is true

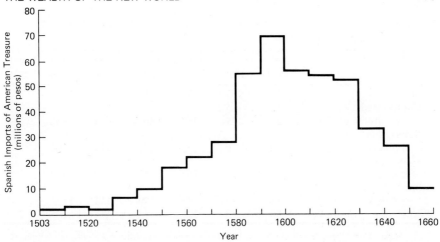

Figure 8.1 Spanish imports of American treasure. [*Source*: Earl J. Hamilton, *American Treasure and the Price Revolution in Spain, 1501–1650* (Cambridge, Mass.: Harvard University Press, 1934).]

that in the first years of Spanish conquest Spanish nobles and merchants did supply financial support for ships and stores, but by 1506 several colonizing Spaniards had accumulated sizable fortunes that helped finance further ventures into Cuba, Jamaica, and Puerto Rico. In turn, investments in Cuba produced wealth that supported a series of mainland expeditions, including the conquest of Mexico. Meantime, a portion of that wealth was beginning to stream toward the treasure-hungry Old World. By the middle of the century, the stream turned to a river and then to a torrent, as shown in Figure 8.1. Compared to the supply of money at the beginning of the century, the influx approximately tripled the total money supply of Europe.

What result would you expect? Far, far too many dollars were chasing what goods were then available. Inflation became the order of the day. By 1600 Spanish prices were 340 percent above their 1500 level. Similarly, England's prices had risen almost 260 percent and French prices 220 percent.

The phenomenal impact of American treasure on European prices, commerce, and growth was analyzed in a pioneering study by Earl J. Hamilton, who argued that *the influx of treasure drove up both prices and wages, but prices more rapidly.* [1] As real wages declined, income and wealth were distributed increasingly in favor of merchants and capitalists. Since these classes supposedly had unusually strong incentives to save and invest, this led to higher rates of capital formation and ultimately to economic growth throughout Europe.

The first part of Hamilton's argument certainly is strongly supported by the evidence. No one can deny that the tidal wave of wealth raised prices. The fall in real wages is clearly shown by the data in Tables 8.1 and 8.2. However, his argument that merchants and capitalists were the greatest beneficiaries of the price rises is much less defensible. Recalling the vital distinction between

---

[1] Earl J. Hamilton, "Prices as a Factor in Business Growth: Prices and Progress," *Journal of Economic History* 69 (Fall 1952): 338–339.

Table 8.1   INDEXES OF PRICE AND WAGE TRENDS IN ENGLAND, 1500–1702
            1451–1500 = 100.

	1521–1530	1551–1560	1583–1592	1613–1622	1643–1652	1673–1682	1693–1702
Total prices	113	132	198	257	331	348	339
Unprocessed agricultural products	132	179	262	402	478	466	518
Assorted industrial products	110	116	150	176	217	200	239
Wood and wood products	87	119	185	259	300	420	395
Imported food products	151	119	146	124	151	—	163
Wages	93	88	125	134	175	205	233

Source: David Felix, "Profit Inflation and Industrial Growth: The Historic Record and Contemporary Analogies," *Quarterly Journal of Economics* 70 (August 1956): 446.

Table 8.2   INDEXES OF PRICE AND WAGE TRENDS IN FRANCE, 1500–1702
            1451–1500 = 100.

	1501–1525	1526–1550	1551–1575	1576–1600	1601–1625	1626–1650	1651–1675	1676–1702
Total prices	113	136	174	248	189	243	227	229
Selected agricultural products	136	163	250	429	259	402	345	315
Assorted manufacturers	96	130	122	144	129	143	133	161
Wages	92	104	103	113	113	127	127	125

Source: David Felix, "Profit Inflation and Industrial Growth: The Historic Record and Contemporary Analogies," *Quarterly Journal of Economics* 70 (August 1956): 446.

absolute prices and relative prices, take a closer look at the two tables. They show that, *relatively* speaking, the chief contributors to the rise in overall prices were not manufactured products but food and agricultural items. During that time, the prices of finished goods were actually rising less than the prices of raw materials.

So who benefited most? It was those who could supply foodstuffs to a rapidly growing population—the landowners. The reason was that the increasing population was putting heavy pressure on relatively scarce arable land, rentals for that land were skyrocketing, and those who gained most from the relative price movements of the period were those who owned the land. The redistribution of wealth was not so much from workers to capitalists as from nonagricultural to agricultural interests.

Again it is important to distinguish between *relative* and *absolute* price changes. The influx of treasure and the consequent increase in the money supply did spur inflation. This had the tendency to push *all* prices higher over time. However, general inflation—a rise in average prices—tells us little about changes in relative prices. Some prices moved up faster than others, and for these differential movements we need to look at the conditions of supply and demand for various goods and productive resources. The general forces of inflation fail to explain differences in relative price movement, but relative price changes lie at the heart of Hamilton's thesis.

The influx of American treasure did not by itself cause a redistribution of income among economic classes or sectors that led to economic development. It did enrich Spain relative to other nations, at least temporarily, but there is little indication that this advantage raised the productivity or soundness of the Spanish economy. The flood of wealth may even have encouraged Spain to undertake the many ill-fated military ventures that eventually led to its decline. With the exhaustion of American mines around 1650, Spain's vital resource influx dried up, and Spain quickly became a second-rate power. No empire of similar dominance has ever undergone such a rapid rise and fall. No other has rested on such a temporary base.

The American Case

America, too, felt the pressure of inflation and deflation during its formative years. We saw earlier in this chapter, and we know from experience, that the soaring prices of inflation can hurt the consumer and anyone living on a fixed income. What about inflation's opposite, deflation?

As the price level fell unexpectedly in the early and mid-1780s, there was growing unrest among debtors in our nation. It is not hard to understand why. Let's say, for example, that farmers had borrowed money to purchase land and tools at a 10 percent rate of interest. Had the price level remained stable, that 10 percent rate of interest would have been paid off in dollars that had the same value when the loan was repaid as when the loan was taken out. The **principal** of the loan—the total amount borrowed—when repaid would also have the same purchasing power it had when it was borrowed. Now look at the situation when we have an *unexpected* fall in the price of goods and services in our economy. Debtors found they had to pay the principal and interest on the loan with dollars that had a higher purchasing power when repaid than when they were borrowed. The actual (real) rate of interest that they were forced to pay for the loans they had taken out before the deflation started was now higher than what was stipulated in the contracts they had signed. Notice that the key to understanding the unrest of debtors during this period of deflation is that the deflation was *unanticipated*. Had it been fully anticipated, debtors would have been willing to pay only a lower rate of interest, and creditors would have been willing to accept that lower rate, knowing full well that they would be paid back in dollars with a higher purchasing power.

In Figure 8.2 we see that the period after the Civil War was one of a drop in the price level, that is, of deflation. In fact, prices *fell* at an average annual rate of 5.4 percent from 1867 to 1879! Farmers and business persons during those years of falling prices cried out, strangely enough, for higher prices. Between 1879 and 1896 prices continued to fall but at a lower rate—1 percent per year. But falling prices or deflation did not mean depression, or declining real incomes, in

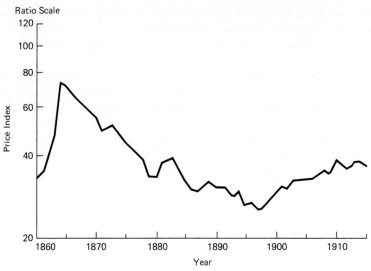

Figure 8.2   The price level, 1860–1915. (*Source*: U.S. Bureau of Labor Statistics.)

the long run. Let's look at the **gross national product** (GNP) for those years. (The GNP is the value of the total final output of goods and services in the economy per year.) Notice that when the price index in Figure 8.2 is compared with the graph of average real GNP per capita in Figure 8.3, there is a slight *negative* correlation.

There was, however, a distinct relationship between changes in the price level and changes in the stock of money during the period. Right after the Civil

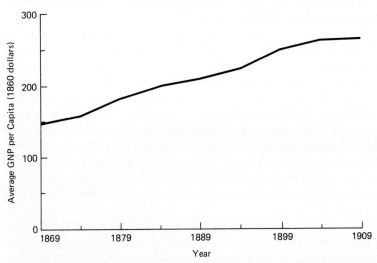

Figure 8.3   Rising standards of living. [*Source*: R. E. Gallman, "Gross National Product in the United States, 1834–1909," in National Bureau of Economic Research, *Output, Employment and Productivity in the United States After 1800* (New York: Columbia University Press, 1966), p. 30.]

War the federal government deliberately reduced the quantity of greenbacks in circulation in order to raise the value of a greenback to a dollar in gold. This exchange **at par** (that is, with $1 in gold exchangeable for $1 in paper) finally happened in 1879. Meanwhile, there were some—primarily farmers—who wanted more, not fewer, greenbacks. In particular, the Greenback Labor party associated more money with higher prices of products and hence higher incomes and a higher standard of living.

What ended the long slide? After the year 1878, we were on a de facto gold standard. That is, gold served as a medium of exchange and as the backing for reserves in the banking system. Hence, the entire money stock was tied to the production of gold, which did not increase rapidly enough to keep up with the need for money for the nation's transactions. Consequently, the economy experienced deflation for three decades. It was only after discoveries of gold in South Africa and the Yukon, plus development of the relatively inexpensive cyanide reduction process—which allowed the gold stock (and, hence, the money stock) to increase faster than the increased rate of output—that the deflation was stopped. Lastly, notice that in the latter period under study (1898–1915) a rise in prices finally occurred.

Before looking at the role of banks in the early American economy, let's take a leap forward in time to examine a phenomenon that has been in existence since 1969. This queer beast does not fit well into the classical description of the short-run relationship between money supply and prices. In general, we equate inflation with excess demand; that is, people try to buy more goods and services than actually exist, thus forcing prices up. However, with lots of unemployment we know that there is *no* excess demand, for unemployed workers imply the opposite.

What we have seen is a hybrid called *inflationary recession,* or "stagflation" (stagnation plus inflation). In the early 1970s an inflationary cycle had been under way in the United States for some time. Inflation continued, and prices remained high, but—strangely—the demand for workers fell off sharply. Men and women lost their jobs. During the early years of the 1970s, while employment steadily worsened, prices hung right on at their peaks. This was certainly an odd situation.

How can we explain stagflation? Basically, three hypotheses are advanced by economists. The first two are straightforward, but they are also of questionable value. The third is much more complex but nearer to the truth.

First, it is charged that over time the labor unions became so powerful that wages increased enough to create unemployment. Thus, both high prices and unemployment resulted.

Second, some argue that during the 1970s competition was inadequate in many markets and entrepreneurs hungry for profits pushed prices far above what they would have been under competitive conditions. Eventually consumers balked and stopped buying. Since the law of demand states that higher prices lead to lower quantities demanded, entrepreneurs who raised prices found that they did not sell as much, and consequently they laid off workers.

Both these arguments make only limited sense. In the first place, such price rises would be triggered by *increases* in the power of the unions or managements, not by the simple existence of such power. There is little evidence that the power of either group, monopolies or unions, has increased noticeably in recent times. Moreover, there would be no way to predict this type of cost-push inflation. In what year could one expect the unions, or business, to assert greater monopoly power? These theories tell us little and are not supported by the facts.

The third explanation has to do with how people perceive the future—with their expectations or anticipations. Let's suppose that workers anticipate that the demand for their labor services will yield them a certain wage rate, depending on what they were used to in the past and on what they see their friends and colleagues receiving. Businesses also have anticipations about the prices they can set on their products in order to maximize profits. In periods of rapidly increasing aggregate demand, such as started in 1965, each year workers and businesses were temporarily fooled. Businesses found that they could raise prices and still sell all the goods and services they had anticipated selling. In fact, at the end of the year they might have found lower levels of inventories than they had anticipated. If so, this told them that they could raise prices. At the same time, consumers were buying, because they too anticipated even higher prices in the future.

Workers, on the other hand, were demanding higher wages and getting them or were switching jobs to obtain them. Many discovered that they could find jobs more easily and at higher wages than they had anticipated. In other words, the demand for their labor services was going up faster in money terms than they expected.

In 1969 and 1970, the government's monetary and fiscal policy was suddenly altered. The growth rate of the money supply was decreased, and federal government purchases fell. These occurrences led to a lower rate of growth in aggregate demand. But business people, who had no idea that this was anything more than a random event, continued to raise prices because they based their predictions of what they could sell on what had happened in the past. At the same time, however, consumers' incomes leveled off. Now they reacted to higher prices by buying less. Inventories started piling up, and layoffs occurred.

Meanwhile, workers still demanded higher wages, for in the past several (inflationary) years they had been accepting wage increases that merely matched increases in the cost of living. Many union contracts were renegotiated during this period. The union leaders wanted not only to make up for the lost real income of the last three or four years, but also to anticipate future erosions of their paychecks by inflation. Hence, they made demands for higher wages. At first business granted them, fully anticipating that they could pass these higher labor costs on to the consumer while maintaining their previous sales records. Such was not the case, however, as both laborers and businesses were caught eventually by an unanticipated change in aggregate demand. Hence, we had a period of rising prices and rising unemployment.

Eventually, though, people started learning, so we saw a decrease in the rate at which inflation was growing until mid-1970. In fact, it appeared that the rate of inflation was abating when President Nixon instituted his New Economic Policy on August 15, 1971. The slowdown in price rise was soon to be reversed as the government's expansionary monetary and fiscal policies, instituted to pull us out of the recession, reinjected purchasing power into the economy and started us off on another inflationary spiral.

We can summarize the most recent price level experiences by stating that since the Vietnam War, inflation has accelerated and become extremely variable on a year-to-year basis. Until the 1960s, we could have considered the U.S. economy fairly immune to peacetime inflation, for there were only two examples of it—in the 1890s and from 1934 until World War II. Clearly, the U.S. experience since the 1960s has been different. Double-digit inflation was common in the 1970s and early 1980s. Next let's look at banking and its effect on the price level.

The First and Second Banks of the United States

The First Bank died when its charter was not renewed, in 1811. The timing of that decision was disastrous, for one year later came the War of 1812. The outbreak of hostilities found treasury finances in disarray, and the lack of a central bank led to a surge of small local banks operating according to inconsistent, unregulated rules of their own. Uneasy about this situation, some people refused to pay off their debts in hard currency (gold or silver). A cry went up for a second national bank, and in 1816 the Second Bank of the United States was chartered, again for a 20-year period.

Although it opened with capital stock three and a half times as great as that of the First Bank, the Second Bank soon ran into trouble. The price of cotton was dropping and farmers were hard pressed to pay back their loans. Instead of countering these problems by expanding credit, the bank in 1818 and through 1819 contracted its deposits. This put pressure on state banks, especially in the West. At the same time, much of America's precious specie was flowing overseas to pay off an enormous national obligation—the price of the Louisiana Purchase. This contracted the money supply in a way that the public did not anticipate.

Finally, the panic of 1819 occurred. The bank completely stopped the payment of specie, and there were bank failures throughout the country. The price level was falling drastically at the same time. However, the extent of this crisis should not be exaggerated in a country that was highly agricultural. True, the commercial sector was hit very hard, but the largely self-sufficient agricultural sector was not. The first president of the bank, who was considered incompetent, was ousted after the panic of 1819. Two later presidents, Langdon Sheves (1819–1823) and Nicholas Biddle (1823–1836), were viewed with more esteem, but Biddle too eventually faced difficulties.

Meanwhile, there were political currents in motion, particularly toward the end of Biddle's appointment. When President Jackson took office in 1829, he immediately began to attack the Second Bank of the United States. He wanted to close it, but a committee formed in the House of Representatives affirmed the constitutionality of the bank in spite of Jackson's request that it do otherwise. During the 1820s, the Second Bank had developed a sort of national currency because it had many branches, and U.S. bank notes were in circulation everywhere. The rate of exchange between U.S. bank notes and all other bank notes was approximately stable throughout the nation. Congress saw this as a good thing, and Jackson's attempt at the time to block recharter on the grounds of unconstitutionality failed.

The Second Bank was unpopular in some quarters. Of course, it was not like a modern central bank. It could not legally regulate the reserves of commercial banks, and the support it could give to others in periods of financial crises was limited. Still, by virtue of its size and the number of branches it had, it could exercise some control over the economy. For instance, it would ask for specie payments for notes from other banks from time to time, to keep them "honest."

Biddle's big political mistake was to apply for a recharter four years before the end of the Second Bank's original charter. His purpose was to get rechartered and at the same time to embarrass Jackson in the 1832 election and maybe cause him to lose it. (Biddle backed Henry Clay in the 1832 campaign.) The recharter was passed in Congress in July 1832, but it was vetoed by Jackson. For Biddle, the scheme backfired.

The demise of the Second Bank of the United States brought with it many changes in the American banking scene. However, what happened after its demise was not entirely a result of that particular event. We are speaking about the inflation of 1835, 1836, and part of 1837, and about the depression from 1839 to 1843. Many historians believe that the inflation was caused by the fall of the Second Bank, which allowed for a rapid increase in the amount of paper currency available through a proliferation of wildcat banks. (These banks got their names from the fact that they were so far out in the boondocks that it was said only wildcats frequented them.) The evidence concerning the increase in the money supply and the increase in prices is fairly impressive. For example, Figure 8.4 shows that the money supply did indeed increase after Jackson's veto in 1832.

At this time Jackson began withdrawing funds from the Second Bank and placing them in state banks called pet banks. Biddle's powers were curbed severely.

But was wildcat banking resulting from the demise of the Second Bank the cause of the sharp money increase? No, wildcat banking with unchecked expansion of credit and paper currency did not occur. The ratio of the bank-held reserves to credit outstanding did not rise. Banks on the whole were fairly cautious, and they did not overlend. What, then, caused the money supply to increase?

The United States was part of an international economy. It adhered to a gold and silver standard, which involved shipments of gold and silver in and out of the country. These formed the basis of our circulating money supply. Moreover, there was a large increase in specie imports from Mexico. Britain and France were also periodically sending specie to the United States. The bottom line of Figure 8.4 shows that there was a tremendous specie jump between 1833 and 1837. Therefore, the demise of the Second Bank alone did not cause the inflation of 1835 and 1836.

Still, the Second Bank was a factor. In the early 1830s people became very trusting of banks, largely because the Second Bank helped maintain sound banking practices. This confidence led to a sharp reduction in the proportion of specie people held as money. Paper money would serve just as well, people believed, as long as the banks were sound. But after the demise of the Second Bank people's

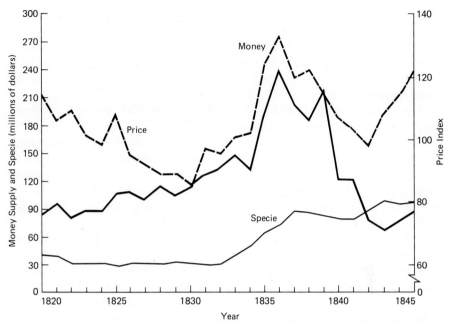

Figure 8.4 Prices and money supply, 1820–1845. [*Source*: Hugh Rockoff, "Money, Prices, and Banks in the Jacksonian Era," in *The Reinterpretation of American Economic History*, Robert W. Fogel and Stanley L. Engerman, eds. (New York: Harper & Row, 1971), Table 1, p. 451.]

confidence declined. The proportion of their money that they wanted in the form of specie went up. And the Specie Circular 1836, requiring that most federal land sales be paid in gold, also increased specie holdings by individuals. People went to the banks for specie, and when some of the banks could not convert bank notes into specie, banking panics ensued. Then nearly everyone wanted to convert their holdings, which put great strains on the banking system. The end result was the worst depression of the century, lasting from 1839 to 1843.

By this time, the effects of a depression, especially one as severe as that from 1839 to 1843, were felt much more acutely by the general population. To some degree, this economic contraction was international in scope, like the one to follow nearly a century later. Particularly hard hit was the new class of workers, those tied to the mills and factories. Mechanization and systematic production controls were just arriving on the American economic scene. To these new pressures were now added sharp declines in employment and **real wages** (wages adjusted for changes in the purchasing power of money) throughout the business downturn. To the hardships of hard work was added the hardship of forced idleness.

Central Banking: The Control of the Money Supply

Another major change came during the Civil War, when a National Banking System was established by legislation. But it was far from perfect. Partly because its method of clearing checks was so costly and inept, the central bank failed to take hold as a national network. As we saw earlier, Congress filled the vacuum in 1913 by passing the act that established the Federal Reserve System. Since then, right up to the present, the power of the Federal Reserve System has been expended to establish and maintain economic stability through regulation of the money supply.

Early in its history, during World War I, "the Fed" played a relatively passive role. Its part was to give full support to the U.S. Treasury in financing the war effort. To expedite the sale of government bonds, the system permitted an abundance of currency and demand deposits to enter the economy. It lowered the interest rate charged to its member banks (the discount rate), encouraging them to borrow more, to build up their reserve funds, and, in turn, to loan out more money. The supply of money in circulation soared: In 1917, money per capita had stood at $225; two years later the figure was $350.

The same thing promptly happened in the American economy as had happened in sixteenth-century Europe when gold and silver flooded in from the New World, and as had happened here during the American Revolution and during the Civil War. A war economy feeds on money, and money fuels inflation. So while the money supply was increasing between 1917 and 1919, the wholesale price index was jumping 20 percent and the consumer price index 35 percent. Figure 8.5 shows the two upward courses. Inflation was again under way.

Now, however, a well-established federal banking system made it possible to check, if not to control, runaway inflation. The governors of the Federal Reserve System have power either to create money or to contract the supply. We have seen how the latter can be accomplished when the system raises the reserve requirements of member banks, raises its discount rate to the banks, or sells government bonds, and opposite actions will "create money" by easing the money supply in circulation.

It is generally thought that government expenditures financed by taxation

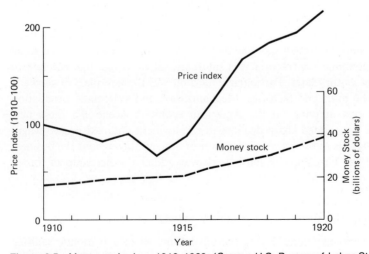

Figure 8.5   Money and prices 1910–1920. (*Source*: U.S. Bureau of Labor Statistics.)

and borrowing from the private sector are not inflationary because both methods have the effect of reducing private purchasing power. If a person pays part of his or her income in taxes, other private expenditures are usually curtailed. If an individual or a business firm decides to lend money to the government by buying a bond, then again individual power, or ability to spend in the private sector, will be reduced. Such is not the case when expenditures are financed by money creation.

People who eventually receive this extra cash do not want to reduce expenditures. Indeed, they want to increase them. Notice that inflation is another form of taxation, but a very special kind. If the price level rises, everybody who holds dollar bills or has a checking account suffers. After all, if you have $100 in the bank and keep it there for a year while the price of everything goes up 10 percent, that $100 has lost 10 percent of its value. It has depreciated by 10 percent. In effect, then, you have paid a 10 percent tax on holding these dollars. There is no way to avoid this tax (except the hypothetical one of trading only in goods, not dollars, which would be extremely costly and inconvenient). Consequently, governments often resort to this type of tax. It is easy to collect and very difficult to avoid. In addition, by using it, government officials can avoid the difficult matter of explicitly legislating new taxes or higher tax rates.

DEFINITIONS OF NEW TERMS

MONEY Money is anything that serves as a medium of exchange, a store of value, or a unit of accounting. In the United States it consists of currency and checking account balances.

LEGAL TENDER Legal tender is currency that must be accepted as payment for a debt or fulfillment of an obligation, or in payment for goods or services.

FIDUCIARY Fiduciary is paper currency that is founded on trust and not backed by some valued commodity such as gold or silver.

FRACTIONAL RESERVE BANKING SYSTEM In a fractional reserve system, each bank holds only a fraction of its deposits on reserve for immediate withdrawal by depositors and uses the rest for lending and investment purposes.

RESERVE REQUIREMENT The reserve requirement is the percentage of deposits that by law must be kept on reserve. For members of the Federal Reserve System, required reserves are kept on deposit in Federal Reserve Banks.

DEPOSIT EXPANSION PROCESS In the deposit expansion process, a dollar deposited with a bank leads to *more* than a dollar on deposit throughout the banking system. The first bank can, by Federal Reserve regulation, loan out a certain portion of its assets. The money it lends is then ultimately deposited in other banks, increasing their assets, and thus the amount they too can loan out—and this leads to still more money on deposit. The process is an ongoing cycle whereby a single deposit "expands" as money changes hands.

DISCOUNT RATE The discount rate is the rate of interest that the Federal Reserve charges its member banks when they must borrow from it in order to meet their required reserves.

DEFLATION Deflation is a continuing fall in the price level.

INFLATION A sustained rise in prices constitutes inflation.

CONSUMER PRICE INDEX The Consumer Price Index (CPI) is an index of prices compiled by the Bureau of Labor Statistics of the U.S. Department of Labor. The index is based on the cost of a market basket of goods and services compared with its equivalent during a base period.

DEMAND-PULL THEORY OF INFLATION The demand-pull theory of inflation explains rising prices by relating them to excess demand on the part of businesses and consumers. Basically, it is a situation described as "too many dollars chasing too few goods."

COST-PUSH THEORY OF INFLATION Cost-push inflation theory holds that spiraling prices are caused by the wage demands of unions, the excessive profit drive of large corporations, or the increasing costs of raw materials.

QUANTITY THEORY OF MONEY AND PRICES The quantity theory of money and prices is one theory that explains changes in prices and income. Basically, if the amount of goods and services in the economy and people's habits concerning how much cash they want to hold are constant, a change in the money supply will lead to an equal change in the price level.

PRINCIPAL The total amount borrowed that must be repaid when the loan becomes due is the principal of a loan.

GROSS NATIONAL PRODUCT The gross national product (GNP) is the value of the total final output of goods and services in a national economy per year.

AT PAR In an exchange at par, a promise to pay is sold for exactly its stated value. Thus if a dollar bill were backed by gold, it would be exchanged at par for a dollar in gold.

REAL WAGES Real wages consist of money wages and payments less corrections made for changes in the purchasing power of money.

The Man Who Faced the Jacksonians

NICHOLAS BIDDLE
(1786–1884)

President, Second Bank of the United States (1823–1836)

Faulty strategy in his fight against President Jackson and the Jacksonians certainly was not in keeping with the brilliant career that Nicholas Biddle had led up until the time he took over the presidency of the Second Bank of the United States in 1823. Biddle came from a prominent Philadelphia family. James Biddle, his father, was a U.S. Naval officer, commander of the *Ontario,* and the man who took formal possession of Oregon Country for the United States in 1818.

Young Nicholas was a precocious student; he entered the University of Pennsylvania at ten and graduated at the tender age of 13. He also received another degree from the College of New Jersey (now Princeton) at age 15. He was a student of the classics and French literature and became the editor of America's first literary periodical, *Port Folio.* In 1815 he helped prepare Pennsylvania's reply to the Hartford Convention, in which numerous proposed amendments to the Constitution had been offered. Most of these proposals attempted to limit the power of Congress and the executive. He went on later to compile for the State Department a digest of foreign legislation affecting U.S. trade.

Among his published works was *A History of the Expedition Under the Command of Captains Lewis and Clark,* which he prepared from the explorers' notes and journals.

By the time Biddle was appointed a director of the Second Bank of the United States in 1819, he was considered brilliant, debonair, and versatile. At the age of 37 he had already been a child prodigy, a writer, a lawyer, a state senator, and a diplomat. And Biddle added to these traits tremendous pride and an uncompromising attitude toward others. The latter two qualities seemed to serve him well when he took over the presidency of the Second Bank.

As president he showed that he could discipline any other bank by forcing it to pay debts to the Second Bank of the United States and its branches in hard specie. But such behavior did not win Biddle many friends in the newer sections of the country or in the Old South.

Biddle's cavalier demeanor did not enhance his chances of winning over President

Jackson's veto of the Bank's charter in 1832. Jackson claimed the Bank was unconstitutional and was merely a monopoly that used public funds to enrich a few already wealthy men. Of course, Jackson's veto prevailed, and from 1834 to 1836 Biddle had his bank concentrate on how to liquidate itself. This, of course, meant moving all of its capital to the East, where the banking center of the nation still lay. However, a state charter was drawn up giving it a new name and allowing it to continue in existence. With this new lease on life, Biddle attempted to maintain the world price of cotton because he felt it was crucial to American credit abroad. His first cotton pool earned a cool $800,000. The second one, however, failed to the tune of over $900,000. The Bank closed its doors in 1841.

Biddle died disgraced and discredited by many, but he left behind principles that could be used later in the formulation of a true central banking system in the United States. Some observers believe that the monetary and banking reforms of Franklin Delano Roosevelt and the original creation of the Federal Reserve System were in part based on some of the principles established by Biddle.

chapter 9

Business Cycles and Unemployment

How is today's economy to be managed to give the greatest good to the greatest number? How are the hands and minds of America's men and women to be put to work? These are some of the problems policymakers must solve. To gain perspective on the relationship between **business fluctuations** and unemployment, let us look at some situations that occurred during the earlier decades of this century.

THE NATURE OF BUSINESS CYCLES

First, what are business cycles? What causes them, and how can anyone trace (or predict) their course? The term itself is somewhat misleading because it implies a certain regularity. Figure 9.1 shows the smooth curves that represent an idealized concept of the business cycle. In contrast, Figure 9.2 shows the actual course of America's business health over the course of a century.

In the idealized business cycle, a boom period is followed by a downturn (colloquially, a bust). The downturn may become a **recession.** The recession leads to a recovery period, followed by a new period of prosperity, which then leads to another downturn. The various phases of the business cycle are useful in describing the state of the nation's economy at any time. By itself, however, such a description does not explain why business is sometimes good and sometimes bad.

In attempting to answer this vital question, economists have developed several theories, each shedding some light on the problems, and even the most improbable of them, such as the sunspot theory, perhaps having some basis in

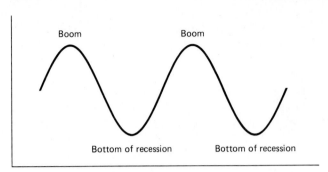

Figure 9.1 An idealized business cycle.

fact. Sunspots are a form of solar activity characterized by great storms on the sun's surface. In the nineteenth century some economists theorized that solar storms might be responsible for downturns in business because these storms affected the weather on earth. Ridiculous? Not altogether so, when we recall that agriculture was the most important factor in the overall economy at the time and that crops depend on weather conditions.

As a matter of fact, throughout most of the nineteenth century there did seem to be a direct relationship between sunspot cycles and agricultural cycles. However, that relationship did not carry over into the twentieth century. Such a theory of business cycles could have been a useful predicting tool had the relationship between weather and business activity persisted. Since scientists today can predict sunspot activity accurately, their predictions might have provided an accurate means of predicting changes in business activity.

The Innovation Theory   An innovation is an invention that ultimately makes good. The great bulk of inventions never really succeed, however interesting and ingenious they may be. Some may quickly go out of date or others may be too limited in their utility. But other inventions become such an essential part of our economy that it is difficult to imagine life without them; the electric light, the telephone, and the automobile are some examples.

The innovation theory suggests that when an invention of this caliber enters the marketplace it leads to a fluctuation in overall business investment. As in-

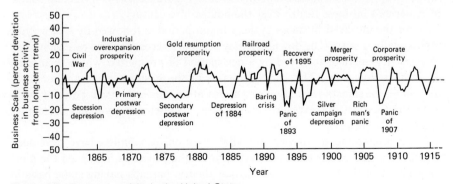

Figure 9.2 Business activity in the United States.

dividuals or firms decide to use the invention ("to innovate"), others are also induced to invest in the new production processes. Business activity takes a sudden upsurge. Eventually, the saturation point is reached. Investment dies down and, with it, overall business activity.

Although the innovation theory has merit in explaining some business cycles, it is weak as a predicting tool. How can people predict when innovations will be made? After the fact, certainly, people can judge which ones have caused a particular increase in economic activity. But although the theory is helpful in some cases in explaining business cycles *after* they have occurred, it cannot predict when changes in business activity *will* occur.

The Psychological Theory   It is possible that people's psychological reactions to changing economic and political events cause changes in business activity. Waves of optimism may be caused, for example, by the prospect of war or peace, or by the prospect of new discoveries of natural resources. As people ride these waves of optimism, the level of business activity tends to follow suit.

However, this type of theorizing, like the innovation theory, is useful in explaining things only after they have occurred. There is little opportunity to use the psychological theory to predict when the next boom or recession will occur. Yet this is precisely what economists want to do with any theory of changes in business activity.

These theories have all fallen into disuse, mainly because they have not helped to explain the many ups and downs in our most recent business activity. Farther on, as we examine some of the actual ups and downs of the American economy in this century, we will also consider some more sophisticated, and more successful, theories that are under current debate. We will find familiar names, like Keynes and Friedman, and terms, like monetarism, cropping up in this discussion. For the present, however, let's consider what happens to *people* when the economy begins one of its periodic downward slides.

UNEMPLOYMENT

When shoppers cut down on buying, businesses find that their stocks of goods for sale do not diminish as fast as in the past. Eventually, they cannot afford to

keep all the workers that they employed when business activity was better. They also cut back on orders to suppliers, thereby reducing derived demand for labor and other factors of production. Producers are then forced to fire or to lay off some members of their work force. Those workers then enter the ranks of the unemployed. This is where the pain of changes in business activity is first felt. The person who is unemployed must rely for survival on savings and government transfers. This is the human aspect of the business cycle that responsible people can never forget. Many know that the level of unemployment in the United States has not always been socially or politically acceptable.

Figure 9.3 depicts the rate of unemployment in the United States over time. You have only to look at the peak labeled 1932 to realize that at that point a recession had deepened into the greatest *depression* in the history of the United States. The rate of unemployment stood at almost 25 percent, meaning that for every three people working, one other was out of work and actively seeking a job that just did not exist. Compared with that high level, more recent rates of unemployment seem relatively mild. Yet few Americans are satisfied to leave willing and competent workers standing idle.

But what is the magical number that constitutes full employment? The answer is not easy. Economists have no way of knowing what full employment really is. Forty years ago, full employment meant that no more than 3 percent of the labor force was unemployed. In the 1960s the number was 4 percent. By the mid-1970s it had increased to 5 percent and by the 1980s to 6 percent.

Why did the number rise? Some economists suggest that it did so because the labor force had become more complex. In a society that has become increasingly technological, it is more difficult for workers who have been laid off to find other jobs.

Types of Unemployment   Government officials, particularly those who work in the U.S. Department of Labor, classify unemployment into several different types. Of course, unemployment means only one thing—not having a job; but there are

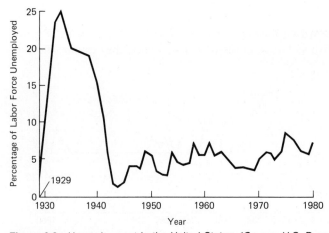

Figure 9.3 Unemployment in the United States. (*Source*: U.S. Bureau of Labor Statistics.)

a number of reasons why workers become unemployed. Economists generally single out the following types of unemployment: frictional, cyclical, structural, and seasonal.

The first, **frictional unemployment,** is caused by high information costs in the system. After all, the world does not provide perfect information. When a worker is fired or laid off, it takes time to find where the best alternative job lies. That time, or friction, is involved in a job search.

A certain amount of friction occurs whenever there is an imperfect match between job vacancies and job applicants. Many economists believe that a large percentage of unemployment is frictional and should not be reduced. After all, searching for and finding a better job is one way a worker can earn a higher income.

Cyclical unemployment is, of course, associated with the ups and downs of business activity we studied in Chapter 8. In a recession or depression, unemployment rises; in a recovery or boom phase, workers are called back and unemployment declines. Cyclical unemployment can be smoothed out when appropriate government policies stabilize economic activity. There have been periods of success in this effort, but there also have been failures. Thus, the elimination of cyclical unemployment in the immediate future appears unlikely.

When the structure of the economy changes, some workers are put out of work. For example, if a new deposit of a basic mineral is found that can be mined at a lower cost than deposits in another region, the workers in the declining area will experience **structural unemployment.** This category also includes the technological unemployment caused by machines replacing laborers, that is, unemployment resulting from automation.

Finally, **seasonal unemployment** is a fact of life in some occupations and in some regions. Apple picking in the Northwest, orange harvesting in Florida, outdoor construction work in the cold northern states, and ski instruction in Colorado are all governed by time of year and climate.

Major Cycles in the American Economy

Business Cycles (1865–1915)

Turning back to Figure 9.2, we see that the period from 1865 through 1915 had its share of ups and downs, although they reached neither the heights nor the depths of the cyclical swings in our own century from 1920 to the present. Figure 9.4 shows that nonagricultural production in America followed similar trends during the same periods. That is, as demand rose and fell with boom or recession, so did nonagricultural output from its base of full production. And in times of recession, people suffered.

Don't be misled by the apparent mildness of those early recessions. They were indeed quite tragic although less so than the Great Depression. The reason is that hordes of immigrants from Europe had been swelling the ghettos of the

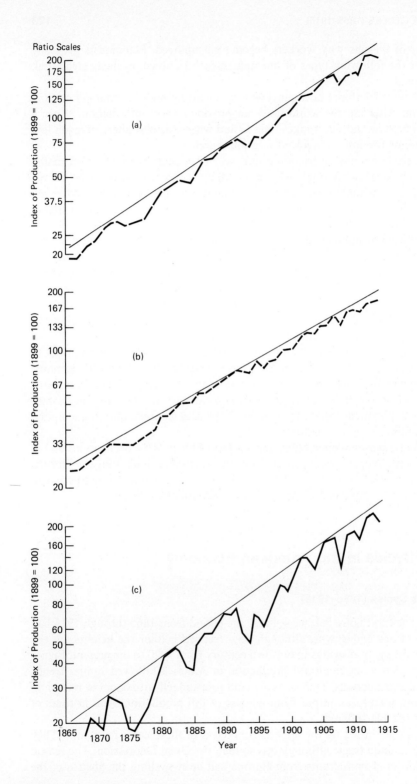

cities during the "good times," and they were the first and hardest hit when workers had to be laid off.

Figure 9.4 also shows an interesting fact about how differently various types of production are affected by boom-and-bust cycles. Note the three classifications of output shown in the figure: industrial and commercial production, nondurable manufactures, and durable manufactures. The peaks in each case indicate the output when resources were fully employed—boom times. The peaks are joined by trend lines, which trace the highest feasible production in each category all during the period. You will see that for each of the types of production there were two extended periods (the 1870s and the 1890s) when production fell well below its potential.

Notice that the dips below the trend line are far more prominent in the case of durable goods than for the other two categories. The reason is simply that durable goods *are* durable—that is, they can be made to serve longer when times are bad. People cannot put off buying food or even, beyond a reasonable point, buying a new pair of shoes, but a person can generally make do with an old kitchen range for a while longer, if necessary; and in the machine shop, a lathe can be propped up for another year when business falls off.

In summary, the period from 1865 through 1915—the beginning of industrialized America's economic cycle—was marked by four major swings and several minor ones, each having much greater impact on durable goods production than on other categories.[1]

In the first cycle the economy swung upward for seven years, peaking in 1872, and then down for four. In those 11 years the decline in output of durable goods from peak to trough was 33 percent.

The second cycle found the economy climbing for six years, until 1882, then swinging down for three and languishing in a depression for four years or more. From peak to bottom, the output of durables declined 25 percent.

The third cycle included two mild recessions and an extremely severe depression that began late in 1892, was interrupted by brief recovery in 1895, but did not hit its trough until 1896. Output of durables fell off 34 percent.

Finally, climbing out of the 1896 depths, the economy struggled through a 12-year period of ups and downs, including two intense, if brief, recessions. Midway through one recession, in 1907, the output of durables abruptly dropped 29 percent in such a short time that the economy suffered an unusual shock. A recovery quickly ensued, and a long upswing of production followed, interrupted by only two short downturns before World War I distorted the whole picture by the demands of war production and a resultant war boom.

[1]See Alvin Hansen, *Business Cycles and National Income* (New York: Norton, 1951), pp. 22–31.

Figure 9.4 Indexes of U.S. nonagricultural production, 1865–1915. (a) Industrial and commercial production; (b) nondurable manufactured goods; (c) durable manufactured goods. During the period of greatest industrial growth, the most volatile sector of production was durable goods, which expanded steeply, although erratically, after the Civil War. [*Source*: Edwin Frickey, *Production in the United States, 1860–1914,* 1st ed. (Cambridge, Mass.: Harvard University Press, 1942). Adapted by Albert G. Hart, *Money, Debt, and Economic Activity,* 2nd ed. (Englewood Cliffs, N.J.: Prentice-Hall, 1953).]

The Roaring Twenties

When the war ended and American troops returned from overseas, they not only found a changing America, they helped to change it further. Farm boys had "seen Paree" and, in the words of the old song, they were not going to be kept down on the farm. For the first time, the *absolute* number of farmers in America declined in this decade.

Incomes grew steadily throughout the decade. Larger proportions of those incomes could now be turned away from food and toward the purchase of services and of such captivating new products as refrigerators, ranges, radios, and—above all—automobiles. A surge in advertising and an initial wave of consumer credit increased the demand for these durables.

Technologies were changing, too, reducing the costs of production as well as greatly widening the choice of goods on the market. This was the decade of the consumer durables "revolution" and of social and moral upheavals as well. Now that people no longer had to dedicate all their mind and muscle to fighting the war, they had time and income for other pursuits. The very air crackled with controversial new issues: suffrage for women; isolationism for the nation; Prohibition. A moral minority had lectured the nation on the evils of alcohol consumption, and the Eighteenth Amendment was made law by Congress and the people. Hard on its heels came the era of speakeasies and flouting the new law. The Capone mob appeared on the scene. Not surprisingly, the decade earned the designation the Roaring Twenties.

Meantime, the vast majority of workers were occupied by the everyday concerns of going to work, paying bills, and making hard choices about economic priorities for their families. But even for the typical family, the comforts of life were available. The automobile in particular opened up vast new opportunities for increased leisure, recreation, mobility—in a word, freedom. By the early 1920s over three million new automobiles were being purchased each year, and by 1929 there were 26 million cars on the road. Although some people did not share in the gains, for many it was a decade of great prosperity.

Over that decade real incomes per capita marched upward at the record rate of 2 percent per year. The growth of productivity was unusually high throughout most sectors—in manufacturing, construction, and even agriculture.

Although output per worker in agriculture increased 26 percent over the decade, largely because of the introduction of the gasoline tractor, which replaced nearly one third of the horses used on farms, many farmers were discontent. The fall in costs did not seem to help them, and farmers in general did not fare well in the 1920s. By comparison with the bonanza years of World War I, they were distinctly worse off.

The broad extension of government powers prompted by World War I was sharply curtailed in the twenties, but in one key area, agriculture, the pressure of government control and intervention remained. The one largely responsible for this situation was Herbert Hoover, who later became president. After serving in the cabinet as administrator of food supplies during World War I, Hoover had directed postwar relief efforts in Europe. Well aware of the vital importance of agriculture, Hoover pressed hard for government measures to support farm prices during the recession of 1920–1921. He especially advocated a federal corporation set up to purchase farm products and to lend money to farm cooperatives. For a short time this program worked, and farm prices were supported by government purchasing, but the Farm Board's budget was too limited, and there were no attempts to curtail supply. Consequently, when farmers began growing more in response to the price supports, excess supplies drove prices down. Nevertheless, these experiences set the stage for subsequent attempts at price supports and supply controls made in the 1930s.

The Great Stock Market Crash

Along with everything else in this high-flying period, the Wall Street market was roaring along in the mid-twenties. Barbers and butlers, janitors and ditch diggers —everybody was playing the market, making money on their money. Increasingly, more and more novice investors were taking advantage of the opportunity to buy on margin, that is, to put up only a certain percentage of the total price of a purchase, with their brokerage houses lending them the balance. Of course they had to pay interest on these loans, but with stocks going up so fast, who could lose?

This question was answered all too promptly, and with shattering results. Figure 9.5 shows the stock market from the beginning of the 1920s to the depths of the depression. By 1929 stock prices were already two and a half times what they had been a mere three or four years earlier. Trading was increasing every day. Something had to give, and it did. In October of 1929, investors started to get jittery. There were reports that economic activity was falling off. With possible

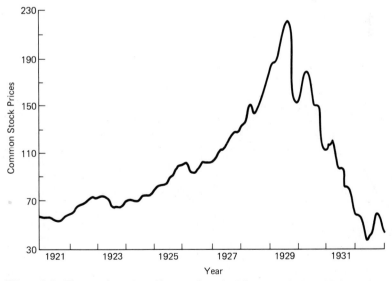

Figure 9.5 The stock market. (*Source*: Standard Statistics Index of Prices of 421 Common Stocks.)

threats of a recession, confidence waned, and people began to sell. Of course, nobody ever anticipated what happened next.

On October 1 the price of an average share fell between $5 and $10. On October 3 the same thing occurred. The next day was no better. Prices kept declining, although the number of shares traded was actually relatively small. Toward the end of the month, when disaster seemed near, business and political leaders tried to intervene in order to stop the precipitous decline. However, on Monday, October 28, 1929, there was a nationwide stampede to sell stocks. In the last hour of trading, over three million shares were traded. In just one day, the value of all stocks fell by $14 billion. The next day was even worse. Blue Monday was followed by Black Tuesday, and newspaper headlines told of once-wealthy investors, now ruined, taking their own lives.

Although stock prices rallied for the first few months in 1930, this was the last major rally that a nation of investors was to see for many years to come. By the summer of 1932, the value of stocks had fallen by 83 percent from their September 1929 prices. For every dollar invested, only 17 cents remained.

It was not long before the entire nation was well into a serious recession, although no one imagined that it would become the greatest depression in the history of the United States. In fact, at the time, the American economist Irving Fisher, who was also a leader in the Temperance movement, optimistically proclaimed that the economic troubles of the United States were bound to be short-lived because Prohibition had made the American worker more productive!

Despite Fisher's optimism, total real output fell continuously after 1929, a rare phenomenon indeed. Real output per capita was falling even more rapidly, since the population was still growing. Figure 9.6 shows that by 1933 actual output was at least 35 percent below the nation's productive capacity. In fact, the

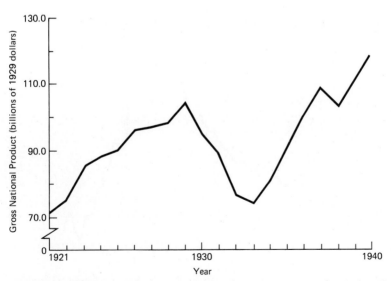

Figure 9.6 Real gross national product. (*Source*: J. W. Kendrick, *Productivity Trends in the United States;* and U.S. Office of Business Economics.)

total output lost during the Great Depression was a little over $350 billion measured in 1929 prices. If the Great Depression had not occurred, America could have built, for example, another 700,000 schools, each costing a half million dollars, or another 36 million homes, each costing $10,000. Never before in peacetime had so much output been lost.

Moreover, the labor force (and with it the actual amount of unemployment) may have been understated. There was a consistent "no jobs for married women" policy throughout the 1930s, and single men were often denied jobs in favor of married men. Additionally, many moved their families into rural areas or onto squatters' land. Instead of looking for a job in the city, they attempted to scrape out a bare existence in the countryside.

This was a poor choice, because even those working good, productive land were having trouble. Farmers in general had missed out on the prosperity of the 1920s, so depression hit them even harder than it did the overall population. By 1932 the net income of farm operators was barely 20 percent of its 1929 level, even though total farm output had risen 3 percent. How could this happen? Falling prices! In the same three years, prices received by farmers had fallen to 40 percent of their already-low 1929 level. Of course, the demand for food is relatively price inelastic. When farmers tried to counter their falling incomes during the early years of the depression by increasing their output, they found they could sell their increasing supplies only by lowering prices even more. After all, it takes a tremendous reduction in the price of corn or wheat to get consumers to buy much more of either. This is always the case when demand for the product in question is relatively price insensitive.

Not surprisingly, farmers became delinquent in paying their taxes and their debts. In 1929 alone there were almost 20 forced farm sales per every 1,000 farms because of failure to pay taxes or debts. This figure had risen by 100 percent in 1932, and even these data fail to reflect what actually happened, because as the depression wore on local tax officials became more and more tolerant of farmers who did not pay their taxes. It usually did not do much good to force a farm sale. Who would buy the farm, and at what price?

The Tidal Wave Spreads   The depression disrupted still another sector—America's commercial banking system. Between 1929 and 1932, more than 5,000 banks, one out of every five, failed and their customer's deposits vanished. By March 1933 the entire banking network had virtually collapsed. It was then that the newly elected president, Franklin D. Roosevelt, took a drastic step to prevent chaos and shore up confidence. He ordered every bank in the nation to close and declared a temporary moratorium on debts. When the banking holiday ended, another 2,000 banks remained permanently closed, and thousands upon thousands of other financial institutions—loan companies, credit unions, and the like—ultimately met the same fate.

During the year 1929 the American populace had saved over $4 billion. In 1932 the nation spent over three quarters of a billion dollars more than it earned. Clearly many individuals were living off their savings. Nor was America the only nation to experience this depression. By 1932 at least 30 million potential workers were unemployed worldwide. The international monetary system was in chaos. The failure of a major bank in Austria, the Credit Anstalt, brought foreign creditors rushing to withdraw their money. This failure set up a chain of unrest that spread across Europe to the nerve center of international banking—London. No country seemed able to maintain the gold value of its currency. No monetary system seemed strong; no nation did either. By the time Roosevelt was inaugurated, the international economy was as much of a shambles as America's, and Hitler was coming into the limelight in a desperate Germany.

What Caused the Great Depression?

Why did what would otherwise have been a normal recession turn into the greatest depression in modern history? The debate continues. One argument is that Americans were living beyond their means, but there is very little evidence for this contention; the productive capacity of the nation was not particularly strained in 1929. Others believe that the situation in the agriculture sector led to the demise of the rest of the economy, but we find little evidence that such a small part of a complex national economy could bring on a severe, prolonged depression. Perhaps it could cause a recession, but nothing of the magnitude of what occurred. There remain two major and, in a sense, competing theories. The first is associated with John Maynard Keynes, originator of **Keynesian economics;** the second with Milton Friedman, the leading proponent of **monetarism.**

The Keynesian Explanation   In 1936, when the nation was still in the depression, there appeared a remarkable book, *The General Theory of Employment, Interest and Money.* Written by John Maynard Keynes, a respected and eminent economist who lived and worked in England, this book raised the possibility that unemployment could persist for a long period. That is, Keynes wrote that unemployment on a large scale might not be corrected by natural forces within the economy. He pointed out that what was necessary to keep full employment was *effective* aggregate demand. He also pointed out that one of the key factors driving the economy was investment. For investment to occur, there had to be savings. In other words, consumers would have to be willing and able to save part of their income if they were to have resources for investment. But, noted Keynes, there might be times when there is not enough effective investment demand to use up all of the private sector's savings. When this occurs, there would be unemployment, for savings as such are useful only when put back into the economy. And money is put back into the active economy only when investors use it to build houses, machines, or buildings.

Proponents of the Keynesian theory of how income and employment are determined point out that during the 1920s the American public engaged in an abnormally high level of saving. According to Keynesian theory, this was dangerous, because unless those savings were put back into the economy by investment, a drop in aggregate demand had to result. Unemployment must then occur.

In fact, during the twenties there was a very high rate of net investment, but such a situation must eventually mean a reduction in the rate of investment as the stock of private capital reaches excessively high levels. At this point the expected profitability of future investment could be expected to fall, with the result that businesses should feel less incentive to increase investment. Unless consumers decrease savings accordingly, the desired level of saving should exceed the desired level of investment. Reduced demand on the part of the entire public should result, as should unemployment. According to this theory, a recession could then begin and could develop into a depression. The government would have to step in to increase effective aggregate demand by appropriate monetary and fiscal policies.

Basically, then, according to Keynesian theory, the Great Depression occurred because of a *collapse in the demand for new capital formation on the part of business people.* That is, there was a *collapse in investment demand.* Investment fell behind saving, reducing output, and thereby causing unemployment. This theory is borne out by all the available statistics. We see in Figure 9.7 that net investment fell precipitously in the years following the stock market crash. But why did the stock market crash occur? Perhaps the reduction in net investment was triggered by something else. At least that is what the other major theory contends.

Milton Friedman and Monetary Theory While not denying that investment decisions by business people relative to saving decisions by individuals may be an important determinant of how the economy moves, the proponents of monetarism, led by Milton Friedman, place considerably more emphasis on what happens to the amount of money in circulation. The following sketch of their theory is simplified, perhaps even oversimplified, but it includes monetarism's most obvious aspects and applies them to what happened during the Great Depression.

Monetarists believe that what occurs in the short run in the economy can

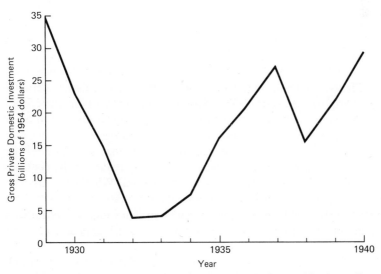

Figure 9.7 The collapse of investment. (*Source*: U.S. Office of Business Economics.)

be determined by how the Federal Reserve System alters the amount of money in circulation. Money, remember, comprises currency and checking account balances. As noted in the last chapter, the Federal Reserve System was chartered before World War I to establish a sound elastic money supply. According to the monetarists, during the Great Depression, the Fed did just the opposite. But why should the amount of money in circulation be important?

The monetarist theory states that people have a demand for money because it facilitates transactions. That is, to live in a world without money would be quite costly, for we would have to resort to barter. Therefore, people keep money in their checking accounts and in their pocketbooks in order to facilitate transactions and to have a temporary store of purchasing power. If the number of transactions goes up, therefore, the amount of money demanded by the public should increase. In other words, there should be some relationship between the level of income and the level of money demanded by the public. And, indeed, according to the monetarists, this relationship not only exists but is fairly stable. Therefore, if the Federal Reserve System increases the total number of dollars, and transactions do not increase, some people will find that they have excess money. In order to get rid of their excess money, these people will attempt to spend it or will buy bonds. This will lead to, among other things, an increase in the amount of goods and services demanded. Hence, if full employment prevails, a rise in prices will occur. If we are not at full employment, this increased demand will lead to a rise in output and employment.

Now, taking the opposite tack, if the Federal Reserve System, sometimes called the *monetary authority,* decides to *decrease* the amount of money in circulation, then some individuals and businesses will find that they have less money than they desire, which is, as we have noted, a function of how much income they make. Accordingly, they will spend less. But when lots of people spend less, the total demand in the economy for goods and services falls, and either prices or output will fall. In any case, money income will decrease, and so will employment.

Using this very simplified version of monetarist theory, we can assess what happened during the Depression. Although the Federal Reserve repeatedly claimed that they had taken action to stimulate the economy, the statistics presented in Figure 9.8 show that the money supply in circulation actually decreased by a third from the start of the recession to the depths of the depression. According to the monetarist theory, this decline could mean only one thing: a reduction in the total demand for goods and services and hence a reduction in output and employment. The monetarists maintain that what would have been just another recession turned into the Great Depression because of the contractionary efforts of the Federal Reserve during this period. Whether or not the Federal Reserve was aware of what was happening is irrelevant. Figure 9.8 shows that the money supply decreased rather than increased. The monetary authorities dealt a crippling blow to an already weak economy and, hence, the depression deepened.

At this point, we should mention the possibility of the reverse causal link between the money supply and income. We find that as incomes fall, banks are

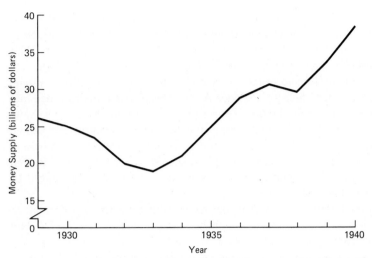

Figure 9.8 The money supply. (*Source*: Board of Governors of the Federal Reserve System.)

less inclined to lend money. Hence, not all of the reduction in the money supply is necessarily the fault of the Federal Reserve. In fact, some observers maintain that the Federal Reserve has the power to pull on the string but cannot push it —can't produce lending. Banks at the time were very reluctant to lend out any of their increased reserves, which meant, of course, that the Federal Reserve would have had to increase reserves even more in order to reverse the decline in the money supply during this period. Moreover, much, if not most, of the decline in the money supply was created by runs on banks (bank panics). These failures were caused to a very significant degree by drastic declines in the value of the banks' capital assets, mainly bonds. The Federal Reserve certainly had the power to strengthen these asset holdings by bond purchases. This move would have restored the banks' solvency, reduced the sense of alarm, and stemmed the tide of bank failures. Sadly, however, the Federal Reserve often sold rather than bought bonds, an action unfortunately characteristic of many countercyclical measures that were misused during the 1930s.

War Again: From Bust to Boom

From the standpoint of unemployment, two decades could not be more unlike than those of the 1930s and 1940s in America. During the whole span of the 1930s, workers and business people had been almost wholly occupied in pulling themselves out of the depression's depths. Hitler's *Mein Kampf* was published in Germany and hardly noticed here. European hostilities erupted in 1939, but even they caused only modest concern on this side of the ocean. To the average American, and to many of the elected representatives in Congress, it seemed all too clear that the nation should mind its own business. Few favored any program of military preparedness. President Roosevelt did succeed in appointing a War Resources Board in 1939, but it quietly closed its doors five months later.

In Europe, however, things were going from bad to worse. When the "invulnerable" Maginot line crumbled before the first major German attack in 1940, France fell to the enemy—and America was shocked into awareness. This was the beginning of a new decade indeed. An Office of Emergency Management was set up in May 1940, succeeded a few days later by a Council of National Defense. By September a Selective Service Act had been passed to draft men into military service, and war production was running in overdrive. Figure 9.9 shows the impressive efforts made to help supply the Allies and to supply the United States itself during those high-pressured first years of the 1940s. From a base of 100 in 1939, the index of war production had soared to 5,600 by 1943. In that year, America was turning out quantities of goods equal to those produced by Italy, Japan, and Germany combined.

When it finally became apparent that America might actively participate in the war, an Office of Production was established to provide for emergency plant facilities if they should be necessary. However, nobody anticipated that the War would reach us so soon, and the Japanese sneak attack on Pearl Harbor on December 7, 1941, caught us shockingly unprepared.

A War Production Board was immediately set up, and government agencies sprang rapidly into being. Dozens materialized, many of them formed jointly with those of our allies. A number of them are listed in Table 9.1. To coordinate efforts as far as possible, an overall Office of War Mobilization was created in May 1943, but by then it was literally impossible to oversee all of the war activities in which the industrial sector of the economy had become engaged.

Labor's Part   To fight the war on many fronts while still turning out great quantities of factory-produced war supplies put an enormous strain on the nation's work force. It was the task of the War Management Commission to provide adequate labor both to the military and to the civilian economy. The draft, of

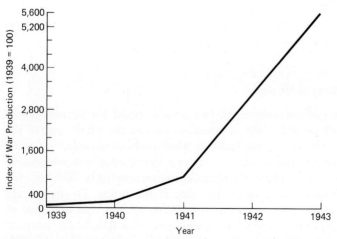

Figure 9.9   The increased war effort. [*Source*: Simon Kuznets, in *National Product Since 1869* (New York: National Bureau of Economic Research, 1954), p. 44.]

Table 9.1 THE PROLIFERATION OF GOVERNMENT AGENCIES DURING WORLD WAR II

Office of Emergency Management	President's War Relief Control Board
Committee of Fair Employment Practice	Selective Service System
Foreign Economic Administration	Joint Chiefs of Staff
National War Labor Board	Office of Strategic Services
Office of Defense Transportation	Joint War Production Committee—
Office of Inter-American Affairs	United States and Canada
Office of War Information	Permanent Joint Board of Defense—
Office of Scientific Research and Development	United States and Canada
War Production Board	Combined Chiefs of Staff—United States, United Kingdom, and Canada
War Shipping Administration	Combined Shipping Adjustment Board—United States and Great Britain
National Housing Agency	British-American Joint Patent Interchange Committee
Federal Home Loan Bank Administration	Munitions Assignments Board—United States and Great Britain
Federal Housing Administration	Joint Mexican-U. S. Defense Commission
Board of War Communications	Pacific War Council
Office of Censorship	United Nations Relief and Rehabilitation Administration
Office of Price Administration	United Nations Information Organization
Office of War Mobilization and Reconversion	
Surplus Property Board	
Retraining and Reemployment Administration	

course, solved the military labor problem. In 1944 and 1945 the men and women serving in the armed forces numbered 11.5 million. On the home front, the civilian labor force took an upward leap as former nonworkers decided to join the war effort, which can be seen in Figure 9.10. Women, retired people, and teenagers who quit school early all began earning paychecks. For these groups, the *labor force participation rate* increased sharply. (Recall that this term de-

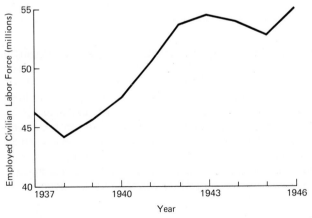

Figure 9.10 The employed civilian labor force during the war. (*Source*: Economic Report of the President, 1966.)

scribes the percentage of the total number of people in any given subsector of the economy who are active in the labor force.) For the total population over 14 years of age, the participation rate jumped from less than 55 percent before the war to about 62.4 percent in 1944. Many of these changes were permanent, especially in the case of working women.

The War Ends Without a Depression Even before the war ended, government officials and other concerned individuals worried about the possibility of a post-war recession. They remembered what had happened after World War I, and they were also well aware of the Keynesian ideas that had become popular in those days (and still are). As argued by Keynes during the depths of the depression, demand must remain high for unemployment to stay low. It appeared that when the war ended there would be a serious drop in demand, because government expenditures would fall drastically. This would lead to a multiple contraction in the level of income, thus leading to high levels of unemployment. Everybody wanted to prevent this result, but nobody quite knew how. What actually happened was just the opposite: Many individuals had high levels of **liquid assets**— that is, large amounts of government bonds and cash—on hand when victory came. They wanted to spend them once the restrictions on the production and sale of consumer durables (such as automobiles, refrigerators, and washing machines) were lifted. This opportunity to purchase new durable goods whose production had been greatly curtailed led to booms in these industries right after the war.

There was also unprecedented activity in the construction industry. Housing units were being speedily built. Lastly, government services contracted somewhat, but not back to prewar levels. Although the unemployment rate did jump from about 1.9 percent in 1945 to 3.9 percent in 1946, the latter figure was a fairly normal peacetime level of unemployment for that time. In fact, it is what was generally called *normal,* or frictional, unemployment in a dynamic economy. It was not until several years later, in 1949, that we actually experienced what could be considered a recession. Nevertheless, Congress passed the Employment Act of 1946, sometimes referred to as the Full Employment Act. It reads as follows:

> The Congress hereby declares that it is the continuing policy and responsibility of the federal government to use all practicable means consistent with its needs and obligations and other essential considerations of national policy, with assistance and cooperation of industry, agriculture, labor and state and local governments, to coordinate and utilize all its plans, functions, resources for the purpose of creating and maintaining, in a manner calculated to foster and promote free competitive enterprise and the general welfare, conditions under which there will be afforded useful employment opportunities, including self-employment, for those able, willing, and seeking to work and *to promote maximum employment, production, and purchasing power* [emphasis added].

In addition, the Council of Economic Advisors was set up to make a continuing study of the American economy and to assist the president in preparing a report on the state of the nation every year. That council still exists today, and the government is continuously engaged in smoothing out economic activity in the United States.

Did World War II Pull Us out of the Depression?   To assess the stimulus of the war on the economy, let us first consider what happened to unemployment. Figure 9.11 shows that unemployment was in excess of 17 percent when hostilities began in Europe. This figure was still almost 15 percent in 1940. It then dropped to an incredible 1.2 percent by 1944. Overall, then, it seems clear that the war effort nearly eliminated unemployment. But something else was happening at the same time, namely, conscription (the draft). The Selective Service Act was passed in 1940, and soon thereafter large numbers of men and women joined or were drafted into the armed services. These people represented a significant fraction of the labor force, as we see in Figure 9.12. Is it accurate, then, to say that the war economy erased the prewar 17 percent unemployment rate because 17 percent of the labor force was in the armed forces at the height of the war? Clearly, a significant and increasing fraction of the labor force was conscripted. Of course, conscription is one way to eliminate unemployment, but it is rather a drastic way. Generally, it is assumed that high production rates create increasing demand for workers, thus eliminating any residue of unemployment. Nevertheless, the output of the economy did expand rapidly during wartime.

Increased Output   Increases in war demand during the early 1940s definitely stimulated aggregate demand. The output of the economy increased at a tremendous rate. As Figure 9.13 shows, total real GNP grew by leaps and bounds from the beginning of the war to its end. But were individuals really becoming materially better off during this period? Figure 9.13 shows that the total amount of government purchases of goods and services skyrocketed during the war. Much of the increase in output actually went to war production, not to enrich the

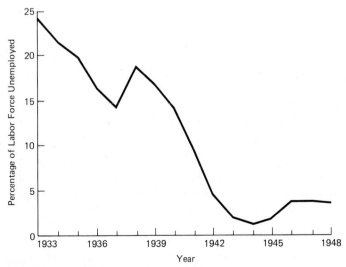

Figure 9.11 Percentage of labor force unemployed. (*Source*: U.S. Bureau of Labor Statistics.)

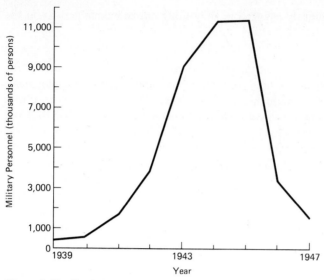

Figure 9.12   Our fighting forces during World War II. (*Source*: U.S. Bureau of Labor Statistics.)

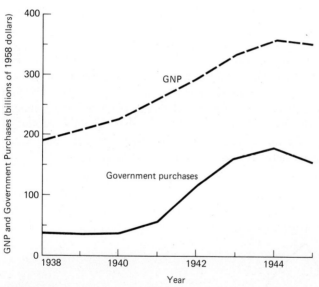

Figure 9.13   Growth of real GNP and government expenditures. (*Source*: U.S. Department of Commerce.)

personal lives of Americans. For example, the trend of per capita personal consumption expenditures for the period 1940 through 1945, as indicated in Table 9.2, is negative. For 1942–1944 per capita personal consumption expenditures were less than in 1941. Moreover, those figures include people in the armed services, a full 5.5 percent of the population. They obviously were not sharing significantly in the increased production of the nation. In short, the private sector of the economy was not very much larger at the end of the war than at the beginning. The depression was over, but people were not as well off as is often

Table 9.2 PERSONAL CONSUMPTION DURING WORLD WAR II
This table shows total personal consumption expenditures in billions of 1958 dollars. There was little rise during this period, and if we look at per capita personal consumption expenditures in 1958 dollars in column 3, we see that in 1942–1944, per capita personal consumption was less than in 1941.

Year	Total Personal Consumption Expenditures in Billions	Per Capita Personal Consumption Expenditures in Billions
1940	$155.7	$1,178
1941	165.4	1,240
1942	161.4	1,197
1943	165.8	1,213
1944	171.4	1,238
1945	183.0	1,308

Source: U.S. Department of Commerce.

imagined. Of course, if we consider the psychological benefit of fighting and winning the war, overall social welfare broadly defined may be said to have increased. The war provided new collective purpose, and certainly people had jobs and the self-respect derived from being employed. Clearly the poorer segments of society were living more comfortably.

What Is Income?   Nevertheless, this brings us to the crucial question: What does income really represent? Does it matter what we produce? Can an armored tank yield satisfaction to the general public? In fact, many argue that such an object is an *intermediate,* not a final, good—intermediate in the sense that it is used to produce what we call *national defense.* As Adam Smith once said, "Consumption is the objective of production." Since World War II, however, politicians seem to be saying that tanks and airplanes are also objectives. Who is right? This is a value judgment. Economics or history cannot answer such a question, but individual reflection will certainly lead most of us to our own conclusions.

America After 1944: Ups and Downs

The end of World War II saw the formation of the United Nations and a renewed commitment to preventing future conflicts. The awesome destructive power of atomic warfare had been amply demonstrated at Hiroshima and Nagasaki. The possibility of worldwide destruction and the end of the human species now truly existed. However, despite the United Nations and the persistent fear of war, the decades that followed World War II were ones of alternating hot and cold hostile actions. Only five years later American men, women, and machines were again engaged in a conflict—the Korean War.[2] After the truce in Korea barely 15 years

[2]Euphemistically called the Korean conflict, in which American forces were merely engaged in a United Nations "peace-keeping mission."

elapsed before American forces were involved in another costly engagement in Indochina. Yet during this time the economy was growing; per capita income was increasing. This can be seen in Figure 9.14, which shows the rise in per capita real GNP in the United States from the end of World War II until the early 1980s. Underlying this long-run trend of increasing prosperity, however, were numerous problems of unemployment and inflation.

Postwar Inflation and Unemployment   The very strict price controls that were in effect during World War II were lifted almost immediately after the war. Consequently, the pressure of repressed inflation that had built up for three or four years was now able to vent itself. Prices rose sharply, and Figure 9.15 shows how the rate of inflation increased dramatically after World War II. Then it slowed as a result of a relatively minor recession at the end of the 1940s. Once the Korean War broke out, however, prices again shot up at a very rapid rate.

Curiously, this price rise occurred even though neither government spending nor the money supply were increasing at very rapid rates during this period. However, people still vividly recalled the effects of price controls and scarcity during World War II. They feared that the same thing would happen during the Korean conflict, and this fear touched off an extraordinary buying spree, particularly for consumer durables and automobiles. The American public bought in anticipation of shortages to come, but few shortages actually developed, since U.S. participation in the war was relatively minor: 5.7 million men and women were engaged during a period of just over three years. There were 157,500 casualties, and the total cost was estimated to be in the neighborhood of $60 billion. The country experimented with a moderate amount of price controls during this war, but the effort was not very extensive, and the effects went largely unnoticed.

After the war, prices rose at very low annual rates—between 1 percent and

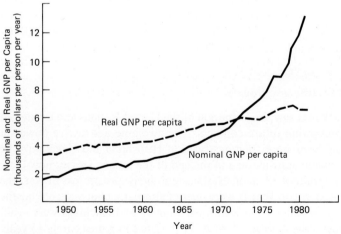

Figure 9.14   Nominal and real per capita GNP over time. (*Source*: U.S. Department of Commerce.)

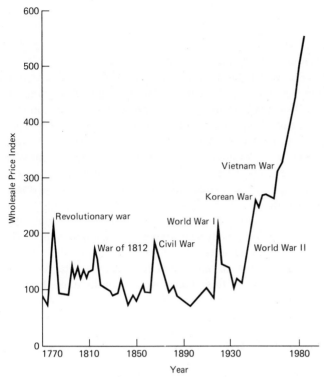

Figure 9.15 History of prices in the United States, 1770–1981. (*Source*: U.S. Department of Commerce.)

2 percent—until things heated up in Indochina. Starting in 1965, the rate of inflation advanced. Not only did this inflation continue, but it worsened as we entered the next decade. President Nixon imposed wage and price controls in 1971, and a modified form of controls was continued for a number of years afterward. They proved ineffective. Price controls will not usually work for long if the underlying monetary and fiscal policies are expansionary.[3] This is exactly what happened during the Korean War, and again in the 1971–1974 period of government wage and price controls. Although since 1971 there have been some periods of monetary and fiscal restraint, the general direction has been expansion-

---

[3] Nearly 2,000 years before the birth of Christ, the ruler of Babylonia decreed that anyone caught violating the empire's wage and price freeze would be drowned. History reports that Babylonia endured more than 1,000 years of such price fixing. In spite of these drastic measures, prices in Babylonia rose.

In A.D. 300, the Roman emperor Diocletian fixed maximum prices on grain, eggs, beef, and clothing. He also set wage ceilings for teachers, lawyers, physicians, tailors, and bricklayers. Anyone who violated such price fixing was subject to the death penalty. But according to a Roman named Lactantius, writing in A.D. 314,

> there was . . . much bloodshed upon very slight and trifling accounts; and the people brought provisions no more to market since they could not get a reasonable price for them; and this increased the dearth so much that after many had died by it, the law itself was laid aside.

ary. In such situations, government controls will be ineffective in holding down prices.

Increasingly, since 1946, we have had not only times of inflation, but also times of inflation concurrent with high unemployment, a situation quite rare in the history of the United States. The levels of unemployment that occurred since 1929 are given in Figure 9.3. There was an immediate but shortlived jump in unemployment soon after World War II, as could be expected with large numbers of soldiers being mustered out. There was another period of exceptionally high unemployment at the end of the decade. We experienced yet another recession some ten years later, when the unemployment rate in 1958 jumped to almost 7 percent. Things improved for a few years, but in 1960–1961 another recession occurred, followed by the longest twentieth-century period of peacetime prosperity, lasting almost a full decade.

The Kennedy Tax Cut   President Kennedy's economic advisors, under the leadership of Walter Heller, argued that a tax cut would give individuals more disposable income. When people spent this additional income, those who received it would also have more to spend, and this process would continue, so that the tax cut would yield a more than proportionate increase in aggregate demand. Increased spending in turn would decrease unemployment, as unemployed workers were hired to produce the additional output demand. Looking at the unemployment record in Figure 9.3, we see that later in the decade it did fall. The tax cut, however, did not actually occur until 1964, when Johnson was president, after Kennedy's assassination. The results of the 1964 Johnson-Kennedy tax cut seemed impressive. However, when the reverse tactic was used a few years later to subdue an overheated economy, it failed to do so.

The Tax Surcharge   One year after the tax cut, the United States had become heavily involved in Vietnam. By 1965, federal expenditures exceeded federal tax revenues, and the country encountered increasingly large deficits. At about the same time, the money supply was increasing at a rapid rate, except for a slight pause in 1966. Whereas it had increased at 3.3 percent per annum from 1961 to 1965, during the period 1967–1969 it increased 7 percent a year. In any event, the Council of Economic Advisors told President Johnson that one way to stop the mounting inflation was to increase taxes. The Council presumed that a reverse Keynesian reasoning would hold: Take more income away from consumers and they will be able to spend less, thus causing a contraction in aggregate demand. Prices would stop rising as fast because people would not be demanding as many goods and services as before. The tax surcharge of 1968 was instituted on this reasoning, but it had little effect on prices, which continued to rise in the next decade.

On to the Eighties   In the early 1970s economists were very optimistic about their power to control the economy, but when President Reagan was inaugurated in 1981 he was confronted with several economic problems inherited from previous administrations: double-digit inflation, a decade of unusually low economic growth, a high average unemployment rate, large budget deficits, and high nominal interest rates. President Reagan confronted the toughest economic times since the 1930s. His administration sought renewed prosperity through a four-part program that included reducing the growth rate of the money supply, lowering tax rates, reducing government expenditures, and deregulation.

Essentially, the Reagan administration adopted an economic policy quite different from the Keynesian approach to the control of spending, unemployment, and economic activity. By mid-1984, sizable tax cuts had been implemented without matching reductions in government spending. The result was record-setting deficits in the federal budget and extremely sharp increases in government debt. The double-digit inflation of 1980 had been overcome, but inflation plus unemployment remained well above the levels of the early 1960s.

DEFINITIONS OF NEW TERMS

BUSINESS FLUCTUATIONS   The ups and downs in overall business activity, as evidenced by changes in national income, employment, and prices, constitute business cycles, or fluctuations.

RECESSION   A period during which the rate of growth of business activity is consistently less than its long-term trend, or is negative, is a recession.

FRICTIONAL UNEMPLOYMENT   Unemployment associated with frictions in the system that may occur because of the imperfect job market information that exists is frictional unemployment. Since workers do not know about all job vacancies that may be suitable, they must search for appropriate job offers. This takes time, during which workers are frictionally unemployed.

CYCLICAL UNEMPLOYMENT   Unemployment resulting from business recessions that occur when aggregate (total) demand is insufficient to create full employment is cyclical unemployment.

STRUCTURAL UNEMPLOYMENT   Unemployment resulting from fundamental changes in the structure of the economy is structural unemployment. Structural unemployment occurs, for example, when the demand for a product falls drastically, so that workers specializing in the production of that item find themselves out of work.

SEASONAL UNEMPLOYMENT   Unemployment due to seasonality in demand or in possible supply of any particular good or service is seasonal unemployment.

KEYNESIAN ECONOMICS   Keynesian economics recommends controlling levels of economic activity (employment and inflation) by changing aggregate demand through taxes and government spending.

MONETARISM   The theory that unexpected changes in the money supply cause fluctuations in real output and employment in the short run is known as monetarism.

LIQUID ASSETS   Liquid assets are assets that are easily exchangeable for cash without a change in their value. The most liquid asset is, of course, cash itself. However, short-term government bonds and savings and loan shares are nearly as liquid.

The Ruthless Businessman Par Excellence

JAY GOULD
(1836–1892)

Railroads and Gold Manipulations

Can you imagine that one man caused a major panic on what Wall Street called Black Friday (September 24, 1869)? It may sound impossible, but it actually happened. That one man was Jay Gould, who with the help of his flamboyant sidekick, Jim Fisk, cornered the market in gold, sold out, and watched it fall. Gold was a very precious commodity after the Civil War, for the issuance of greenbacks, which could not be redeemed at par in specie, brought great speculation in all precious metals. However, the growth of confidence in the government, improvement in the U.S. trade balance, and perhaps the postwar prosperity brought the price of gold down again in terms of greenbacks. By 1869, $131 in greenbacks bought $100 of gold. Gould bought $7 million worth, helping send the price up to $140. Since Jim Fisk seemed to have similar ideas, they banded together and started to buy all the gold they could, with as much money as they were able to get out of a Tammany Hall-controlled bank called the Tenth National. At the same time, however, they were worried about the $80 million in gold that the U.S. Treasury held, part of which could be thrown on the market at any time, causing them great financial loss.

To forestall that day, Gould befriended the man who had married President Ulysses Grant's middle-aged sister. To make sure this man used his influence correctly, Gould bought him $2 million in gold bonds on margin, so if the price of gold continued to rise, Grant's brother-in-law could reap sizable profits. When Major Dan Butterfield was named Assistant U.S. Treasurer at New York, he, too, suddenly had somewhere around $2 million in gold bonds in his account, purchased, of course, by Gould.

By September of that year, Gould and Fisk really did have a corner on the entire gold market, when the price of gold was at $141 in greenbacks for $100 in gold. When Gould got wind that the president was going to force the U.S. Treasury to unload its holdings of yellow metal, he quietly started selling out, as did all of his associates, while simultaneously acting and talking like a bull. The price of gold first went up to $150, then to $164 in greenbacks, for $100 of gold.

Finally the president ordered the U.S. Treasury to sell $5 million in gold immediately. In 15 minutes, the price fell 25 points. Gould and Fisk were already in their headquarters, guarded by police and their own men. Gould alone made $11 million. Kindheartedly, he announced his regret over the Black Friday panic. And Assistant Treasurer Butterfield sanctimoniously pointed out that only speculators had lost money.

No one had ever dreamed that little Jason Gould, who was born in Roxbury, New York, the son of poor hill farmers, would become a great American financier. He first started working for a blacksmith, then became a clerk in a country store. He learned the rudiments of surveying and obtained enough education before his twentieth birthday to write the *History of Delaware County and Border Wars of New York.* Before he was 21 he had $5,000 in capital, with which he joined hands with a New York politician and opened a large tannery in northern Pennsylvania. He abandoned the tannery, became a leather merchant, and finally found where he had a special genius—speculating in small railroads.

His notoriety became immense during his battle with Cornelius Vanderbilt over the Erie Railroad. While they were attempting to bring the price of Erie stock down, Fisk and Gould found a printing press in the cellars of the Erie offices and turned out phony stock certificates. Eventually, they did get control of the Erie, the stock of which they successfully "watered."[4] The money he made on the Erie and other speculative ruthless adventures was Gould's starting capital for cornering the gold market. The public scandal was so great that Gould was finally ejected from his control of the Erie on March 10, 1872. At that time his fortune was estimated to exceed $25 million.

Furthermore, he went on to still greener pastures. He took over the Union Pacific Railroad, became its director, and remained in virtual control until 1878, at the same time buying control of the Kansas Pacific. Then in 1879 he bought control of the Denver Pacific, Central Pacific, and Missouri Pacific. In another seemingly unscrupulous deal with the Union Pacific and Kansas Pacific, he made a stock deal that supposedly netted him $10 million. Gould was the epitome of the ruthless American businessman. He apparently had few friends, but some observers point out that he was a warm and kindly family man, enjoying the diversions of books and gardening. He died of tuberculosis at age 57 with an estate of $70 million.

---

[4]The term *watering* comes from the practice of salting cattle just before they go en route to market and not allowing them to drink until just before being weighed.

chapter 10

War, Depression, and the Rise of the Public Sector

When the government enters into any economic activity, we refer to that participation as taking place in the *public sector* of the economy. You are aware of many things the government does at national, state, or local levels. It provides schools, roads, fire and police protection, and the like. Hundreds of thousands of people are employed in governmental work at various levels. The government is also a big buyer of goods and services, for which money must be paid out. So, like any individual citizen, the government has to have sources of income. Indeed, the federal government is the biggest business in the world, dealing in millions of dollars almost as petty cash and primarily in billions. (A billion dollars, if put into dollar bills laid end to end, would reach around the world at the equator four times.) The 1982 federal budget was approximately $700 billion. How are such sums raised?

GOVERNMENTAL INCOME

Basically, there are three ways in which the government finances its outlays: taxation, borrowing, and money creation.

Taxation   In the American economic system there are dozens of different taxes. They are levied on property, on income, on sales, on inheritances, and on many other activities. Essentially, however, there are three general types, or systems, of taxation. Any specific tax can be put into one of these categories.

   1. **Proportional taxation.** Under a proportional tax system, a fixed percentage of every dollar earned is levied on the taxpayer. When income goes

up, the taxes go up. When income goes down, so do the taxes. If the proportional tax system rate is 20 percent, then 20 cents is paid in taxes for every dollar earned.

2. **Progressive taxation.** Like the proportional tax system, a progressive tax system requires the taxpayer to pay more taxes as earnings increase. The difference is that the percentage of tax—the tax *rate*—increases as income increases.

3. **Regressive taxation.** Contrary to progressive taxation, the regressive tax system levies a *smaller* percentage tax on additional income. Suppose, for example, that all government revenues were obtained from a 50 percent tax on food. Since relatively less of family income will be spent on food when a family has high income, the wealthy would pay a smaller percentage of their total income in taxes.

Of the many kinds of federal tax, the personal income tax is an example of a progressive tax. To some degree, however, this aspect is reduced by the current allowance for deductions. For example, many people think that a person in the 50 percent tax bracket pays 50 percent of all income to the federal government in taxes. This is not the case, even for an honest taxpayer. Fifty percent may be paid on the last, say, $15,000, but certainly not on all the income earned in a given year.

When taxes are levied, individuals must pay them out of their money income, after which they have less money with which to purchase goods and services. The amount of spending on goods and services by households and businesses must therefore fall by the amount of the taxes paid. Thus, total spending in the private sector is less than it would be without taxes. This creates a gap between the total output in the economy and private expenditures. The government uses tax revenues to purchase the commodities that are not sold in the private sector. In other words, the government fills the gap.

Like individuals, corporations pay income taxes. Originally, the corporate tax rate was a flat (proportional) 1 percent of total taxable corporate profits after a fixed deduction allowance. Not until 1936 was a progressive tax schedule for corporations put into effect, and by 1950 a more complex system, including surtaxes, was adopted.

Borrowing   Like any citizen, the government, when it spends more than it takes in, must resort to borrowing—either from its own citizens or from sources abroad. In our own day, the national debt has become a household word and a topic for headlines.

As any borrower knows, interest must be paid to the lender; and when a nation indulges in **deficit spending**—buying more than taxes can pay for—interest keeps building up. This is true whether the borrowing is from outside sources or from government bonds sold to Americans.

The negative difference between government expenditures and receipts can be financed by the issuing of government bonds; in this way the government borrows from the private sector. When the government borrows, the private sector transfers purchasing power to the government (and the national, or public, debt increases). This method of government finance has been used increasingly in recent years and is extremely prevalent today.

Money Creation   It is also possible for the federal government (but not state and local governments) to create new money. It does not actually print the money, although it could. Rather, the Federal Reserve Bank buys new U.S. bonds from the Treasury. The process is somewhat more complicated than simply printing money, but the effects are the same—more command over resources for the public sector and less for the private sector.

GROWTH OF THE PUBLIC DEBT

The public debt has grown continuously for many years. However, the total public debt alone is not what we should look at to analyze the burden of the debt. Let's consider the per capita public debt as shown in Table 10.1.

We see that in 1945 the nominal public debt (expressed in current dollars) per capita was $1,849. In 1970 it was less than that, about $1,806. When we look at the *real* public debt (that is, the public debt corrected for inflation) per capita, the decrease in recent years is even more drastic. Look at Figure 10.1: We see that the real public debt per capita actually fell by more than one half from 1945 to 1980. Thus, although the total may be rising, the amount per capita has been falling until very recently.

How Big Are the Annual Interest Payments on the National Debt?   Let's consider the size of the interest payments on the public debt (the value of federal government bonds outstanding). In Figure 10.2, we see interest payments as a percentage of gross national product (GNP). Even though interest payments in

Table 10.1   THE PUBLIC DEBT OF THE FEDERAL GOVERNMENT
Here we show the gross public debt and the gross public
debt per capita in both nominal and constant 1967 dollars.

Year	Total (billions of dollars)	Total Real (1967 billions of dollars)	Per Capita (dollars)	Real per Capita (1967 dollars)
1935	28.7	63.9	226	503.3
1940	43.0	90.9	325	687.1
1945	258.7	454.6	1,849	3,249.6
1950	257.4	362.0	1,697	2,201.1
1955	274.4	344.3	1,660	2,082.8
1960	286.3	322.8	1,585	1,786.9
1965	317.3	357.3	1,631	1,836.7
1970	370.9	317.8	1,806	1,547.6
1975	544.1	337.5	2,472	1,533.5
1976	631.9	370.6	2,939	1,723.8
1977	709.1	390.7	3,270	1,801.6
1978	780.4	399.6	3,577	1,831.5
1979	833.8	383.0	3,784	1,738.2
1980	914.3	353.8	4,108	1,589.8

Source: U.S. Office of Management and Budget.

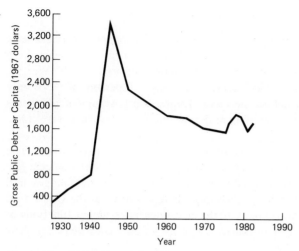

Figure 10.1 Per capita public debt of the United States in constant 1967 dollars. (*Source*: U.S. Department of the Treasury.)

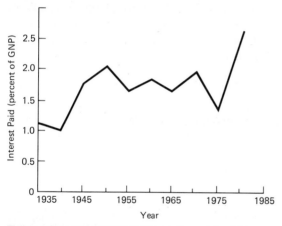

Figure 10.2 Interest payments on the public debt as a percentage of GNP. (*Source*: U.S. Department of Commerce.)

absolute terms have been rising steadily since before World War II, as a percentage of GNP they have not gone much above 2 percent for the last two decades.

We shall find in Chapter 11 that the federal budget deficit has been getting bigger and bigger in recent years. Therefore, interest payments expressed as a percentage of national income is rising. Note, however, that as long as the government borrows from Americans, the interest payments will be made to Americans. In other words, we owe the debt to ourselves. Some people are taxed to pay interest given to other (or the same) people. The public debt cannot be dismissed out of hand as an insignificant policy issue, however. One reason is that not all of the interest payments are made to Americans. There has been an increase in the foreign holdings of the public debt, which today account for 9 percent of that debt, a percentage that seems to be growing.

GOVERNMENTAL OUTGO: GROWTH AND LEVELS

Figure 10.3 expresses total government purchases of goods and services as a percentage of GNP from 1890 to the present. Notice that in recent years there is a definite upward trend. Until the Great Depression and World War II, government purchases of goods and services exceeded 10 percent of GNP only during World War I. Just before the Great Depression government purchases were only 8.2 percent. At the beginning of the twentieth century, they were closer to 6 percent.

Prior to 1917, state and local government was the most important level. The federal government did little more than pay for national defense, finance a few public works projects, and pay the salaries of members of Congress, judges, and the few thousand employees who worked in such departments as the U.S. Postal Service. State and local governments performed most government functions at that time, and they depended primarily on property and sales taxes for their revenues.

Both the state and local levels grew in the 1970s faster than the federal government. In particular, local and state expenditures on sewers, roads, schools, and welfare programs have increased dramatically. However, both local and state governments have for some time been more than overshadowed by the federal government. Let's examine the role of the public sector in the growth and development of the American economy.

Public Sector Issues in American Finance

The Revolutionary War

An urgent problem faced America during and after the Revolution: How could the war be paid for? In fact, the total cost of the Revolutionary War for the new nation was only $100 million—probably less than 10 percent of the national income per year from 1775 to 1783—but the Continental Congress had great

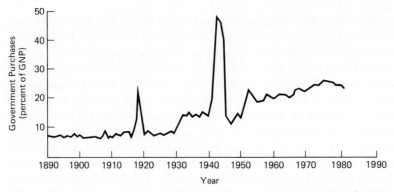

Figure 10.3 Rising government purchases. (*Source*: U.S. Department of Commerce.)

difficulty raising that sum. The very weak Articles of Confederation did not give the Continental Congress the power to tax, and thus it had to borrow. It was able to borrow almost $8 million in gold from abroad, over three fourths of it from France and the remainder from Holland and Spain. Domestically, about $10 million was raised through loans from individuals and businesses. Attempts to requisition money from the new states raised only $6 million, because each state tended to ignore the request, letting others carry the load.

To make up the rest, the Continental Congress authorized an issue of almost $200 million in paper currency during the four-year period commencing in 1775. But during that period this paper money actually accounted for little more than $40 million in terms of gold, since nobody was sure whether these "continentals" were going to be redeemed in gold or silver after the Revolution, and Congress was not empowered to declare that they were legal tender. Instead, it merely asked the states to penalize persons who refused to take them in exchange for goods and services.

By 1781 continentals were worth one five-hundredth of their original face value. Part of this devaluation was caused by people's lack of faith in the government, but a large part was caused by the tremendous increase in the number of them issued. Recalling our earlier discussion of money and inflation, you will know what happened to prices in this period: They rose out of sight.

Shays's Rebellion and the Need to Revamp the Articles of Confederation

By 1786, in the City of Concord, Massachusetts, the scene of the one of the first battles of the Revolution, there were three times as many people in debtors' prison as there were imprisoned for all other crimes combined. In Worcester County, the ratio was even higher—20 to 1. The prisoners were generally small farmers who could not pay their debts. In August 1786 mobs of musket-bearing farmers seized county courthouses and did not allow the trials of debtors to continue. The rebels encouraged Daniel Shays, a captain from the Continental Army, to lead them. Shays's men launched an attack on the federal arsenal at Springfield, Massachusetts, but were repulsed. The rebellion did not stop there but continued to grow into the winter. Finally, George Washington wrote to a friend, "For God's sake, tell me what is the cause of these commotions? Do they proceed from licentiousness, British influence disseminated by the Tories, or real grievances which admit to redress? If the latter, why were they delayed until the public mind had become so agitated? If the former, why are not the powers of government tried at once?"

What Shays's Rebellion did was to demonstrate the weakness of the government under the Articles of Confederation. In order for the nation to grow and prosper, a stronger central government was essential, so the Constitutional Convention, which originated as a commercial convention, was convened in Philadelphia in May 1787. The completed Constitution went into effect in March 1789. It was a critical factor in the economic development of the nation.

The Constitution of the New United States

One of the major weaknesses of the Articles of Confederation had been the inability of the Continental Congress to levy taxes against a national population. Without the power to tax, the United States could never have achieved an organized central government.

Sections 8–10 of Article 1, set forth the main economic provisions of the Constitution. These sections affirm the inviolability of private property and the right of the federal government to tax, to control money and credit, and to restrict commerce. In each case the constitutional provision is to be held paramount over all laws passed by the several states.

Like taxation, control over money and credit was essential to a strong central government. State banks were allowed to continue, but the federal government now held the reins. It was empowered "to coin money, regulate the value thereof, and of foreign coin, in addition to fixing the standard of weights and measures."[1] Implicit in this section of the Constitution was the ability of the federal government to issue a national currency. Eventually this was important for the development of commercial activities and of a market in which the buying and selling of debts and shares in companies could occur (a *capital* market). The Constitution also allowed the federal government to redeem the debts of the "several" (individual) states. This further allowed a capital market to develop.

The Constitution also decreed that import duties should be the same for all the states and that there would be no export duties. These provisions were intended to ensure that the states did not establish barriers to trade among themselves. This was a way of fostering interregional, as well as intraregional, trade. The Constitution effectively gave the federal government the right to police interstate commerce, which was at that time limited mainly to coastal trade. In this way a newly forged public sector took over its duties and authority.

Government Finances and the Civil War

On the eve of the Civil War the South was prosperous, and its future looked bright. There was a single cloud, however: In the North thousands of people considered slavery immoral and said so, and the newly elected president openly shared their views. It seemed only wise for a South dominated by slaveholding interests to sever the ties that bound it to an abolitionist North. It wanted independence, and it was willing, if necessary, to gain it by force of arms. In short, the South seceded out of economic strength, not weakness. The North had a different objective: to hold the nation together. To achieve its goal it had to conquer the secessionists. We shall see that, in both North and South, the public sector grew rapidly during these war years.

Shortly after the first engagement, the North set up a naval blockade of southern ports. This was a disaster for the South, which had engaged in extensive trade with the Northeast and with foreign ports. At the beginning of the war only

[1]This power was the basis for the legislated conversion to the metric system of measurement.

one tenth of the total value of manufactured products used in the South were made there. Self-sufficiency was costly and difficult; trade was important. Despite these and myriad other problems, the southern economy supported a large army for four years of extremely heavy fighting.

Among the South's greatest problems was the shifting of productive resources out of cotton—no longer a useful industry because the output could not be traded for needed manufactured goods and foodstuffs—into providing foodstuffs and supplies for the armies, as well as other manufactured goods for the civilian population. To this end, cotton production was cut back sharply in 1862. The government did not need to enforce this cutback. After all, southern cotton growers were not going to increase production if they could not sell their product. They quickly shifted their capital into areas where relative rates of return were higher. Reduction of the crop continued. In 1863 it was well below one million bales, as compared to four million a few years earlier; and in the following years output was halved again. Tobacco production was also reduced, again because the surplus over what was consumed in the South could not be sold.

Entrepreneurs made a valiant effort to produce substitutes for the manufactured goods that the South had previously imported. A noteworthy achievement was the development of homespun cloth.

Was the South Defeated from Within?   Many observers of the defeat of the Confederacy maintain that the government policy of inflationary finance and its inept handling of foreign trade caused the downfall of the South during the Civil War. However, the evidence in support of this view is mixed.

Trade policies   In retrospect, the Confederacy appears to have made a number of mistakes in trade policy. The northern blockade really did not take effect until 1863 and 1864, so before then—that is, during the first two years of the war—the South could have continued exporting cotton to obtain needed munitions, manufactured items, and foodstuffs. However, the Confederate government discouraged any export during this period, so that out of a four-million-bale crop from 1861 to 1862, only 13,000 bales were reported to have left the South. The Confederate government reasoned that by withholding cotton from the North and foreign countries (especially Britain), it could compel support for the Confederacy from abroad. Obviously, the South would have been better off had it exported as much cotton as possible in order to obtain supplies for the army and the civilian population.

Inflationary finance   The Confederate government, of course, somehow had to obtain part of the civilian output for use in fighting the war. Foreigners were unwilling to lend very large sums to the Confederacy and, certainly after the northern blockade on trade came into effect, there were very few import duties that could be used to support the war effort. The South did appropriate a certain amount of federal government property and that of Union citizens when the war broke out. The most noteworthy acquisitions were the Harper's Ferry arsenal and the naval shipyard at Norfolk. There was a certain amount of confiscation of privately produced goods in addition to internal taxes and loans. However, these measures accounted for less than one half of the total outlays of the Confederate government during the war. These outlays were estimated then at about $3 billion. How was the rest made up? By **inflationary finance.** That is, the Confederacy issued large amounts of paper notes (printed money). Figure 10.4 shows an index of commodity prices in the South that rose from 100 in January 1861 to 9,210 in April 1865. An index of the stock of money grew from 100 in January of 1861 to 2,000 in April of 1865. These data constitute a typical instance of **hyperinflation**—a dramatic, overwhelming increase in the price level over a short period of time. As prices begin to rise very rapidly, consumers start anticipating this rise: They realize that their dollars—in this case, Confederate notes—are going to lose purchasing power because of inflation. This means that it becomes more expensive to hold cash, and so people attempt to spend their dollars before they lose value. In this way, people bid prices up even faster than would occur otherwise.

The Confederacy also faced a problem not encountered by most countries during hyperinflations: Toward the end of the war, it was assumed that Confederate notes would have a zero exchange value if there was a Union victory. Clearly, a Confederate dollar would be worth little or nothing if the South lost the war; this is the main reason that the inflation in the South reached astronomical proportions by the end of 1864.

The Union War Economy   The outbreak of the Civil War meant immediate losses to many northern merchants, since none of the $300 million in debts owed

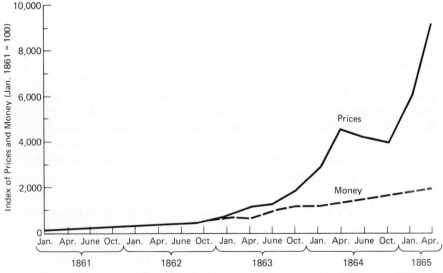

Figure 10.4 Inflation in the Confederacy. [*Source*: E. M. Lerner, "Money, Prices, and Wages in the Confederacy, 1861–65," *Journal of Political Economy* 63 (February 1955): 29.]

by southerners were to be repaid. Moreover, most of the cotton textile factories soon became idle. In 1861 over 6,000 business failures were reported by Dun, a forerunner of Dun & Bradstreet. Also, banks started to fail; for example, 80 percent of the 110 banks in Illinois closed their doors. But by 1863 a minor war-related boom was under way in the northern states.

Military labor   About 15 percent of the labor force was involved in the Union military effort. There had to be some way to procure these men. In 1863 the North passed the Enrollment Bill for troop conscription. However, this system of draft was quite different from our recently defunct system of conscription. It allowed those who were drafted the alternative of paying someone to go in their stead. Thus, even though the method of conscription was somewhat arbitrary, the final determination of who would go to war was quite flexible.

Obviously those whose civilian incomes were relatively high found it useful —indeed, advantageous—to hire replacements whose civilian incomes were relatively low. Apparently many of the less well-to-do found the "bribes" advantageous, since they accepted them.

This method of conscription tended to trade off equity for efficiency, a scheme some may view as unfair or unjust. Nevertheless, it is clear those whose incomes are high suffer a greater dollar cost if they are drafted than those whose incomes are low. From an economic point of view, then, it is more efficient for high-income earners to pay low-income earners to fight, because income is generally (although not always) a reflection of a person's productivity in the economy. Therefore, if high-income people are left to do their jobs and low-income people fight the war, the total output of the economy will be higher than otherwise. In a situation like this, fairness and efficiency conflict. The North's means of manpower procurement emphasized the latter.

Financing the Northern effort   As we have noted, in 1861 there was an immediate financial panic as banks suspended specie payments and business failures occurred. The federal treasury was almost empty; federal credit hit a low point as the government itself suspended specie payment. The Union had to finance the war somehow, and it did so by increased loans, taxation, and paper money.

1. *Loans.* With respect to this form of war finance, J. Cooke, a Philadelphia banker, floated many loans for the government. He popularized bond issues by emphasizing the advantages of the investment and the patriotic duty of the citizens of the North. Over $2 billion was raised in this manner. Cooke's fee was 1 percent on sales up to $10 million and three eighths of 1 percent on sales that exceeded that amount. He made a mint.
2. *Taxes.* The North probably used taxation to raise funds more than did the South. Excise taxes were raised in 1862 and extended to numerous goods and services. They produced almost $300 million. The Morrill Tariff, passed in 1861, raised another $300 million; the country's first income tax produced about $55 million.

3. *Money creation.* As in the South, large amounts of paper money were created. Almost half a billion dollars in U.S. notes, also called **green-backs,** were issued. These bills were not backed by gold or silver; the government merely promised to redeem them. Their value fluctuated wildly in terms of gold. By 1864 the rate of exchange was one greenback for 40 cents of gold. By the same year the price index had risen to twice its pre-1860 level.

Northern industry during the Civil War   Although some new manufacturing occurred during the war that would not have occurred otherwise, total output in the North was hardly greater during the Civil War than it was before or than it would have been without the war. There are no extensive data for the period, because federal censuses are taken only at ten-year intervals. However, New York and Massachusetts did take censuses for 1865, and these show that in both states there were declines in real output between 1860 and 1865 and between 1855 and 1865.

Further evidence supports the view that there was little growth in the economy during the war years. Generally, the Civil War era was not one of intensive capital investment. Estimates of residential construction during this period indicate that after the war there was twice as much residential building as during the war. Moreover, sales of McCormick reapers showed a boom after the war, not during it. Nor was there a surge in what are usually called *war industries.* For example, the iron needed for small-arms production during the war was only 1 percent of the total U.S. iron output during the four years starting in 1861; one small factory could have produced this amount. At the same time, the iron used to make railroad tracks *decreased* by seven times this figure. Another war industry was the manufacturing of boots for servicemen. However, at the same time that more boots were needed for Union soldiers, fewer boots were sold to the South. For example, in Massachusetts employment in the boot and shoe industry fell from almost 80,000 to 55,000 during the Civil War. Output fell from 45 million pairs to 32 million.

Government expenditures   Some have argued that large government expenditures caused a rapid increase in the manufacturing sector, especially in the north. This, however, was not true. Government expenditures went mainly for bounties, salaries, and food—especially beef—and for various types of small arms. In any event, the total amount of northern government expenditures during the Civil War represented a minor part of the total output, and these expenditures were generally substitutes for what the private sector would have spent anyway. In other words, the private sector did not spend as much, and this was because the government obtained part of its income through loans, increased excise taxes, the new income tax, and inflationary finance.

The Civil War and Long-Run Economic Growth   Despite the short-run disruptions caused by the war, early students of the Civil War were convinced that it spurred economic growth and industrialization in the long run. For example, historians have argued that the Civil War was necessary in order to rid Congress (especially the Senate) of the southern voting bloc, which opposed legislation allegedly essential to economic development. After the withdrawal of the southern bloc, the all-Republican Congress passed a series of economic measures, one of the most significant of which was the National Banking Act.

The National Banking Act Prior to federal legislation in 1863 and 1864 establishing a national banking system, banking in America was largely unregulated. State bank charters were easily obtained just about anywhere. The publicly stated intent of the National Banking Act was to establish a unified national banking system. However, the original legislation that provided for the chartering of national banks was based on the banking charters of the day—in almost all respects. The result was *not* a national banking system; nor was it the creation of a nationwide network of banks that would foster economic development by greatly expanding credit markets and credit availability.

Congress enacted banking legislation (specifically, the National Banking Act) primarily, although not exclusively, in order to increase the government's borrowing power during the war. It did this by requiring all national banks to invest a portion of their capital in government bonds. It turned out that the capital necessary to open a national bank was substantially more than most banks, especially those in rural areas, actually had. As a result, the system of national banks did not become established as the sole institution for banking throughout the United States. In agricultural areas, the average capital of nonnational banks was less than the *minimum* required to open, or be transformed into, a national bank, and national banks were forbidden to make real estate loans. Moreover, state-chartered banks had their note issues taxed by the federal government. These conditions hindered the growth of rural banks. The consequence was higher rural interest rates in the South and West.

Even in 1900 there were still about 9,000 nonnational banks as opposed to about 4,000 national banks. Because of the differential treatment of nonnational banks, which slowed their growth, it seems likely that the effect of the National Banking Act was actually to discourage the starting of new banks.

A unified reserve system A positive consequence of the national banking legislation was that the 4000 nationally chartered banks were linked through a reserve system that provided a legally sanctioned formal mechanism for transferring funds between banks. This system tended to promote a more efficient allocation of loanable funds throughout the country. In other words, it was easier for funds to go to areas where they could yield the highest reward—areas where the *rate of return* on investment would be highest. This generally meant the transfer of bank funds from agricultural to industrial uses, which helped funnel credit to areas that required large amounts of capital, such as railroad investment and large-scale industry. Contrasting its positive and negative effects, we see that the National Banking Act enhanced but was not critical to the economic development of the United States.

Giving away land In 1862 the Union Congress passed the Homestead Act, which provided that 160 acres of federally owned land could be acquired by a settler if he agreed to live on it or cultivate it for at least five consecutive years. What effect did this act have on the distribution of land in the United States and, consequently, on the development of our open spaces? The amount of new land put into cultivation after the Civil War that was attributable to homesteading was less than 20 percent of the total new acres taken up until then. The rest was either purchased from federal, state, or local governments or was given away in the form of land grants to railroads.

Many historians maintain that the Homestead Act caused a reduced growth of national product during this period because it caused farmers to use inefficient amounts of capital and labor on tracts of land that turned out to be too small. Remember that the Homestead Act provided only 160 acres. By the time it was passed, in 1862, most available land was pretty far west. Although some good land remained, most of it was prairie land and good for little more than grazing sheep or cattle. As any rancher will attest, 160 acres of grassland is not much for grazing purposes and in fact will supply only about 15 or 20 cattle with forage.

Helping out the railroads   Land grants to railroads were another possible way in which the government disposed of land in the public domain. Other railroad subsidies were also given out during this period, and again we must ask whether federal land grants sharply affected the growth rate.

Remember that during the war the construction of new railroad mileage virtually stopped. But the federal government had established a policy of subsidizing railroads by giving them land grants along their rights-of-way. Five railroad systems received 75 percent of these subsidies: the Central Pacific; Union Pacific; Atchison, Topeka and Santa Fe; Northern Pacific; and Texas and Pacific railroad systems. The subsidy to the Union Pacific Railroad, which obtained land grants by the acts of 1862 and 1864, did indeed turn out favorably. The **social rate of return**—the returns to the investors plus the positive spillover benefits to society —on that investment was relatively high. So the government subsidies were indeed justified from a social point of view. However, the increase in national income made possible by the Union Pacific was only 0.01 percent. Similar computations have been made for the Central Pacific Railroad, with similar results. Although these numbers certainly leave room for doubt, it appears that legislation allowing subsidies to a few railroads provided positive but very minor impetus to growth. It seems likely that the railroads in question would have been built eventually even without the land grants. Such an alteration in the timing of construction due to the subsidies would have had negligible effects on national income in the long run.

World War I: The First Modern War Effort

With the assassination of Austrian Archduke Franz Ferdinand in Sarajevo, in 1914, war broke out in Europe. Soon the Great War spread to most of the rest of the world. The Central Powers, Germany and Austria-Hungary, were fighting against the Allies—France, England, and Russia. In 1914 America was in the throes of a recession. Unemployment had reached an uncomfortable one million the year before. From the very beginning America attempted to stay out of the conflict. In fact, the Democrats used a slogan for President Wilson's reelection that would soon be contradicted by events: "He kept this country out of the war." That was in 1916. In April 1917 the United States declared war on the Central Powers. War production and preparation for war had started earlier, and supplies had been made available to the belligerents as early as 1914. It was not unlike an earlier time, in 1793, when, as a neutral country, we were able to trade with both parties to the conflict. After the first shock of war, our exports increased by leaps and bounds. The trade surplus for each of the years 1914 and 1916 was over $5.2 billion. Other countries made up for this deficit vis-à-vis the United States by liquidating investments, shipping us gold, and borrowing from us. In some cases we were never repaid, particularly for the loans made to Germany. Nonetheless, most observers have concluded that our preparation for the war and entry into it pulled us out of a serious recession. By 1916 most of our unemployment had vanished.

World War I was the first modern war—one fought with formidable weapons that required large amounts of capital, supplies, and manpower, and that involved, at least indirectly, the entire industrial economy of each modern nation involved. War had become expensive. Whereas the Civil War cost the Union $3.5 billion, the Great War cost the United States alone $33.4 billion. It was a period of increased government powers. Government spending after World War I was significantly higher than before. Federal revenues, for example, were only $750 million when we entered the war, but almost $5 billion after it.

Manpower and Production   Of course, the war had to be fought with soldiers. Although the United States did not use large amounts of its available labor force for the actual fighting, the total number of Americans who finally served during the conflict numbered almost five million—about 5 percent of the population. In addition, another three million were needed for war production. Although unemployment was lowered during this time, most of the civilian population did not become materially better off, because a significant fraction of our labor, capital, and resources was expended for the war effort. The actual standard of living fell during the war period. Industrial production did not increase very much after an initial spurt when hostilities broke out in Europe. Industry produced about 1 percent more from 1916 to 1917, but in 1918 and 1919 it produced less than it had several years earlier. Because we were using up part of our real output for the war effort, fewer consumer goods and services were available to the private sector, particularly since production did not significantly increase during the height of the hostilities.

Were We Unprepared?   It may seem that we were totally unprepared for the war effort because the president was relying on his ability to keep us out of the war in order to be reelected. However, this is not a completely accurate view. As early as 1915 the Naval Consulting Board had an Industrial Preparedness Committee, and it became a full-fledged Committee on Industrial Preparedness in 1916. This organization was financed solely by private contributions, although it was officially an arm of the federal government. By late 1916 there was a new organization, called the Council of National Defense (CND). President Wilson said that the purpose of the CND was to organize "the whole industrial mechanism ... in the most effective way." In February 1917, even before we entered the war, the CND set up a Munitions Standards Board, Eventually the CND was to designate an entire system of food control, censorship of the press, and purchasing war supplies. Finally, a couple of months after we joined the Allies, a War Industries Board was established to take control of much of the economy. Figure 10.5 shows what a complicated control mechanism was imposed on the economy by the rigors of war production and distribution.

Controls   War always creates an atmosphere conducive to expansion of government powers. The Great War was no exception. In fact, we might view World War I as a period that generated much of the administrative machinery that set the stage for many of the government control mechanisms instituted during Roosevelt's New Deal.

The War Industries Board took its job seriously. It soon became the coordinator and allocator of commodities and allowed the fixing of prices and the setting of priorities in production. Bernard Baruch became head of this vast bureaucratic organization in March 1918. Baruch was an obvious candidate, for he had been an earlier supporter of our entry into the war and had presented a scheme for wartime industrial mobilization to the president in 1915, well before most people thought we might enter the conflict. All of the leaders of the various departments in the control mechanism for war mobilization were from big business, and, as can be expected, they looked out for their own. For example, in the granting of

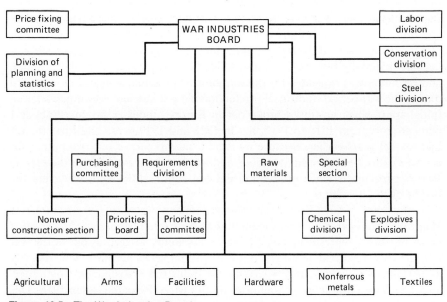

Figure 10.5   The War Industries Board.

war contracts, there was no competitive bidding. The big-business-dominated War Industries Board handed out contracts as it saw fit, often ignoring costs and efficiency in the process.

Price fixing   Since wars have generally been associated with inflation, the government sought to establish price-fixing mechanisms to control inflation. However, the methods of war financing made inflation inevitable. Nonetheless, a Price-Fixing Committee of the War Industries Board was formed. Naturally, the public was told that the committee would set maximum prices so the consumer would not be hurt.

Price fixing in the agriculture sector was presided over by Herbert Hoover. Instead of direct control over food, his Food Administration used a vast network of licensing agreements. Every producer, warehouser, and distributor of food had to obtain a federal license from the Food Administration. The licenses were used to control prices, because they were granted only if the licensees set prices to allow "a reasonable margin of profit." The goal, it would seem, was not lower prices, but rather to stabilize and ensure higher noncompetitive prices. Certainly this was the end result, and any competitor who tried to increase profits above prewar levels by price cutting was threatened with the loss of its license. And when direct price controls were applied, a maximum was not set, but rather a *minimum*. For example, the Food Control Act of 1917 set a minimum price of $2 a bushel on the 1918 wheat crop. This figure was later increased 25 cents in the summer of 1918.

Other forms of control   The government completely took over some industries, such as the railroads. At the beginning of the war, the railroads agreed to form a Railroads War Board and to cease competitive activities. However, the desire for higher profits was stronger than the railroad managers' patriotic impulses. Price cutting became common, and more and more overt forms of competition appeared. Finally, President Wilson seized the railroads on December 28, 1917, placing them under direct government control. Many important railroad personnel were appointed to leading positions in the Railroad Administration. Soon there were numerous rules for compulsory standardization of locomotive and equipment design and for the elimination of duplicate passenger and coal services. Additionally, no railroads were allowed to solicit new business. All of this was done even before the Railroad Administration was legalized by the Federal Control Act of March 1918.

The entire system of controls was more or less dismantled after the cessation of hostilities. However, the stage had been set for collective action linking government and business in a cooperative atmosphere. This was similar to, but on a vastly different scale from, government involvement in early nineteenth-century transportation mediums. This cooperative atmosphere was to prevail again years later, during Franklin Delano Roosevelt's administration.

Financing World War I   As can be seen in Figure 10.6, federal expenditures rose rapidly during the period under study. But federal expenditures do not just happen. Even the government has faces **budget constraints**: If government expen-

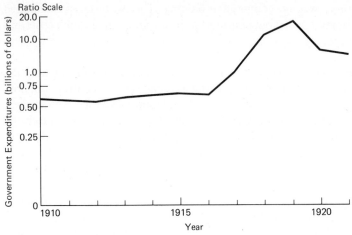

Figure 10.6   Rising government expenditures. (*Source*: U.S. Department of the Treasury.)

ditures are increased, they must somehow be financed. As discussed earlier in this chapter, the government generally finances its expenditures in three ways: by taxation, borrowing from the public, or money creation.

Taxation   Taxation is the most obvious manner in which the government pays for its expenditures, but none of our major wars has been completely financed by taxation. The Great War was no exception, although Congress continuously increased tax rates in an effort to offset its increased expenditures. Moreover, there was a change in the entire tax structure during the war, emphasizing more direct taxes and more progressive tax rates. For instance, in 1916 the maximum personal income tax rate was raised from 7 percent to 15 percent, and the maximum corporation rate was raised to 14.5 percent. In 1917 there were increases in estate taxes and again in personal and corporate income taxes. The maximum rate on personal income taxes went up 67 percent, and the normal corporation rate rose from 2 percent to 6 percent, with the maximum excess profits rate going up to 60 percent. This still was not enough, so the Revenue Act of 1918 (which was eventually passed in February 1919) increased the maximum personal rate to 77 percent, the normal corporation tax rate to 12 percent, and the maximum excess profits tax rate to 65 percent. Ultimately, taxes provided about one third of the revenues needed for the war effort.

Borrowing from the private sector   When the government spends more than it receives, it may borrow by selling government bonds to the public. The federal government took full advantage of this option during World War I. In addition to its regular bond sales, which occur all the time in today's dynamic economy, it instituted four Liberty Loan drives, and one postwar drive, called a Victory Loan. A total of $19.1 billion was raised in this manner. In fact, the government's increased bond sales were, and still are, a postponement of the inevitable, a disguised form of increased taxes. After all, when the government sells a bond, it obtains money from individuals, owners of banks, or corporations. In return, it promises to pay interest for a certain number of years and then pay back the original price of the bond, called the *principal*. But how does the government pay the interest? Out of revenues. Where does it obtain revenues? From taxes. This means that when the government runs a deficit and makes up for it by selling bonds, it is increasing the *future* tax liabilities of the nation.

Of course, it is obvious that one cannot get something for nothing. If someone gives up part of his or her income to buy bonds so that the government can increase its expenditures, that person has to be paid a reward. And the reward is the interest rate, which we can call a reward for waiting. So we have these options: Either pay taxes today to finance government expenditures, or pay higher taxes in the future to pay for those government expenditures. Lastly, the money used for government finance (bonds) is diverted from elsewhere, leaving less for private investors and consumers.

Money creation   The last method of government finance is money creation. It was resorted to during the Revolutionary War, when continentals were printed; it was used during the Civil War, when Confederates notes and greenbacks were issued; and it happened again during World War I. By this time, however, a more formalized machinery for money creation had been established—the Federal Reserve System.

The Great Depression and the Growth of the Public Sector

There are many myths about what happened before the election of President Franklin D. Roosevelt and what happened after. In the main, many observers contend that Hoover was a complete laissez-faire president who was unwilling to attempt any government intervention to pull the economy out of a deepening recession. On the other hand, many contend that President Roosevelt took Keynesian economics to heart and attempted by every means necessary to stimulate the economy through federal programs designed to increase aggregate demand. Both of these common notions are misleading. We have already referred to the interventionist attitude that Hoover had exhibited during World War I. That attitude was to continue during his time as secretary of commerce and, more important, during his first three years as president.

Hoover, the Government Advocate   Hoover was both a mobilizer and an economic planner during World War I. During the 1920s, he was a persistent advocate of government-business partnership in stabilizing industry. In fact, Hoover campaigned for reelection in 1932 on a platform of past government intervention into the private business affairs of the nation. He said, "We might have done nothing. That would have been utter ruin. Instead, we met the situation with proposals to private business and to Congress of the most gigantic proportion of economic defense and counterattack ever evolved in the history of the Republic."

He was not exaggerating much, for as soon as the stock market crashed in

1929, he started putting his program into operation. He called a series of White House conferences with the leading financiers and industrialists of the day. He had them pledge, for example, that they would not reduce wage rates and that they would expand their investments. His theory was that the way to prevent recession was to maintain the purchasing power of the working people. How better to do this than by not reducing their wages?

The error of keeping wages up   What Hoover ignored during this period was that if prices are falling and wages stay the same, then real wages are rising. Just as with any other good or service, the demand for labor is negatively related to its price. If labor's price—the real wage rate—goes up, a lower quantity will be demanded. If there is unemployment, an explicit program to keep real wages up will lead not to more employment, but rather to less, which is exactly what happened. Only in 1932, after several years of severe depression and extensive unemployment, did money wages begin to fall. Meanwhile, between 1929 and 1933 real wages advanced, while by 1933 unemployment reached 25 percent.

Expansion of public works   In December 1929 Hoover proposed to expand public works by some $600 million. In 1931 he was instrumental in passing the Employment Stabilization Act, which established an Employment Stabilization Board. This board was allocated $150 million to expand public works during the depression. Hoover was not content to stop there. He instituted the start of the Boulder, Grand Coulee, and Central California dams, and also signed a treaty with Canada in order to build the Saint Lawrence Seaway. Hoover was the first president to actively promote extensive public works.

Finally, in January of 1932 Hoover created the Reconstruction Finance Corporation (RFC). It was modeled after the old World War I Finance Corporation, which extended emergency loans to business. The U.S. Treasury furnished the RFC with half a billion dollars, and it was allowed to issue bonds up to another $1.5 billion.

Also, even prior to the depression, Hoover had established a Federal Farm Board, which was ready to take action as soon as the depression began. Its first big operation was to cartelize wheat farmers into cooperative marketing units in order to withhold wheat stocks, thereby causing a rise in prices. This move did not work well. Persuasion was not adequate to induce wheat farmers voluntarily to limit their wheat production. Then the Grain Stabilization Corporation was set up. It was supposed to purchase enough wheat to prevent the price of wheat from falling. However, supplies were too great, and prices fell.

A change of heart   Finally, in the last year of his administration, Hoover changed course. Many advisors had encouraged him to continue his efforts to increase the scope of government intervention in the marketplace and to increase the amount of cartelization among industry leaders. When he declined, he was labeled a laissez-faire president, although this label does not reflect what actually happened during the first three years of Hoover's administration. Franklin Roosevelt was nonetheless able to capitalize on it and become president for the remainder of his life.

The New Deal   Roosevelt's sweep into office allowed him to push through Congress a massive amount of legislation in the first 100 days of his administration. Space limitations prevent us from giving the details of every program that America's thirty-second president instituted; we can, however, look at the major ones.

It must be noted that Roosevelt did not take office with the idea that government deficit spending was a necessary stimulus to economic recovery. In fact, only later in his administration did he come to believe that deficit spending was the route to prosperity for a gravely depressed economy. Many of his speeches suggest that he was convinced that a balanced federal budget should be maintained. Nonetheless, he wanted to start numerous programs to put the country back on the road to recovery.

Using Hoover's ideas   Many of Roosevelt's ideas were merely extensions of Hoover's. Roosevelt felt that it was necessary to increase worker's wages in order to increase purchasing power in the economy and to reduce drastically tumbling prices owing to "cutthroat" competition. Therefore, he was convinced that a new system of cooperation among workers, businesses, and the government was necessary. Hence, the National Industrial Recovery Act (NIRA) was passed, and the National Recovery Administration (NRA) was formed. Its basic purpose was to allow collusion among businesses to prevent price cutting. Those businesses that joined in the national recovery effort were allowed to post the Blue Eagle emblem to identify themselves.

For labor, section 7a of the National Industrial Recovery Act allowed for collective bargaining by employees. This was a great impetus to the union movement, which had started many years before.

From the very beginning, a considerable portion of the population opposed the National Recovery Administration and its obvious monopolizing tendencies. Finally, on May 27, 1935, the Supreme Court, in the Schecter case, declared that the NIRA was unconstitutional.

Farm programs   The Federal Farm Board had already been set up with an appropriation of a half billion dollars to be used to stabilize the prices of the three major commodities in the program: wheat, cotton, and wool. The Farm Board soon ran out of money, though, in attempting to keep the price of these commodities high. The major replacement for the Farm Board was brought about by the Agriculture Adjustment Act of 1933. It established within the Department of Agriculture the Agricultural Adjustment Administration (AAA). Its stated goal was to support farm prices and to control the production of farm products. These measures were reinforced and extended by the Bankhead Cotton Control Act, passed in 1934, as well as the Curr-Smith Tobacco Control Act. Both of these acts levied fines on farmers who produced more than their quotas. Many farmers who signed agreements to limit production were given benefit payments by the government.

From the very beginning the programs of the AAA provoked scandal. "The murder of six million little pigs" occurred after a survey showed young pigs to be extremely numerous, indicating that in the near future so much pork would be available that prices would plummet. The Farm Bureau, the National Corn Hog Committee, and the Farmers Union recommended the slaughter of six million pigs; the owners were paid for the pork by the Federal Surplus Relief Corporation. In another incident, AAA farmers provoked outrage by plowing under 11 million acres of cotton.

At this time, the Commodity Credit Corporation was formed. It was allowed to make *nonrecourse loans* to farmers, who used cotton as collateral. In other words, the farmers would turn over to the Commodity Credit Corporation cotton in exchange for a stipulated price that was above the market price. Farmers were not obliged to repay the loan, but if they chose to do so, they could get their cotton back. The Commodity Credit Corporation is still in operation.

Nonfarm relief programs and Social Security   Numerous other programs were instituted during the New Deal. Many were aimed at providing employment for the impoverished. There were the Civilian Conservation Corps (CCC), the National Youth Administration (NYA), the Civil Works Administration (CWA), and the Works Progress Administration (WPA). None of these programs lasted, but they did provide jobs for a certain number of people during the depression, and similarly designed and motivated programs are being implemented today.

One program that did last was Social Security. The Social Security Act, signed by Roosevelt on August 14, 1935, provided one of the most important social insurance programs in the history of the United States. Its major aspects were unemployment and old age insurance plus survivors' benefits. It started out small, enabling the federal government to provide grants to states to help them fund their old age assistance programs. There were also grants for aid to dependent children and to the blind.

These were the first major entitlement programs. They were to become the main source of the growth in government in the 1970s and 1980s.

The Social Security Act levied a basic tax on payrolls of all employers; initially it was 1 percent but it rose to 3 percent after 1937. Although it is not clear how effective the Social Security Act's provisions were during the program's early years, today we have ample evidence of how the Social Security system works. All workers who are covered start paying Social Security the minute they start making money, no matter how little. The basic rate in 1980 was 6.65 percent for the employer and the employee alike, applied to the first $29,700 of earned income; these figures are scheduled to climb steadily in the future.

However, employers do not bear the cost of their 6.65 percent. Since the employers' payments are part of their costs of hiring, they accordingly offer lower money wages to workers than if there were no Social Security payments. The employee indirectly pays the Social Security tax because the Social Security payment is ultimately a tax on labor income. Of course, it is redistributed to older, retired workers; but those who are paying view it simply as a payroll tax.

Furthermore, it is not, strictly speaking, a guaranteed insurance program. Death benefits can be small or even zero unless the deceased leaves a long-lived widow or minor children. Moreover, Social Security payments are voted on by

Congress. We can never be certain that Congress in the future will be as generous as it has been in the past. Nevertheless, the program remains visible and is one of the major social insurance programs in existence today.

Aggregate demand   Despite all the fanfare, it is not really clear that the programs enacted during Roosevelt's days in office had much effect on aggregate demand. To decide this point we must consider not only the programs that were instituted, but also the way they were paid for and other programs that were dropped.

During his campaign, Roosevelt had criticized Hoover for the large budget deficits that had accumulated after the crash of 1929, and in fact Hoover's administration had the largest federal deficit in the history of the United States prior to Roosevelt's election. Once elected, Roosevelt told Congress that he did not want the country to be "wrecked on the rocks of loose fiscal policy," and deficits during the depression years were indeed small. In fact, in 1937 the total government budget, including federal, state, and local levels, had a surplus of $0.3 billion. During this time, taxes were repeatedly raised. The Revenue Act of 1932, passed during the depths of the depression, brought the largest percentage increase of federal taxes in the history of the United States except for periods of war.

Fiscal policies, then, were actually very weak, and even perverse. At the same time that the federal government was increasing expenditures, local and state governments were decreasing them. If we measure the total of state, federal, and local fiscal policies, we find that, as compared to what the government was doing prior to the depression, they were truly expansionary only in 1931 and 1936; and these two years were expansionary only because of large veterans' benefits that were passed by Congress in both years—despite the vigorous opposition of both Hoover and Roosevelt. In 1933, 1937, and (although to a lesser degree) 1938, fiscal policy was quite a bit less expansionary than in 1939.

So although Roosevelt's administration has often been characterized as expansionary, it was not. The New Deal's primary achievements were reform and the establishment of clearly delineated government control over more aspects of American economic life.

World War II

As we have pointed out repeatedly, the government must finance its war expenditures. It has three ways to do so: taxation, borrowing from the private sector, and money creation; and all three were used in World War II. Federal expenditures from 1939 to 1945 grew enormously, as did the federal government's deficit—the difference between federal expenditures and federal tax receipts. In 1945 the deficit reached an astounding $53.9 billion, more than one half of federal expenditures in that year!

Taxation   As early as January 1940 Roosevelt asked for additional taxes to pay for anticipated war expenditures. How did Congress respond? In June 1940 it merely lowered personal income tax exemptions and added slightly to the personal income tax surtax rate. It also charged a little more to corporations and made some nominal increases in gift, excise, estate, and other assorted taxes. Nevertheless, tax receipts quickly fell behind expenditures. In October 1940, when it was obvious that the fighting was intensifying rather than subsiding, an excess profits tax was passed, with rates ranging from 25 percent to 50 percent. The corporate profit rate was raised to a maximum of 24 percent. About one year later, the maximum personal income tax rate went up to 77 percent and the corporate rate to 31 percent. The next year taxes were raised again, the personal tax to a maximum of 88 percent and the corporate to 40 percent. In addition, the maximum excess profits rate on corporate profits was now 90 percent. The following year (1943), when the president asked Congress for even more taxes, it refused. However, a year after this request Congress increased the maximum marginal tax rate on individuals to 90 percent.[2] Still, only 61 percent of the entire war effort was financed by taxation.

Selling Bonds Because of the growing government deficit, bonds had to be sold. Just as there were Liberty Loans in World War I, there were Liberty Loans in World War II. In fact, the U.S. Treasury conducted seven of them, plus one Victory Loan. All told, during this period loans from the private sector accounted for 28 percent of government expenditures, leaving 11 percent to be made up by money creation.

Money Creation The Federal Reserve System agreed to help the Treasury. Its primary objective was to ensure the Treasury adequate funds to meet all government expenditures. In March 1942 a special committee in the Federal Reserve System asserted its desire to prevent a rise in the interest rates of government bonds. So from then until 1951, the Federal Reserve tried to keep the interest rate at a very low level: 2.5 percent on long-term bonds, and 0.375 percent on 90-day Treasury bills. To maintain these low rates of interest, the Federal Reserve had to stand ready to buy all the government bonds offered when interest rates started to rise above the support level. At that time anybody could exchange cash for government bonds. But every time the Federal Reserve bought a bond, it increased the base on which the money supply rested. It is not surprising, then, that the money supply grew 12.1 percent a year from 1939 to 1948 as a result of the Federal Reserve's bond purchases. The Federal Reserve had essentially abandoned control over the monetary system during this period of bond support. This is clearly seen in Figure 10.7, which shows what happened to the money supply from the latter part of the 1930s through 1950.

Price Controls Whether from an excessive demand by the government for war production or from the increased amount of money that the Federal Reserve was putting into circulation, mounting pressure on prices soon resulted. Many knew

[2]The *marginal tax rate* is the rate at which additional income is taxed. Note that it can be very different from the average tax rate.

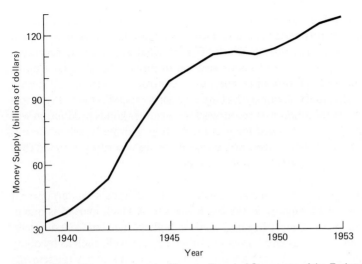

Figure 10.7   The money supply. (*Source*: Board of Governors of the Federal Reserve System.)

this was going to happen, but nobody wanted it. Hence, the Price Control Act of January 1942 established the Office of Price Administration. By mid-1943, fully 95 percent of the nation's foodstuffs were rationed, and maximum prices and rents had been established. The Anti-Inflation Act of October 1942 then established the Office of Economic Stabilization. Its purpose was to limit wages and salaries and to curb prices and rents not yet controlled. At the height of price controls, these two offices, along with the Office of War Mobilization, created in 1943, were assisted by almost 400,000 volunteer "price-watchers" throughout the country. As a result of this national effort, wholesale prices rose only 14 percent from November 1941 to August 1945. Figure 10.8 shows what happened to prices before, during, and after World War II.

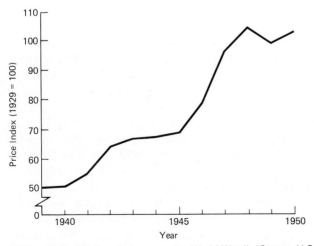

Figure 10.8   Inflation during and after World War II. (*Source*: U.S. Bureau of Labor Statistics.)

Repressed inflation   Price controls were not new to Americans, of course; but the effects of controls were little understood. Because prices were prevented from rising, there occurred during World War II what is known as **repressed inflation.** That is, the shortage of goods relative to money did not show up as inflated prices because of rationing and price controls. Nevertheless, during World War II individuals obviously had more cash to spend. Hence there was pent-up demand; yet the amount of resources for consumer goods production was limited, since so much was needed for war production. Normally, when there is excess demand for goods or services, prices rise; but price controls prevented this. Queuing and rationing became common practices.

Black markets   There are many ways in which individuals can circumvent price controls. One is by buying on the black market. A **black market** is one in which goods and services are (illegally) sold at higher than controlled prices. Individuals can obtain goods and services in other ways as well, such as by doing favors for the supplier of a rationed good or service, or by making arrangements for under-the-counter payments in addition to the stated price. It is not clear how much of this actually happened during the war, but many accounts indicate that illegal or semilegal dealing was rampant. When controls were finally lifted after the end of hostilities in 1945 prices soared, as Figure 10.8 clearly reveals.

This response to the removal of controls further supports the contention that repressed inflation occurred during World War II. When prices were allowed to rise, they did, indicating that they would have risen all along in the absence of controls. Moreover, it took considerable bureaucratic effort to police controls during the war, despite the strong patriotic spirit that prevailed at the time. Although moderately successful during World War II, such measures have been ineffective in peacetime, and the inevitable inflationary burst ultimately came after 1945.

The Nixon Administration and Price Controls

Let's conclude the chapter by looking again at a later use of price controls. Under President Richard M. Nixon, price and wage stabilization programs, known as Phases I–IV, were put into effect starting in 1971. Phase I was a 90-day freeze on all wages and prices commencing August 15, 1971. Phase II, initiated in November 1971, reduced the number of controls. It lasted until the end of December 1972. Phase III, announced in January 1973, set acceptable increases in wages at 5.5 percent, those in corporate profits at 1.5 percent. In Phase III most price-control categories were shifted to voluntary restraints. This triggered renewed inflation. Phase IV was instituted in August 1973. The price freeze on all items except beef, gasoline, and diesel oil ceased. Phase IV gradually ended when all but a few price restraints were removed in April 1974.

If we look back at prices during 1971–1974, we find that prices were rising more rapidly than they had before the imposition of controls. Of course, this does not mean than Nixon's price stabilization program caused the rise. What it does mean is that if the underlying causes of inflation are not addressed, inflation will continue no matter what the government tries to do. During Phases I–IV federal monetary and fiscal policies were, on the average, quite expansionary. That is, there were large amounts of government spending and a significant increase in the money supply. For much of the time, it was a case of "too many dollars chasing too few goods." Of course, this demand-pull theory of inflation cannot explain all that occurred during the period.

People who experienced Nixon's price stabilization program can attest to the ineffectiveness of its wage and price controls. People find a way to circumvent controls when doing so is in their own interest. Just from a practical standpoint, can you imagine how difficult it would be for any government official to control every single price in the economy? There are literally hundreds of thousands of items and millions of prices. How could anyone ever hope to control even a significant portion? Whatever may be the appropriate method of stemming inflation, wage and price controls have their fatal drawbacks.

DEFINITIONS OF NEW TERMS

PROPORTIONAL TAX   A tax system in which, as an individual's income goes up, the tax bill goes up in exactly the same proportion is a proportional tax. It is also called a flat rate tax.

PROGRESSIVE TAX   A tax system in which, as a person earns more income, a higher percentage of the additional dollars is taxed is a progressive tax.

REGRESSIVE TAX   A tax system in which additional income lowers an individual's tax rate is a regressive tax.

DEFICIT SPENDING   Federal government spending that is in excess of government tax revenues is deficit spending.

INFLATIONARY FINANCE   Inflationary finance, which usually occurs during wartime, involves the issuance of large amounts of money to help finance government expenditures.

HYPERINFLATION   Hyperinflation is a consistent rise in the price level that attains astronomical rates, such as a 1,000 percent increase in a month.

GREENBACKS   Greenbacks were U.S. bank notes that were not backed by gold or silver; they got their name from their color.

SOCIAL RATE OF RETURN   Social rate of return is the rate of return on an investment that takes account not only of the benefits to the private investor but also of any other benefits that society obtains.

BUDGET CONSTRAINT   The constraint that an individual, a government, or even the world has on its spending capacity is a budget constraint. People are limited in how much they can spend by their budget constraint. So, too, is the government, except that it has the means of expanding its budget constraint by selling bonds and by creating money.

REPRESSED INFLATION   Repressed inflation is inflation that is not allowed to manifest itself in rising prices. The symptoms of repressed inflation are shortages, black markets, under-the-counter payments, and discrimination against certain classes of consumers.

BLACK MARKET   The black market is an illegal market where goods and services are exchanged at prices that exceed legally controlled maxima and are transferred illegally.

A Wall Street Whiz Becomes Wartime Economic Czar

BERNARD MANNES BARUCH
(1870–1965)

Financier and Economist for the Government

In 1940 the National Defense Advisory Commission had a meeting with Bernard Baruch. The country was worried about the possibility of war. What to do in such an event was foremost in everyone's mind, at least everyone's in the government. Baruch urged the members of the NDAC to form industrial committees, establish priorities, and impose price controls, all under the centralized authority of a single agency. Such a recommendation from the former Wall Street whiz was not unexpected. After all, during World War I he had headed the War Industries Board, which controlled much of American economic life during the hostilities.

Baruch didn't start out as a government economist and advisor. He was the son of a well-known physician and writer on medical subjects, who lived in Camden, South Carolina. The Baruch family soon moved to New York, where Bernard eventually won his B.A. degree at the College of the City of New York. He then entered the brokerage house of A. A. Housman & Company. He spent literally hundreds of hours poring over industrial and railroad manuals. In fact, his employer freely predicted his failure as a "customer's man." Failure he was not, however. Eventually he became a member of the firm and started negotiating some of the largest industrial mergers to occur in the United States. He soon had the esteem and confidence of Rockefeller, the Guggenheims, and a number of other financiers of the day. He was brought to the attention of President Wilson and this started him on his long career of government service.

In 1916 the president invited Baruch to sit on the Council of National Defense. He was made commissioner of raw materials, minerals and metals. Finally he sold his membership in the New York Stock Exchange and never again returned to private business.

Baruch's penchant for assisting in producer organizations, which were later to engage in numerous anticompetitive practices, started at the very beginning of his government career. In the raw materials field, he got cooperative committees of highly placed executives to assemble trade information and to facilitate the business-government partnership that Baruch was to be so fond of in the future.

When the Council of National Defense organized the War Industries Board on July 28, 1917, Baruch was named a member. During this time the operations of the various war agencies seemed to be little coordinated, at least in the eyes of President Wilson. There seemed to be a need for the creation of a "war cabinet" with autocratic powers, so the president made the War Industries Board independent, with Baruch as chairman. The board was clothed with full power of enforcement for all of its rulings. Bernard Baruch became the industrial dictator of wartime America. The operations of the board affected practically every phase of the nation's economic life. Price fixing seemed to be a major occupation. Accordingly, the prices of aluminum, cement, copper, cotton, cotton linters, hides, leather, hemp, lumber, platinum, sand, gravel, crushed stone, steel wool, and zinc were fixed.

There was also a distinct desire to reduce "wasteful" duplication. Hence, the board under Baruch's iron hand regulated the style and color of clothes, reduced the number of types of such items as paints, farm implements, tires, furnaces, refrigerators, sofas, metal beds, and spring wagons. The War Industries Board also waged a campaign to eliminate "unnecessary" delivery service. At one extreme, the War Industries Board's activities were thought to simplify and standardize manufacturing methods to the end of saving labor, materials, and costs. However, many critics of Baruch's methods pointed out that he was helping stifle competitive forces within the nation's economy.

Baruch's organizational methods were simple: When he wanted an industry to do something, he commandeered the industry's heads to Washington jobs. He paid little attention to precedent, and never allowed his mind to be lost in the mazes of organization charts. Nor did he allow his purposes to be thwarted by government red tape. When he had a goal, he proceeded by the shortest possible route.

For all of Baruch's efforts on the War Industries Board, President Wilson gave him the Distinguished Service Medal.

After the war the president got a firm "no" when he asked Baruch to become secretary of the treasury. Instead, the president was able to get him on the commission to attend the peace conference in Paris, where the former financier became the sole American member of the economic drafting committee. His work has been severely criticized, for he single-handedly wrote many of the sections that outraged certain domestic observers. For example, he specified that all alien property taken over by the United States during the war should remain under the control of Congress.

Then Baruch went into semiretirement, devoting himself to the study of what he called "practical" economic questions, both national and international. He wrote reports on the defects in the business side of farming and suggested remedies. He advised the American Farm Bureau Federation and attempted to get the financial world interested in the business troubles of American farmers.

Although retired from the world of Wall Street that he knew so well, Baruch nonetheless kept his keen insights: he began liquidating all his stocks as early as 1928 and putting the proceeds into gold. He died a very rich man.

chapter *11*

International Trade

WHY TRADE?

America would be a radically different place if there were no international trade. **Imports** and **exports**—the coming in and going out of all types of goods—affect the life-style of Americans far more than we usually realize.

Although the share of imports in our economy is only about 10 percent of our total national economic activity, the list of imported items in everyday use is impressive. Without shipments from abroad we would have no tea, coffee, chocolate, pineapples, bananas, or spices. Today we also bring in nearly 90 percent of our radios, over 90 percent of our motorcycles, and a large share of our automobiles and optical goods, among many others.

On the other hand, the world looks to the United States for agricultural products and many manufactured goods. One third of America's mined sulfur is sold to foreign nations, as is one fourth of our grain and tobacco, one fourth of our textile and metal-working machinery, and one fifth of our national cotton crop. The business of exporting employs between three and four million Americans.

Why do people exchange money for goods and services? Usually because the value they place on a good or service is at least as great as the value they place on the amount of money they give up to obtain that good or service. In other words, they voluntarily engage in economic exchange with others because doing so makes them better off. If it did not, they would not make the exchange.

If you question whether trade, or exchange, among individuals is beneficial, think how you would live if you could not exchange with someone else—if trade were prohibited. All people would have to become self-sufficient. They would have to grow their own food, make their own clothes, and furnish their own recreation. Life would be hard and most likely dull.

Just as trade between individuals tends to enhance the lives of those who engage in it, so does trade among the states benefit the parties to such exchange. Americans have access to a huge variety of products that would not be available if trade among the 50 states were prohibited. In fact, interstate commerce was perceived to be necessary and desirable by the drafters of the U.S. Constitution, who prohibited any taxes on interstate trade. Article I, section 9, paragraph 5 of the Constitution reads, "No tax or duty shall be laid on articles exported from any state," and the next paragraph declares that

> no preference shall be given by any regulation of commerce or revenue to the ports of one state over those of another; nor shall vessels bound to, or from, one state, be obliged to enter, clear, or pay duties to another.

Finally, article I, section 10, paragraph 2 reads as follows:

> No state shall, without the consent of the Congress, lay any imposts, or duties on imports or exports, except what may be absolutely necessary for executing its inspection laws; and the net produce of all duties and imports, laid by any state on imports or exports, shall be for the use of the Treasury of the United States; and all such laws shall be subject to the revision and control of the Congress.

If you still doubt that Americans benefit from trade among the several states, ask yourself what life would be like if the state in which you reside were prohibited from buying goods from other states. Suppose you lived in Delaware; how much fresh fruit might be obtainable? Or suppose you lived in Oregon; how many new automobiles would be produced there?

Unrestricted trade among the states, then, is an accepted part of the nation's economic activity. It would be difficult, if not impossible, to demonstrate that any American is worse off because **free trade** (trade without restrictions) among the states is permitted.

Free trade allows individuals to specialize in whatever enables them to make the highest profits—whatever yields them the greatest income and satisfaction for the use of their time. The same is true for states and for nations.

Some politicians seem unaware of these principles. They complain about foreigners "underselling" American industry by offering relatively cheap goods for sale in the United States. Nevertheless, when free trade exists among nations, each nation can specialize in producing and marketing whatever enables it to get the highest reward. It can exchange with other nations the goods it specializes in producing for the goods that other nations specialize in producing.

Because nations have different collective tastes and different collective resource bases, we can reasonably conclude that trade among nations will always yield gains to the traders. Furthermore, the more trade there is, the more specialization there can be, which leads to increased output.

COSTS OF TRADE

Trade has costs, however. For example, if in the United States one state has an advantage in producing agricultural crops, other states may not be able to survive as centers of agricultural production. Farm workers in these other states will suffer decreases in their incomes. Eventually, they may have to find other work.

As tastes, supplies of natural resources, and prices change throughout the world, countries might find their trading advantage in some exports slipping. When this happens, some people may experience severe hardships. An example of a changing advantage in world trade is the production of steel. In recent years Japan has become increasingly competitive in steel products in the world market. As Japan has become more competitive, U.S. steelmakers have been hurt. American steel companies—including their stockholders and employees—are feeling the effect of Japan's ability to produce steel products at low prices.

ARGUMENTS AGAINST FREE TRADE

The arguments against free trade therefore have some merit. However, many of these arguments are incomplete. They point out the costs of trade without considering the benefits; nor do they consider possible alternatives for reducing costs while reaping benefits.

Protecting Infant Industries   Many nations believe that if a particular industry is allowed to develop domestically, it can eventually become efficient enough to compete in the world market. Using this reasoning, they favor placing restrictions on imports in order to afford domestic producers time to acquire experience and to develop their own techniques. This idea of protecting infant industries against foreign competition has some merit, and the United States has used protective **tariffs** (taxes on imports) to protect a number of American industries in their infancy.

Such policies can be abused, however. Often protective import restrictions are not removed after an infant industry has matured. The people who benefit from this situation are obviously the stockholders (owners of the companies) and perhaps the employees in the industry that is being protected from world competition. The people who lose out are consumers, who must pay a higher price than the going world price for the product in question.

Providing for National Security   It has been argued that the United States should not rely on foreign sources for many products. Those who hold this view point out that in times of war the United States might not be able to rely on those sources, and that therefore it should strive to build up its own industry instead.

A classic example of this belief involves oil exploration. For reasons of national defense, President Dwight D. Eisenhower instituted during the 1950s an oil **import quota** system. At first voluntary but then mandatory, the system restricted the amount of foreign oil that could be imported into the United States. Eisenhower's idea was to force American oil companies to undertake more exploration for American oil. In time of war, the United States would then have a ready and available supply of oil for tanks, ships, and planes. Taking a long-run perspective, we realize, however, that we used up our domestic supplies of oil more rapidly because of this policy.

Keeping the National Economy Stable Many people argue that foreign trade should be restricted because it introduces an element of instability into the American economic system. They point out that foreign trade activity goes up and down. Its ups and downs add to the ups and downs in the domestic employment rate.

If this argument is followed to its logical conclusion, however, trade among the states should be restricted as well. After all, changes in the volume of trade among certain states can cause unemployment in some states. Although displacements are sorted out over time, workers suffer during the adjustment period.

Nonetheless, when a country allows itself to become specialized in one crop through extensive free trade it invites problems. In such a case the country's economy is at the mercy of any severe price changes affecting that crop. For example, if Brazil's economy relied only on exporting coffee to the rest of the world, that nation would be in serious difficulty if the price of coffee on the world market were to drop. Furthermore, when a country specializes completely, it becomes much more dependent on other nations. In times of war or emergency, this may pose a problem. Traditional trade routes might be disrupted, thus depriving the dependent country of critical materials.

International Trade in Economic History

The roots of international trade go far back in time. America was not even a name when daring traders first began to venture along the overland routes between Europe and the East. By the late 1300s the northern Italian city-states of Venice, Florence, Genoa, and Milan were sending out accomplished overland traders; and it was from northern Italy that Marco Polo set out on his journeys to China, seeking new avenues of commerce. By their superior know-how, commercial skills, and locational advantages, Italian traders were able to dominate most of the world's long-distance trades.

In contrast to the earlier centuries of the Middle Ages, the late sixteenth century was a time of material expansion. This period witnessed the growth of trade, both in volume and in value. In long-distance trades the most important items were expensive manufactured products: light cottons from India and China and jewel-toned rugs from Persia. Even delicate items such as glass from Damascus and porcelain from China were carried on the long routes to the markets of Europe. Another extremely important item in the long-distance trade was spices, such as cloves, nutmeg, ginger, and cinnamon. These were eagerly sought to rescue European diets from monotony, and pepper was vital as a meat preservative in warm climates.

Short-distance trade within Europe was burgeoning as well. Here again Italian merchants reigned supreme, especially in the handling and delivery of Mediterranean goods. A brisk traffic in grain, salt, salted fish, and other bulk commodities such as cheese, wine, and oil arose in the late fifteenth century. By this time the Mediterranean had become a bustling trade arena.

Clearly, the type of commodities carried on long-distance trades was quite different from those on short-distance trades. The commodities from distant areas were typically expensive relative to their bulk and weight. This characteristic was due to the high land transportation costs. No cheap water route had yet been discovered to Asia. Nevertheless, Europe was reaching out, and voyages to the more distant areas were taking place as the decades passed. Of the many motives spurring Atlantic exploratory voyages, the primary one was to tap the riches of the long-distance trade from Asia. The most vigorous adventurers in this endeavor, however, were not the Mediterranean city-states. Why should they seek out new paths, when they were already comfortably astride the traditional routes?

The Atlantic Pioneer

The great Atlantic pioneer of the time was Portugal. Indeed, it was almost an accident of history that an Italian sailor in the employ of Spain made the most significant of all the landfalls. By the time Columbus set sail in 1492, Portugal could already claim more than seven decades of Atlantic exploration and discovery. It was Portugal that discovered Madeira and the Canary Islands, settled the Azores, and made important voyages along the western coast of Africa. Since as early as 1415 the series of Portuguese adventures had been given firm and persistent backing by Prince Henry the Navigator, the younger son of the king of Portugal. For almost four decades, he led Portugal through a rich period of exploration, and each new probe into the Atlantic added to seafaring experience and to the stockpile of knowledge about winds and currents. New trades developed in the islands, and in Africa new discoveries were made as the Portuguese relentlessly pushed farther and farther south along the African coast. Finally, in 1488, Bartholomew Dias reached the Cape of Good Hope. He might have sailed on into the Indian Ocean, but a mutinous crew prevented further exploration. Nine years later Vasco da Gama reached India by the all-water route. The rate of return on the capital invested in that expedition approached 6,000 percent—certainly a lucrative investment. There can be little doubt that in the perspective of the time da Gama, not Columbus, had made the more praiseworthy and rewarding discovery. By the turn of the century, Portugal controlled a rich trading realm. The cargoes of spices from Asia, gold, ivory, and slaves from Africa, and sugar from the Atlantic Islands near Africa all swelled her coffers.

Of course, the all-water route to the East Indies offered military possibilities as well as economic opportunities. The traditional vessels of the Indian Ocean were no match for the well-armed ships of Portugal. Taking advantage of their military superiority, the Portuguese frequently tried to block the flow of goods to the Italian city-states in the Mediterranean and to win trading concessions from rulers in the East. It was their ambition to monopolize the trade from the Far East. Despite disruptions, however, trade flow along the traditional routes persisted. Moreover, Portugal's military excursions in the Far East, although intermittently successful, proved extremely costly in the long run, and its goal of complete monopoly was never realized. In the process, Portugal's limited resources were severely strained, and many soldiers, slaves, and ships were lost. Actually it was not until 1600 that the preeminence of Venice in the eastern trade was destroyed. This coup, accomplished by the Dutch East India Company, was effected by economic means: by superior efficiency in shipping and in commercial organization. More advanced military technology and greater strength also helped, but they played a secondary role.

Shifts in the Center of Wealth

As the realm of Portuguese trade expanded, the relative economic position of the Mediterranean began to slide. The volume of trade in the Mediterranean continued to increase in absolute terms throughout the sixteenth century, but not in proportion to the size of the Atlantic trade. The centers of commerce and wealth and the balance of power were shifting steadily to the nations bordering the Atlantic Ocean.

In addition to Portugal's seafaring adventures, which initiated new southern and far eastern trades, other developments in the North Atlantic were reinforcing the shift of European economic activity. New discoveries of fishing grounds, such as that resulting from John Cabot's expedition from England to Newfoundland in 1497, spurred fishing activity in the North. The main force of northwest European expansion, however, was in the older, established trades. To a disproportionate degree, trade expanded in the cold-zone products—grain, salt, salted fish, woolen cloth, furs, iron, timber, and naval stores. These bulky staple items could withstand the high cost of transportation, since they were transported almost entirely by sea, and unlike the Asian all-water trade, in which vessels were typically full only on the return to Europe, the trade between the Baltic and the northwestern Atlantic regions fully utilized ships in both directions. This had the effect of lowering the average cost of freight and thereby encouraging trade, even in these heavy, bulky products.

As markets widened and trade increased throughout Europe and the rest of the world, greater regional specialization in production took place. Areas increasingly specialized in products that they could produce most efficiently and traded these for other goods produced more cheaply elsewhere. In this way, there were gains from exchange, and people became better off in terms of material wealth. In addition, the growth of market exchanges during this period encouraged greater division of labor. Individual workers slowly but steadily took on specialized tasks, instead of performing all the tasks necessary to produce an item from start to finish. As each worker specialized in one or a few steps of the line of production, output per worker increased.

Antwerp

As the volume of trade increased in sixteenth-century Europe, Antwerp became the center of trade among the city-states of northern Italy, Germany, England, and Holland. It was the distribution point for German wares of silver, copper, lead, and zinc, and for Italian, Flemish, and English manufactures. Both its shipping and commercial services flourished; like a magnet, it attracted merchants from all over Europe.

The rise of Antwerp was linked to the rise of the Atlantic trade. Its commercial superiority was determined primarily by its willingness to enforce contracts and reduce risks of exchange and by its advantageous location. As they formerly had on the Italian city-states, the great crossroads of trade now converged on Antwerp. New discoveries of copper, lead, zinc, and silver deposits in southern Germany, Hungary, and Poland further stimulated trade throughout western Europe. The expansion of population and growing urbanization also increased demand. Moreover, insurance coverage became more common, and market exchanges became less risky. By the late fifteenth century the Netherlands had become one of the most densely populated and economically advanced areas in Europe.

Antwerp's zenith was reached around 1560, when its population exceeded 100,000. In the West, only Paris, London, and Seville matched or surpassed Antwerp in size. Trading activity was continuous throughout the year, but four lengthy trade fairs annually provided periods of financial settlement.

Wars and the division of the Netherlands between 1572 and 1585 finally ended Antwerp's supremacy. Its decline paralleled the weakening prosperity of central Europe, which had been sapped by peasant wars in religious and dynastic struggles throughout the middle of the century. By this time, the value of silver was decreasing, and the silver mines of central Europe were greatly depleted and becoming less productive. Now, for the first time, precious metals from America became truly critical in the economic landscape of Europe. The flow of Spanish-American silver and gold made Cadiz the new trade center. In addition, it provided the sinews of war and whetted the Spanish Crown's appetite for empire.

The voyages of discovery, together with the swelling tides of commerce, exerted heavy pressure on the balance of power in Europe. By the late sixteenth century, dramatic shifts had already occurred. The minor short-run effects of the discovery of the New World were giving way to significant long-run effects. Although contemporary Europeans were only mildly impressed by Christopher Columbus's discovery, later observers were beginning to realize what time has confirmed: Columbus had given Spain an empire that made it the envy of Europe.

The Colonization of North America

Colonization was pursued for the purpose of strengthening the parent nations, and it greatly affected the balance of power among them. As we observed with regard to Spain, and as we know today, the basis of international power is determined by economic strength. At the time of British colonization in North America, the policies of **mercantilism** were the order of the day.

Mercantilist policies were based on the belief that the more wealth a nation had, the more power it had. Wealth and precious metals were viewed as one, and in order to increase the inflow of precious bullion, governments encouraged exports and discouraged imports. When exports exceeded imports in value terms (a favorable balance of trade) the difference was paid in gold or silver (specie). Accordingly, government intervention took the forms of taxing goods coming into a nation, of expanding colonial territory, and of providing incentives to encourage the sale abroad of domestically produced goods. In other words, there was an attempt to force exports from the mother country to be greater than imports. However, mercantilist precepts ignored the principle that both parties gain from voluntary trade, whether the trade be between individuals, states, or nations. From our vantage point, we might say that the goal of government intervention should have been increased exports and imports—an increase in trade with all nations. But in the hostile world of that era, it was thought best to develop and trade with a nation's own colonies. Trade with other nations was perceived to be risky, since it entailed the possibility of being cut off from needed goods by war (which was frequent) or by an adverse change in policy.

Mercantilism and the Navigation Acts   Although the Netherlands was the supreme maritime nation in the seventeenth century, by around the turn of the eighteenth century the English had surpassed the Dutch on the high seas. How was this accomplished? A series of ocean battles was important, but a primary factor was the English Navigation Acts, devised to exclude the highly efficient Dutch shippers from trade within the British Empire.

The Navigation Act of 1661 was directed at shipping; it restricted all British Empire trade to British (including colonial) ships. A foreign ship could deliver goods to England, but only from its own country, not from its colonies or elsewhere. A British ship was defined as one built, owned, and at least three-quarters crewed by British (including colonial) citizens.

Other acts in 1660 and 1663 regulated the movement of many goods. Imports into the colonies from continental Europe were required to pass through England first. Certain items, such as salt and wine from Spain, were excepted and could be shipped directly. Most of the vast array of colonial imports from the continent, however, had to be landed in England and then reloaded before being shipped to America. In addition, key colonial products were to be shipped only to England. At first only tobacco, sugar, and indigo were affected, but later other products, mainly naval stores such as pitch, tar, turpentine, masts, and yards, were added to the list. These items were called **enumerated articles** and could be reexported to the continent only after landing in England. Of course, this procedure made transportation and other distribution costs much higher.

Some of the mercantilist controls encouraged production of certain "essential" items. Other laws actually prohibited production. Indigo and some of the naval stores were subsidized by a per-unit bounty. Various other manufactures were outlawed. For instance, the production of finished woolens outside of England was outlawed in 1699. Later, in 1732, imports of fur hats (mainly beaver) from the colonies were forbidden, as was finished iron in 1750.

British Trade Controls and the American Revolution

Although a simple tabulation of the mercantilist restrictions on colonial trade might lead us to think that the colonists were being exploited, this conclusion is not necessarily correct. Would the colonists have been better off if they had been independent at an earlier date? That is, would their level of material well-being have been higher? To address this question, we must first assess the costs of the restrictions and then consider the benefits of membership in the British Empire.

Manufacturing Restrictions   The least consequential of the mercantilist restrictions were those on manufactures. It is hardly surprising that these were imposed by Parliament in response to pleas from various vested interest groups at home (the English woolen, hat, and iron manufacturers). They wanted to stop "undesirable" competition elsewhere in the British Empire. Actually, the Woolen Act was aimed primarily at Ireland, but it addressed the colonies as well. American colonists were allowed to produce homespun woolens (bedding and garments), and they imported fine linens and fabrics. This arrangement was quite satisfactory to the colonists and would have come about with or without the law. The English and other Europeans could produce these items more cheaply, so for the colonists the law was superfluous.

The restriction on fur hat production in the colonies hurt New York hatters, but this was a small group. Overall, it was inconsequential.

Interestingly enough, the restrictions on the production of finished iron were also harmless, because the law was ignored with impunity. Twenty-five "illegal" iron mills were established between 1750 and 1775 in Pennsylvania and Delaware alone, despite the ease of detection.

Given the overwhelming comparative disadvantage of the colonies in most types of manufactures, these restrictions were not a significant hardship. At most, they were a minor nuisance. There is little reason to infer exploitation from these restrictions.

Shipping and Trade Restrictions   The controls on shipping had mixed effects in the colonies. Tobacco planters and other producers lost out after 1660 because cheap Dutch shipping was no longer available. But colonial shippers gained, as did colonial shipbuilders. Shipping became a major commercial enterprise in New England and the middle colonies, and shipbuilding developed into the most important colonial manufacturing activity. By 1775 one third of the British merchant marine had been built in the colonies. Considering both those who were hurt and those who gained, it is likely that colonial products benefited, on average, from the controls on shipping. After independence, when American shipping was treated as foreign by the British, its exclusion from British Empire trade had catastrophic consequences; American shipbuilders were severely hurt, too, because American-built ships were then classified as foreign.

The most costly features of the Navigation Acts to the colonists were those influencing the movement of goods. By requiring colonial imports and enumerated articles to pass first through the mother country, England made her own ports more active. Of course, this was precisely the purpose of the acts; but they also raised the costs of distribution, which hit at the pocketbooks of the colonists, both coming and going.

The procedure used to estimate these burdens is a tedious one. Essentially, the problem is to figure out how prices and quantities would have changed for goods forcibly routed through England if their direct free movement had been allowed. If direct shipment to the continent had been permitted, the prices received for and quantities sold of colonial exports would have been higher. Similarly, if goods had come in directly, colonial imports from the continent would have cost less and been more plentiful.

Of course, after the Revolution direct shipment was allowed, and a number of scholars have studied price adjustments resulting from this change in order to assess the magnitudes of these burdens.[1] These adjustments range from 1 to 3 percent of colonial income; that is, colonists averaged less income by a couple of percentage points because of the trade restrictions.

Benefits of Being a Colony   Some of the specific benefits of British mercantilist regulation, such as the bounties on indigo, naval stores, silk, and, to a lesser extent, lumber, have already been mentioned. Although the direct payments to colonists in bounties do not indicate the actual net gain to them, we can get an upper estimate on the benefit from bounties. The data obtained by Lawrence Harper show that the bounties paid on colonial products totaled about £65,000 or, at the approximate exchange ratio of pounds to dollars in those days, $325,000.[2] This benefit is dwarfed by an even larger one, which came from military protection.

Before the Revolution, the colonists had little to do with the protection of their property and life. Almost all such protection was provided by the British government. In the beginning, the British helped fight the Spanish, the Indians, and the French. Moreover, American ships were allowed to sail to the Barbary Coast without fear of the infamous Barbary pirates, for Britain had in effect bought off the pirates from attacking its own ships as well as the ships of its colonies. One measure of the benefit of British protection to the colonies is obtained by looking at what the new government spent for national defense after independence. Its annual outlay was in excess of $2 million, and this amount grew with the population. Had the colonists become independent earlier, they would have had to provide for their own military and naval protection. They would have borne the burden of defense alone.

Additionally, Britain took care of much of the administrative work in the colonies, which did not, for example, have to conduct their own foreign policy, or pay for missions abroad for ministers. When these benefits are compared

---

[1]These studies are surveyed by Gary M. Walton in "The New Economic History and the Burdens of the Navigation Acts," *Economic History Review* 24 (November 1971): 533–542.

[2]Lawrence Harper, "The Effect of the Navigation Acts on the Thirteen Colonies," in *The Era of the American Revolution,* R. B. Morris, ed. (New York: Columbia University Press, 1939).

with the costs, any net burden is reduced to insignificant proportions, at least on average.

The Revolution and Its Aftermath

Exploitation or Self-Determination?   Although there is agreement among many historians that the colonies were exploited by England, this view is based largely on the indirect routing of goods forced by trade controls. These controls, however, were never mentioned in the list of grievances sent by the colonists to the British Crown. Furthermore, they were more injurious in the seventeenth century than in 1775, and the colonists had lived quite harmoniously with the Navigation Acts for more than a century. Expectations, land values, and values of other assets had long since been adjusted to account for the costs imposed by the acts. There is thus little if any connection between economic exploitation of the colonies and the American Revolution, which was spurred by a broader range of political issues—the conflict over who was to rule.[3] In any case, British economic, political, and military influence in North America did not end with the Revolution.

Peace and Trade Adjustments   When peace was resumed after the Revolutionary War, the Treaty of Paris gave the United States all the territory west to the Mississippi between Canada and Florida, in addition to the right to navigate the Mississippi. (Of course, this right was worth little, since at that time Spain controlled the mouth of the river, at New Orleans.) Additionally, the United States received fishing rights within British territorial waters in the North Atlantic.

Except for these highlights, there were few bright spots. The United States suffered many economic hardships stemming from the war and independence, and the Articles of Confederation added to the difficulties because of its weak political framework.

The first major peacetime goal was to reopen trade with overseas areas. Here the United States faced great problems, for American ships could no longer trade legally with the British West Indies, and ships built in America lost this market in England because of the Navigation Acts.

Overall, exports did not bounce back to their former levels, and yet imports were vital, because Americans were far from being self-sufficient. Consequently, there was a deficit in the U.S. balance of trade with the rest of the world, since the value of exports remained below that of imports. In order to pay for this excess of imports over exports, the United States temporarily shipped large amounts of specie—gold and silver—to other countries. The result was a reduction in the U.S. money supply and with it a fall in prices. This caused many American merchants grave concern because they had not anticipated the intensity of the *deflation* that occurred after the Revolution. Moreover, they were hurt when the

---

[3]For a more complete analysis of the causes of the American Revolution, see Gary M. Walton and James F. Shepherd, *The Economic Rise of Early America* (London: Cambridge University Press, 1979), Chapter 8.

British resumed large-scale exports to the United States. In fact, the British were accused of **dumping**—that is, selling their goods in our country at prices below cost. This undercut domestic production.

What happened in the United States was a "depression" between the years 1785 and 1786. It was limited primarily to the commercial sector, and we must be careful not to equate the depressions of those years with depressions (or recessions) of more modern times. Today a depression is usually felt by the vast majority of Americans, but in the eighteenth century most of the population was engaged in farming. The fall in prices hurt people, but few became unemployed. Changes in business activity were not generally catastrophic.

The export sector, however, did suffer. The real value of exports per capita right after the war was probably less than one half of that just before it. As Table 11.1 shows, the annual average of real exports per capita fell by 30 percent between 1768 and 1772 and between 1791 and 1792, and this lower level was still evident after several years of business recovery in the late 1780s. Most of the difficulty, as Table 11.1 indicates, was with southern staples. The markets of Europe and elsewhere had stagnated.

In addition, the United States had not yet secured much political power internationally. Few countries accepted the United States as a viable nation in the world economy. As a result, trade discussions and treaties were less fruitful than they might have been.

Recovery and the Growth of Shipping   The situation at the end of the 1780s was one of incomplete economic recovery from the depression of 1785 and 1786. In 1789 the French Revolution began. Then, in 1793, the French and English became embroiled in war. The series of battles between the two archenemies lasted until 1815. Of necessity, both the British and French quickly relaxed their normal mercantilist restrictions. As their demand for our goods increased, American export activity soared; by 1795 exports of American goods had doubled over their 1793 level.

In addition, British and French ships, which normally carried cargo, were now deployed on sterner business. American shipping was prepared to fill this void, and the United States quickly became one of the main shipping countries in the world. Because it was a neutral power, the United States also began to **reexport** numerous trade items. Goods from other nations were shipped to the United States and then reshipped to the belligerents. For example, in 1790 the United States reexported only 3 percent of the goods imported, but by 1805 it was reexporting 60 percent.

As shown in Figure 11.1, the reexport trade grew by leaps and bounds. Of course, total exports did, too, until certain political events in 1807 prevented further U.S. trade expansion. In 1790 almost 60 percent of U.S. trade was carried in American ships; in the years 1805 and 1806 it was nearly 100 percent. This was, in fact, an era of unusually intense commercial and trading activity, as well as shipping activity. For American commerce, the war in Europe was fortunate, at least initially. It stimulated the U.S. economy and brought prosperity to American business and workers.

**Table 11.1   AVERAGE ANNUAL REAL PER CAPITA EXPORTS FROM
COLONIES AND REGIONS OF THE 13 COLONIES,
1768–1772, AND FROM STATES AND REGIONS OF THE
UNITED STATES, 1791–1792**

Pounds Sterling; 1768–1772 Prices

The difficulties of adjusting to independence and new
peacetime circumstances were felt unevenly throughout
the nation. The 30 percent decline in real per capita
exports for the entire United States between 1768 and
1772 and 1791 and 1792 was largely due to catastrophic
declines in the export of the major southern staples. The
northern states fared better than the southern states in
their ability to recover.

Origin	1768–1772	1791–1792
New England		
New Hampshire	0.74	0.23
Massachusetts	0.97	1.14
Rhode Island	1.39	1.72
Connecticut	0.50	0.62
Total:	0.82	0.83
Middle Atlantic		
New York	1.15	1.51
New Jersey	0.02	0.03
Pennsylvania	1.47	1.34
Delaware	0.51	0.44
Total:	1.01	1.11
Upper South		
Maryland	1.93	1.51
Virginia	1.72	0.91
Total:	1.79	1.09
Lower South		
North Carolina	0.38	0.27
South Carolina	3.66	1.75
Georgia	3.17	1.17
Total:	1.75	0.88
Total, all regions:	1.31	0.99

Source: James F. Shepherd and Gary M. Walton, "Economic Change After the American
Revolution: Pre- and Post-War Comparisons of Maritime Shipping and Trade," *Explorations in
Economic History* 13 (October 1976): 413.

Nevertheless, the prosperity of these times was not necessarily a basis for
long-term development. There was no similar increase of prosperity in the interior
of the United States, and a large nation cannot generally grow merely by becoming an efficient shipper for the rest of the world. Yet the profits made from
commercial endeavors during this period were a major source of investment funds
that financed later development, and the market sector of the economy was
growing in importance.

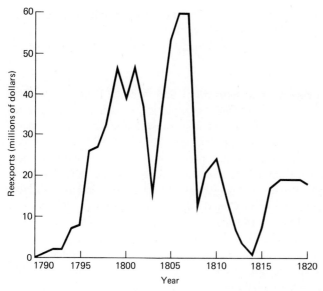

Figure 11.1 Reexport cycles. (*Source*: *Historical Statistics*, p. 538.)

The End of the Commercial Boom   England and France made a temporary peace during 1803, and the U.S. commercial shipping boom ended abruptly. When the European powers started fighting again, they renewed the economic stimulus for American shipping, until both belligerents decided to deny neutral ships entry to enemy ports. Nearly 1,500 American ships were seized after 1805 until Congress enacted the Embargo Act late in 1807. This act prohibited American vessels from sailing to foreign ports, in the hope of forcing England and France to respect American neutrality. The results of the embargo were impressive indeed. As shown in Figure 11.1, reexports fell drastically; similarly, total exports dropped by almost 80 percent when the embargo was enacted. Pressure from merchants, sailors, and commercial interests led to the repeal of the act in 1809. Instead, the Non-Importation Act was passed, prohibiting trade specifically with Great Britain, France, and their territories.

Nevertheless, further difficulties ensued, and eventually the War of 1812 erupted. During this primarily naval war between the United States and England, the British navy blockaded the entire coast of the United States and seized more than 1,000 American ships. Exports fell to practically nothing.

The Resurgence of Foreign Trade

After the second war with England, trade rebounded, and it continued to grow through midcentury. It was later, however—between 1860 and 1920—that the pattern of international trade underwent extensive changes and assumed its modern characteristics. From new parts of the world came an ever-growing flow of foodstuffs and raw materials to support the growing urban populations and feed the furnaces and fabricating plants of industry. In exchange went the manufactured products of the industrial countries, chiefly Great Britain, Germany—and the United States.

Advances in Communication, Transportation, and Metals Processing   Two major forces dominated the changes. One was rapid improvements in communication and transportation. For example, the first transatlantic cable began operations in 1866, a railroad spanned the American continent by 1869, the Suez Canal was opened in the same year, and dramatic productivity gains in ocean transportation occurred over the last half of the nineteenth century. Especially important was the development of railroads in various parts of the world, making available great quantities of cheap grain from Canada, Australia, Argentina, Russia, and the midlands of the United States. In the late 1870s and early 1880s, refrigeration on vessels made possible the shipment of meats, then dairy products, and finally fruits. To these were added the products of the tropics—rice, coffee, cocoa, vegetable oils, and tapioca. The shipments of grains were also of great importance in stimulating the worldwide distribution of foods.

Transportation was not the whole story however. Great Britain, Germany, and the United States rose to industrial supremacy during the nineteenth century, in large measure because they had coal and iron in abundance. England, which until 1875 was the leader in manufactured goods, lost ground to Germany and the United States in the last quarter of the century. The volume of British trade continued to increase, but England's chief role became that of a world financial leader. The United States surged to the front in iron and steel production; Germany and the United States became leaders in the applied fields resulting from scientific efforts—the electrical, chemical, and machine-tool industries.

During the decades around the turn of the century, the countries of the world became divided for at least a century into two groups—those that possessed political and economic power and those that did not. The tropical and subtropical countries of Africa, Asia, and South America, although drawn into world trade as sources of raw materials and as buyers of cheap factory products, remained at low levels of income per capita and developed little industrial power. In the temperate zones, in the United States, Canada, Australia, New Zealand, and Argentina food production advanced ahead of population growth, and income per capita rose rapidly. No other area, however, was comparable to that of the United States.

The Balance of Trade

Because 1864–1896 was a period of falling prices, the dollar values of U.S. foreign trade increased less than the physical volume of trade. On the other hand, 1896 –1914 was a period of steady increases in prices, and from 1914 to 1920 sharp inflationary pressures occurred. Thus, the physical volume of trade between 1896 and 1920 did not increase at all close to the amount indicated by the dollar figures.

Nonetheless, because of World War I there was a remarkable increase in trade, especially in exports between 1914 and 1920. Merchandise imports typically had exceeded exports until 1875. From 1875 on, exports exceeded imports in every year except three; from 1894 on, there was no year in which the value of goods exported from the United States did not exceed the value of goods imported into the country. We say that in those years the United States had a favorable **balance of trade.**

There were also major changes in the kinds of goods exchanged. On the export side, the most striking change was the fall of raw materials from three fifths the value of exports at the end of the Civil War to less than one fifth the value of exports by 1920. Crude foodstuffs grew to nearly one quarter of the total exports for the five-year period 1876–1880, reflecting the advance into the West by the railroads, and then declined until 1915. Manufactured foodstuffs also rose to one quarter of total exports for the period from 1876 to 1880, held this proportion for nearly three decades, and then dropped in relative importance until World War I brought a small revival. A third important trend was the sustained rise of **semimanufactures** and **finished manufactures.** These categories refer to manufactured goods, the former group including products that will require further manufacture before they are used. In the 1915–1920 period these two categories accounted for about half of the total value of exports.

The opposite movements, although not as marked, occurred on the import side. Crude materials jumped from one tenth the value of imports after the Civil War to two fifths the value of imports during the World War I years. The chief crude materials imported—those that were necessary to a great industrial structure but that could not be found in the United States—were rubber, tropical fibers, and metals such as nickel and tin. Imports of foodstuffs showed uneven ups and downs, but did not change materially over the half century, as Americans imported coffee, tropical fruits, and olive and coconut oils that could be produced domestically only at great cost. Imports of semimanufactures increased somewhat, but finished manufactures declined in importance as American productive capacity grew.

Finally, trade linkages altered as well. Europe became a more important customer of the United States than ever before after the Civil War, but American exports to Europe began to decline about 1885. During the 1870s and 1880s, Europeans were the recipients of more than four fifths of all U.S. exports; by 1920, this figure had dropped to three fifths. Meanwhile, the United States remained Europe's best customer. But the sharp decline in the proportion of American imports from Europe during the years 1915–1920, a result of wartime disruption, permanently reduced this trade.

In the first 20 years of the twentieth century, American foreign trade grew in Asia and Canada, and an interest in the Latin American market was just beginning. On the import side, the Asiatic countries and Canada were furnishing a great part of the crude materials that were becoming typical U.S. imports. South America had already achieved a substantial position in coffee and certain key raw materials for Americans.

Table 11.2   U.S. INTERNATIONAL PAYMENTS BY PERIODS
(Billions of Dollars)

Period	Net Goods and Services	Net Income on Investment	Net Capital Transactions
1850–1873	−0.8	−1.0	1.6
1874–1895	1.7	−2.2	1.5
1896–1914	6.8	−1.6	−0.7
1915–1919	14.3	1.4	−14.1

Source: *Historical Statistics of the United States, Colonial Times to 1970* (Washington, D.C.: Government Printing Office), pp. 865–869.

Factors Offsetting the Favorable Balance of Trade   The best way to summarize the history of American foreign trade is to examine a series of international balance of payments statements. The **balance of payments** shows the flow of money into and out of the United States in payment not only for goods, but also for services, securities, gold, and other items.

If American exports exceed American imports, we have seen that there is a favorable, or *positive,* U.S. balance of trade. We might expect the export of goods also to increase the U.S. balance of payments, and indeed it does—goods flow out of the United States, and currency flows in to pay for them. We can see in the first column of Table 11.2 that the United States had a slightly unfavorable trade balance between 1850 and 1873. Between 1874 and 1895 the balance of trade shifted to favorable, becoming markedly favorable between 1915 and 1920.

But items other than merchandise enter into the international balance of payments. Suppose the United States increased its imports of gold. American dollars must pay for that gold, and the result will be a negative amount in the U.S. international balance of payments. And if Americans purchase the services or securities of other nations, it is just as if the United States had "imported" those things, and those "imports" will appear as negative amounts in the balance of payments.

Table 11.2 shows the changes that occurred in several major accounts of the U.S. international balance of payments between 1850 and 1919. It helps us see how, as the years went by, the people of the United States offset their consistently favorable balance of commodity trade.

The Civil War and the years immediately following saw a continuation of high levels of income and imported goods and services. Moreover, U.S. firms were paying foreigners substantial sums on their *previous* investments in American business enterprises. Table 11.2 shows that a total of $1.8 billion was paid out by Americans over the years 1850–1873. Residents of the United States could enjoy this net inflow of goods and services and pay interest and dividends on existing foreign investments largely because foreigners continued to make *new* invest-

Unilateral Transfers	Changes in Monetary Gold Stock	Errors and Omissions
0.2		
− 0.6	− 0.4	
− 2.6	− 1.3	− 0.6
− 1.8	1.2	− 1.0

ments in American businesses, usually in American railroads. Another balancing item during this period was the $200 million in foreign currencies brought or sent to the United States and changed into dollars by immigrants and their families. Such payments are called *remittances.*

From 1874 to 1895 the American price level fell more than price levels abroad, so exports were stimulated more than imports. In addition, American agricultural commodities were available to the world market in greatly increasing quantities. When we consider that the manufacturing industries of the United States were also becoming progressively more efficient, it is hardly surprising to find that exports increased so fast. During these years, the favorable *trade* balance was reduced by the growing tendency of Americans to use the *services* of foreigners. Even so, Americans had net credits on current account of $1.7 billion, and foreign investors sent another $1.5 billion into this country. Offsetting the credits were more than $2 billion in payments to foreigners, and on balance remittances began to reverse themselves as immigrants sent substantial sums back to friends and relatives in their countries of origin. To make up the balance, the United States imported gold.

During the prosperous years of 1896–1914, the United States became an international economic power. The favorable balance of trade grew to over $9 billion, but this figure was cut to less than $7 billion by purchases of services from foreigners. Interest and dividend payments to foreign investors, remittances of immigrants to their families, a slight reversal of the capital flow, and an inward gold flow secured a balance of payments.

A Major Creditor   Finally, World War I brought change in the balance of payments of the United States. The last rows of Table 11.2 show the great jump in the favorable balance of trade created by the hefty demand for American war materials. Until the United States entered the war in 1917, European nations financed their purchases in the United States by selling their American securities and by shipping gold. When the United States finally joined the side of the Allies, continued large purchases of American goods were made possible by U.S. government loans to the Allies of nearly $10 billion. At this point in international relations, the United States did not think of *giving* assistance to its friends. It was expected that the loans would be repaid, but just how Europeans would repay the loans was not made clear. During the war, Americans, as private citizens, began to invest heavily in other countries; in these years they received more income in the form of interest and dividends than foreign nationals received from the United States. At last, the United States had shifted from a debtor position to the position of a major creditor. Although the capital flow reversal had preceded World War I, the effect was to involve the United States in world matters on an unprecedented scale throughout the twentieth century.

The Growth of Protectionism After 1861

The Infant Industries Argument Revisited   Even before the time of Alexander Hamilton, the first prominent American leader to advocate high protective tariffs to stimulate U.S. manufacturing, it was realized that the growth of certain industries could be facilitated by tariff protection. Historically, however, it has usually been the case that even after such industries have matured, the tariffs are retained. Some of the history of the protectionist attitude in the U.S. economy can be seen in Figure 11.2, which shows that the two decades prior to the Civil War were

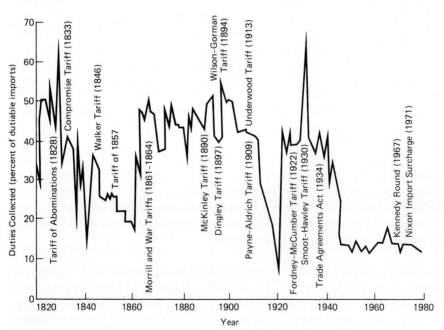

Figure 11.2   Tariff rates in the United States since 1820. Tariff rates in the United States have bounced like a football, and, indeed, in Congress, tariffs represent a political football. Import-competing industries prefer high tariffs. In the twentieth century, the highest tariff we have had was the Smoot-Hawley Tariff of 1930, which was almost as high as the 1828 Tariff of Abominations.

characterized by a relatively low tariff policy. The Republicans, however, came into power in 1861 committed to making sure that there were higher duties to "protect" American manufacturers. Since there were no southern congressmen to oppose them, the Republicans raised the tariff even before Lincoln took office. Then, using the excuse that they needed to generate more war revenues, they raised the tariff still higher. By 1867 the average duty on imports was 47 percent. Even though the tariff was raised substantially during and after the Civil War, it is not at all obvious that northerners benefited, nor that economic growth in general was increased. No doubt some manufacturers benefited, and no doubt the economy as a whole, especially consumers, suffered.

Just before 1900, tariff rates reached a post-Civil War high with the enactment of the Dingley Tariff. Although they then declined sharply, rates rose once more during the 1920s. In 1930 they peaked with the enactment of the Smoot-Hawley Tariff. We see in Figure 11.2 that in historical perspective our average tariff rates in recent years have been comparatively low.

Distortions Caused by Tariffs   It is clear that in almost all cases a tariff causes a distortion and a misallocation of resources. After all, the highest economic value from scarce resources is obtained by using them where they have the highest comparative advantage. If other countries can produce goods at a lower price than U.S. producers, consumers can take advantage of the lower price if they want to maximize their economic welfare. Of course, certain industries may be hurt in the short run, but others end up producing goods for which other nations do not have a comparative advantage. We export the latter and import the former. The results are gains from trade, which is why so many economists (and consumers) are against protective tariffs.

It is ironic, and clearly counter to the infant industries argument, that major U.S. steel and automobile corporations today are calling for tariff protection against Japanese steel producers. But then, perhaps it would not surprise Andrew Carnegie, the great steelmaker of the late nineteenth century.

DEFINITIONS OF NEW TERMS

IMPORTS   Imports are goods and services purchased from other countries.

EXPORTS   Exports are goods and services sold to other countries.

FREE TRADE   Free trade is trade without restrictions.

TARIFF   A tax on imported goods is a tariff.

IMPORT QUOTA   An import quota is a limit placed on the quantity of a certain good that is allowed to enter a country.

MERCANTILISM   Mercantilism denotes a set of governmental policies that, from the sixteenth to the nineteenth century, were used by European countries to direct commerce so as to maximize power and wealth for certain groups that held political power.

ENUMERATED ARTICLES   Enumerated articles were colonial exports that could be shipped only to England; after unloading, shipment elsewhere was permitted.

DUMPING   The selling of goods in foreign markets at greatly reduced prices that fall below cost is the practice of dumping.

REEXPORTS   Goods produced in a foreign area, imported from there, and then exported to another country are reexports.

BALANCE OF TRADE   The balance of trade of a country is the value of the goods it exports less the value of the goods it imports. If the balance of trade is positive, or favorable, exports exceed imports.

SEMIMANUFACTURES   Manufactured goods that will require additional processing before they are used are called semimanufactures.

FINISHED MANUFACTURES   Goods that have been manufactured from raw materials and are ready for use are called finished manufactures.

BALANCE OF PAYMENTS   The balance of payments is the amount of its currency that enters a country less the amount of its currency that leaves the country. The balance of payments is increased by the export of goods, services, securities, gold, and other items.

The Great Steelmaker

ANDREW CARNEGIE
(1835–1919)

Industrialist and Scientific Philanthropist

"A messenger boy of the name of Andrew Carnegie, employed by the O'Reily Telegraph Company, yesterday found a draft for the amount of $500. Like an honest little fellow, he promptly made known the facts, and deposited the paper in good hands where it awaits identification" (news clipping from the *Pittsburgh Dispatch,* November 2, 1849).

Five hundred dollars was indeed a lot of money for the son of a Scottish weaver— it represented ten years' wages. Later in life it would represent merely what Andrew would earn every ten minutes of every day. The saga of Andrew Carnegie has indeed inspired generations of schoolchildren. At age 12 the young immigrant worked in a cotton mill for $1.20 a week. Then he moved into the telegraph department of the Pennsylvania Railroad, where he quickly became the private secretary of its head. He started investing, first in a small oil company, and then in the Woodruff Palace Sleeping Car Company. Soon the young man was building railroad bridges, iron rails, and the like. Carnegie also made a small fortune in oil and took several trips to Europe selling railroad securities. His operations in bond selling, oil dealing, bridge building, and the like were so dashing and successful that conservative Pittsburgh businessmen regarded him as somewhat of a Young Turk. By 1873, however, Carnegie thought that steel was the new American industry. He began his famous policy, which he described as "putting all my eggs in one basket and then watching the basket." He was then 38 years old. His business life for the next three decades was to some extent a microcosm of the industrial history of the United States for the same period. During this time he was a staunch advocate of tariffs for infant industries; but he considered them wicked "when used merely to swell the profits of an established business." Even before he retired, he advocated the removal of tariff duties on imported steel. (As well he might, since his firms could produce at lower cost than the British!)

Industrialist Andrew Carnegie rose to power in the steel industry during the period after the Civil War, which has been characterized as one of uninhibited exploitation and cutthroat competition. Even Calvinist attitudes were insufficient to excuse what was happening. Carnegie found his philosophical underpinnings in the English writer Herbert Spencer, who applied the fundamental principles of Darwinian evolution to society. His thesis was that of social Darwinism—in the struggle for existence, survival went to the fittest, whether it be in business or economics. And the fittest had to become the wealthiest. When Carnegie read Spencer, he found an idol. The industrialist said that when he read Spencer's *First Principles* in 1862, "light came as in a flood and all was clear." Carnegie and other businessmen of the day used Spencer as an argument against government intervention and against the rise of unions. However, during this period big business, in conjunction with the government, was active in attempting to throttle free competition.

In 1868 the steelmaker wrote a memo to himself: "Thirty-three and an income of $50,000 per annum! Beyond this never earn—make no effort to increase fortune, but spend the surplus each year for benevolent purposes. Cast aside business forever, except for others." He did not follow his advice until he was 66, but then he engaged in what he called *scientific philanthropy.* The major projects worth giving money to were universities, free libraries, hospitals, and parks, in that order, in addition to swimming baths and churches, which ranked low on his list.

Carnegie retired after the sale of his steel company to the new United States Steel Company in 1901. Of the $250 million he got, he left a $5 million pension and benefit fund for his trustworthy employees. He did not stop giving from that moment. Over $60 million of his money went into almost 3,000 free public libraries around the world. The size of Carnegie's gift depended on the town's population; it averaged $2 per person. (This formula left some small towns with an uneconomical library that had to be closed down; nobody ever thought of pooling the funds for regional libraries.)

Giving away money seemed to be as hard as making it. "Pity the poor millionaire, for the way of the philanthropist is hard," he wrote to a newspaper in 1913. After working for ten years at giving away $350 million, he realized that no one man could do such a big job; the Carnegie Corporation in New York started with an endowment of $125 million. It was the first modern philanthropic foundation administered by trustees who were skilled in their different areas. Carnegie chose only trustees who had been good businessmen.

He died in 1919 after fulfilling his personal pledge of giving away just about everything he had accumulated.

chapter *12*

Income, Wealth, and the American Past

From the earliest colonial times until the present, extreme differences in income and wealth have existed in America. During the 1940s and 1950s, the percentage of income going to the poorest 20 percent of Americans changed very little, remaining between 5 and 6 percent. Because most Americans were earning more and living better, many people thought poverty no longer existed in the United States.

A book published in 1962 significantly changed that view. It also provided the incentive for President Lyndon B. Johnson's War on Poverty. The book, *The Other America,* was written by Michael Harrington, who lived among the poor in order to gather data about poverty. In *The Other America* he wrote about a world of slums, desolation, bitterness, discrimination, and hopelessness. He wrote about old people living alone in run-down tenement rooms. He stressed the need to use sociology as well as economics in order to reach a better understanding of poverty and poor people.

Harrington contended that the poor constitute a subculture. He also pointed out that most poor believe no one cares about them. Their world is isolated from the mainstream of American life, and they are totally alienated from the values of middle-class America. Because the poor are mainly concerned with day-to-day survival, they are not inclined to try to understand or to integrate themselves into middle-class society.

THE OFFICIAL DEFINITION OF POVERTY

In 1959 the president's Council of Economic Advisors originally set a poverty line of $3,000 income a year, regardless of family size. In 1965 it redefined poverty to take into account family size. That definition, worked out by a Social Security

Administration statistician who devised a formula for establishing the minimum adequate standard of living, is still used today. The statistician based the formula on a nutritionally adequate "economy food budget" for various family sizes drawn up by the Department of Agriculture in several of its household consumption surveys. The official poverty line changes according to the number of persons in the family. In addition, the poverty line is updated annually to reflect changes in the cost of living.

Is Poverty Absolute?   If the original poverty line of $3,000 a year were carried back to, say, 1935, we would find that one third of all Americans were poor in that year. By 1955 one in five would have been classified as poor, and today something like one in 20. Clearly, if we were to keep $3,000 as the limit, even with adjustments for inflation, there would be very few poor in a few more years. That is, very few adults would receive any less than $3,000 (in adjusted dollars) a year. The poverty line, however, does not remain stable. Poverty is a relative concept. Today's official poverty income would have been considered opulence 200 years ago. Moreover, the poverty-line income in the United States is greater than the average income level in most other countries in the world.

Nevertheless, as long as the distribution of income in this country is not more or less equal, there will always be relative poverty, by definition. There will always be some individuals and families whose income is greater than that of others. Hence, in a realistic sense, relative poverty is impossible to eradicate. Yet this matter of the unequal distribution of income is linked closely with the problems of the poor and the drive to eliminate poverty in America. Let us take a look at standard income distribution statistics at the end of the 1970s.

INCOME DISTRIBUTION

First let's divide the population into fifths according to the total distribution of income and consider the fifth receiving the least income. In Table 12.1 the percentage of national income going to the various fifths of the population is given for the period right after World War II and for 1979. There is relatively little change in the measured money income distribution over that period of time. The fifth of the population receiving the smallest percentage of money income still

Table 12.1   DISTRIBUTION OF INCOME

Families	Money Income Share (%)	
	1947	1979
Top 20 percent	43.1	39.2
Fourth 20 percent	23.1	24.8
Third 20 percent	17.0	17.1
Second 20 percent	11.8	13.1
Bottom 20 percent	5.0	5.8

Source: U.S. Bureau of the Census.

appears to receive not much more than 5 percent of the total. The richest fifth of all Americans still receives approximately 40 percent of national money income. The conclusion that many critics of government welfare programs reach is that neither the progressive nature of our federal personal income tax system nor the massive money **transfers** that the U.S. government has engaged in have succeeded in changing the plight of the 20 percent of our population who receives the least income.

Indeed, some observers, such as M.I.T.'s Lester C. Thurow, believe that the United States is still plagued with relatively large inequalities in the distribution of economic resources. "The richest 10 percent of our households receive 26.1 percent of our income, while the poorest 10 percent receive only 1.7 percent."[1] To Thurow, this means that the wealthiest 10 percent of U.S. households receive 15 times as much income as the poorest 10 percent. He compares this with Sweden, where the ratio is 7; Japan, where the ratio is 10; and Germany, where the ratio is 11. Both the Congressional Budget Office (CBO) and a number of academic researchers disagree with Thurow's conclusions and with the data on which they (and our Table 12.1) are based.

The Wrong Measure of Income   The statistics that come from the Census Bureau measure what is called *money income.* These distribution-of-income estimates comprise only actual monetary income (including money transfers from the government) that households receive. The standard of living of a family is not, however, solely a function of money income. If a family receives a rent subsidy, Medicare or Medicaid, food stamps, and so on, that household has a higher real standard of living than is indicated by its money income alone. It turns out that since 1966 a very large share of total government transfers to the poor has taken the form of these *in-kind* benefits rather than direct cash payments. The average total of such in-kind benefits for the ten years since 1966 has been something like $40 billion a year. When the CBO took these transfers into account, it came up with some startling conclusions about the number of poor in America in 1977. Instead of the 26 million reported by the Census Bureau, the CBO contends that there are only nine million. The Census Bureau figures show that 15 percent of Americans 65 and over are living in poverty; the CBO believes that only 4 percent are. According to CBO director Alice M. Rivlin, "The nation has come a lot closer to eliminating poverty than most people realize." The Rand Corporation did a study of New York City's welfare families and found that their in-kind benefits raised 80–90 percent of them above the poverty line, even though officially they are still counted as poor.

Economist Edgar Browning has recomputed the Census Bureau distribution-of-income figures to take account of in-kind transfers to the poor. In Table 12.2, we see the dramatic changes that such calculations bring about. The 20 percent of the population receiving the least money have more than doubled their share of national income, to over 12 percent, since World War II.

[1]*Newsweek* (February 14, 1977), p. 11.

Table 12.2 **FAMILY INCOME PERCENTAGES**

Family	Total Income Share (%)	
	1947	1974
Top 20 percent	42.3	31.9
Fourth 20 percent	23.0	20.9
Third 20 percent	16.8	18.4
Second 20 percent	12.6	16.1
Bottom 20 percent	5.3	12.6

Source: Edgar K. Browning, "The Trend Toward Equality in the Distribution of Net Income," *Southern Economic Journal* 43 (July 1976).

But There Are Poor Just because the fifth of the population with the least money income have dramatically improved their lot since World War II does not mean that poor people do not exist in the United States, and certainly there is widespread (a high percentage of) poverty among certain portions of the population: blacks, single women with dependent children, and others. Nevertheless, to the extent that we accept a *relative* definition of poverty, there will always be some poor people. Whether or not we can go as far as George Washington University economist Sar A. Levitan, who stated that "if poverty is defined as a lack of basic need, it's almost been eliminated," is an open question. We can nonetheless point out that the problem of poverty has not been ignored in this country, and a variety of methods of transferring income to those who truly need it is certainly well established.

THE DEMAND FOR LABOR AND INCOME DIFFERENCES

One way to analyze the problem of poverty is to discover why there are such extreme differences in income among households in the United States. Today the fifth of all workers receiving the least income get only 5.5 percent of the money income in the United States, whereas the top fifth gets about 40 percent.

As discussed in Chapter 4, the price of labor—wages—is determined like the price of most things in the economy, assuming, of course, that there are no restrictions in the labor market. The price of labor is determined by the interaction of the supply of and the demand for labor. Basically, the demand for labor is a function of how productive each worker is. A worker's productivity is affected by (among other things) intelligence, schooling, experience, and training.

One reason some people are poor is that they are not as productive as other individuals. They may lack innate characteristics that would enable or dispose them to be more productive, they may have been denied adequate schooling or training, or they may simply choose not to be productive. Other individuals are poor because they have been denied access to jobs that are open to others in the society. In other words, racial or sexual job discrimination can prevent a worker from being paid according to his or her productivity.

As we know, the price of anything is determined not only by demand but also by supply. The supply of workers who have few skills—those who are classified as unskilled—is quite large relative to the demand for such workers. This means that the price unskilled workers can charge for their services is relatively low. Hence, one reason many poor people earn low wages is that they lack the skills that are in high demand. That is, they have only skills that are in great supply. The equilibrium wage rate for these unskilled workers is low, so they are classified as poor.

THE ELIMINATION OF POVERTY

The preceding analysis suggests several ways in which poverty might be eliminated. The first, obviously, is to improve the productivity of poor people. This is being done by manpower training programs, job corps where unskilled poor people are taught new skills, job retraining programs for those who have skills that are no longer in demand, and improved educational opportunities for minority groups.

These are the direct ways of influencing the future productivity and earning power of relatively poor people in American society. To the extent that these programs are successful, they enable retrained workers to make higher incomes. But what happens in the interim? What about the poor who cannot be retrained? What about women who have children and no income-earning husband? Many are helped, at least partially, by existing **welfare programs**.

Welfare programs are one means of providing purchasing power to the poor to buy essentials. Most welfare payments are made through programs that are partly or largely federally funded. Approximately 10–12 million Americans receive some form of welfare each month. Welfare payments are not given out to just anyone, however. In fact, many poor people do not receive welfare. They cannot pass what are called *means tests.* These tests are used by welfare agencies to compare a budget plan with the potential resources of those who apply for aid. Furthermore, in the past, many poor could not obtain public assistance because they failed to meet state or local minimum residency requirements. However, these requirements have been voided by the U.S. Supreme Court as unconstitutional. Then, too, many poor do not know they are eligible. Others do not apply for benefits because they feel shame at taking what they view as charity.

A Negative Tax   Although most Americans agree that poverty should be eliminated, today's complex, often ineffective, welfare system not only often fails to help those in need, it often benefits many who are not in need. And it sometimes appears that certain programs have helped give rise to a class of welfare recipients who are content to remain unemployed.

Inescapably, any plan will cause some reduction in the incentive to work. This is the cost society must bear for any type of income redistribution, a goal the society considers worthwhile. Yet there is much room for improvement in public assistance programs, and alternatives to the current situation must be found.

One alternative to the present welfare system is a **negative income tax**. The negative income tax is not a tax but a government payment to low-income citizens. It uses the personal income tax system to set up a series of payments to citizens and tax receipts by the U.S. Treasury according to a schedule based on family size and actual income earned. The plan would not require setting up a new system. It could be an extension of the fully computerized system that already exists.

The case for a negative income tax   Many economists favor a negative income tax. They point out that it would not require the massive bureaucracy that now exists for administering public assistance, food stamp, and other programs. Hence, many of the resources now spent for this huge bureaucracy could be spent on other priorities, or used to provide the negative tax (the government payment) to needy families. Such a tax system might also restore dignity to the poor. Most welfare recipients must now fill out endless forms and generally submit to the inquiries of an occasionally insensitive welfare bureaucracy.

The case against a negative income tax   On the other hand, many economists oppose a negative income tax, pointing out that it might cost "too much." In particular, if for political reasons such current welfare programs as food stamps and subsidized housing cannot be dismantled, then the negative income tax would just be one more facet of the welfare system. These critics contend that it would not really simplify the existing bureaucracy.

They also contend that any effective negative income tax would have a strong **work disincentive effect.** That is, the payoff for returning to work would be so small with an effective negative income tax program that many who could work would nevertheless decide not to do so.

Inequalities: The Historical Perspective

"With liberty and justice for all" summarizes an American ideal. But does "justice for all" refer merely to equal rights before the law, or does it mean more—equal rights to good health, to job security, equal pay, equal leisure; in short, does it mean total equality?

Some people believe that the distribution of income that results from participation in a market economy such as ours is inherently unjust, and that income should be distributed equally. Actually, in the earliest years of colonial life in America, the goal of strict economic equality was earnestly pursued.

Jamestown Revisited

The Jamestown colony in Virginia originally operated as a collective, in terms of both communal production and shared consumption. Belief in the ideals of fairness and equality, however, was not shared by all. Many individuals inevitably shirked assigned tasks, and the human characteristic of self-interest offset incentives to work and to innovate. To see why, consider the following hypothetical case.

Suppose that one out of 100 equally industrious workers suddenly decides to work half as hard as the others. As a result, daily output falls by 0.5 percent. If each worker receives an equal share of the total product, the one who shirks loses almost nothing in consumption, yet his work is markedly easier. Others follow suit, and with each new shirker, the total product continues to decrease. Alternatively, suppose one worker decides to work twice as hard as his or her peers. Total output then rises by about 0.5 percent. For twice the effort, however, this worker receives hardly anything more to consume. In such circumstances, greater work effort is not likely to occur. Now suppose that there are various tasks to be done, and one worker thinks of a way to perform a task better and more quickly. With collective production methods, the worker gains little, for the time freed is not rewarded to this person alone; for the sake of equality, it must be used to help others in other tasks. As a consequence, collective production methods and shared consumption often lead to relatively low levels of output and limited growth, especially when material gain is the main incentive to work.

Such was the situation in Jamestown in the early years. Single men complained of working, without due reward, for other men's wives and children. The strong and industrious were aggrieved at obtaining no more in food, clothes, and supplies than those capable of much less work. Wives considered tasks benefiting others than their own families a form of enslavement. And since land was owned in common, incentives to care for and improve it were generally lacking. Only with private holdings could individuals expect the *full* return for their efforts to improve the land.

Despite the introduction of tobacco in 1612, which led to commercial production for market, the organizational difficulties stemming from collective enterprise resulted in continued complaints and low levels of output per worker. The clash of the egalitarian ideal with the economic reality of individual self-interest could not be ignored. By 1614 the first step toward private holdings (with 3-acre limits) had been taken. In 1619 the **head-right system** mentioned in Chapter 1 was introduced. This program granted 50 acres of land to anyone paying his or her ocean passage to Virginia. Another 50 acres could be obtained if the person paid the way for someone else. In 1623, the year of the "royal investigation," all holdings were converted to private ownership. The noble but difficult era of economic equality in America was over.[2]

Inequality in the Colonies

Differences in ability, inheritance, legal status, work effort, and just plain luck soon led to a distribution of wealth in the 13 colonies that was far from egalitarian. Not only did differences in people's wealth sharply accent the differences in social class in the colonies, epitomized in the contrast between master and slave, but

[2]Although eventually abandoned, collective activity in early New England had fewer negative results. Undoubtedly, this was because of a more cohesive society there, based on common religious principles (Puritan beliefs). Similarly, the Mormon pioneers, and to a degree their descendants, fruitfully combined collective enterprise with individual motivation. Again, these successes apparently result when strong religious or social forces tend to counter individual motivation based on self-interest.

they also revealed very sharp differences in the possibilities of obtaining wealth among the major geographical regions.

As shown in Table 12.3, in the years just preceding the American Revolution the southern colonies were more than twice as wealthy (per free person) as the middle colonies and New England. This higher relative standing shows up not only in the category of slaves, where we might expect it, but also in all the other components of wealth.

Although we do not have precise documentation of the distribution of wealth in the southern colonies, it seems fairly obvious that the greatest degree of wealth inequality prevailed there. Southern whites averaged the highest wealth holdings per free person in the entire 13 colonies. At the same time, the South domiciled 90 percent of the nation's slaves. In the late colonial period Virginia's population, for instance, was 45 percent black; in South Carolina 70 percent of the population was black. Despite their large numbers, the share of total wealth going to those in bondage was only a tiny fraction of the whole. The blacks in Virginia probably received less than 10 percent of the wealth; in South Carolina they might have held a little more than 10 percent. Yet, as just noted, their proportions of these populations were 45 percent and 70 percent, respectively.

A more systematic view of wealth distribution is possible for New England and the middle colonies. In these regions, slaves were few, and most people had the legal right to share at least potentially in the economic opportunities provided by work and enterprise. As Table 12.4 reveals, however, the distribution of wealth per free person in New England and the middle colonies was far from equal. In New England, the poorest half of the population had only 11 percent of the wealth, whereas the richest tenth had almost four times that much. The degree of inequality was less striking in the middle colonies, but clearly, economic equality did not exist there, either.

Table 12.3 AVERAGE PRIVATE PHYSICAL WEALTH PER FREE PERSON, 1774
New England—New Hampshire, Massachusetts, Rhode Island, and Connecticut; middle colonies—New York, New Jersey, Pennsylvania, Delaware: southern colonies—Maryland, Virginia, North Carolina, South Carolina, Georgia.

	New England	Middle Colonies	Southern Colonies	All 13 Colonies
Land	£27	£28	£ 55	£38
Servants and slaves	0	2	58	21
Livestock	3	5	9	6
Farm tools and household equipment	1	1	3	2
Crops and perishables	1	3	5	3
Consumer durables	4	4	6	5
Other	2	3	1	2
Totals:	£38	£46	£137	£76

Source: U.S. Bureau of the Census, *Historical Statistics Colonial Times to 1973,* Series Z (Washington, D.C.: U.S. Government Printing Office, 1976), p. 1175.

Table 12.4 DISTRIBUTION OF PHYSICAL WEALTH IN NEW
ENGLAND AND THE MIDDLE COLONIES IN 1774

	Total Wealth (%)	
Cumulative Proportion of Wealth Held by	New England	Middle Colonies
Poorest 10% of population	< 1	< 1
Poorest 20% of population	1	2
Poorest 50% of population	11	23
Richest 20% of population	60	47
Richest 10% of population	40	32

Source: Alice Hanson Jones, "Wealth Estimates for the New England Colonies about 1770," *Journal of Economic History* 32 (March 1972): 119, and "Wealth Estimates for the American Middle Colonies, 1774," *Economic Development and Cultural Change* 18 (July 1970).

Trends in Inequality in the Colonial Period   One scholar, Jackson Turner Main, provides evidence that there was growing inequality in wealth and income as a result of the very process of colonial settlement and economic development. In Main's opinion, the increasing commercialization as frontier areas were transformed into subsistence farming areas and ultimately, in some instances, into urban areas resulted in greater inequality in the distribution of colonial wealth and income.[3]

Other studies also suggest a growth over time in the inequality of the colonial distribution of wealth within regions.[4] The inequality was greatest in the major urban centers, such as Boston. Comparing two Boston tax lists, James Henretta found that the top 10 percent of Boston's taxpayers owned 42 percent of the wealth in 1687, whereas they owned 57 percent in 1771. Bruce Daniels surveyed many New England probate records and therefore was able tentatively to support Main's contention that as economic activity grew more complex in the colonies it tended to produce a greater concentration of wealth. Apparently, as subsistence production gave way to production for markets, the interdependence among producers generated or was accompanied by greater wealth inequalities. This was true both in older and in more newly settled agricultural areas. Alternatively, large established urban areas, such as Boston and Hartford (Connecticut) exhibited a fairly stable (although very unequal) distribution of wealth throughout the eighteenth century until 1776. Smaller towns showed less inequality, but as they grew, their inequality also increased.

Especially high levels of affluence were observed in the port towns and cities where merchant classes were emerging. Particularly influential were the merchant shipowners who were engaged in the export-import trade and who were

[3]Jackson Turner Main, *The Social Structure of Revolutionary America* (Princeton: Princeton University Press, 1965).

[4]James Henretta, "Economic Development and Social Structure in Colonial Boston," *William and Mary Quarterly,* 22 (January 1965), pp. 93–105; and Bruce D. Daniels, "Long-range Trends of Wealth Distribution in Eighteenth-Century New England," *Explorations in Economic History* 11 (Winter 1973–1974), pp. 123–135.

considered to be in the upper class of society. In addition, urbanization and industrialization produced another class: a free labor force that owned little or no property. Obviously, occupation differences and property ownership were major factors in widening the gap between various social groups in the colonies. Of course, race and sex were also factors. Typically, women owned far less property than men, and women's opportunities to gain wealth were sharply restricted. Similarly, the growing use of indentured and slave labor after 1675 furthered the rise of wealth inequality in the colonies.

It is a statistical curiosity, however, that throughout most of the colonial period up to 1775, a growing concentration of wealth did not occur in the 13 colonies as a whole. Although there was increasing inequality within some regions and localities, the areas in which there was a lower concentration of wealth—the rural and, especially, the new frontier regions, which contained over 90 percent of the population—grew faster than the urban areas, thus offsetting the growing inequality of the urban centers.[5] Whatever the details, substantial inequality of wealth was a fact of economic life long before the age of industrialization and the rapid and sustained economic growth of the nineteenth century.

Income Distribution in the Pre-Civil War Period

Between 1774 and 1860 there was a sharp advance in the concentration of wealth. In 1774, 12.6 percent of total assets were held by the top 1 percent of free wealth holders, and the richest 10 percent held slightly less than one half of total assets. By 1860 the wealthiest 1 percent held 29 percent of U.S. total assets, while the top 10 percent held 73 percent.[6] In short, the share held by the richest 1 percent more than doubled, and that of the top 10 percent jumped by almost one half of its previous level. There are no statistical peculiarities to these measures, and their broad impact may be emphasized: "The movement toward wealth concentration occurred within regions, within given age groups, among native and foreign born, and within rural and urban populations."[7]

The famed world traveler and commentator Alexis de Tocqueville (1839) warned of this growing concentration, and feared that the rise of an industrial elite would destroy the basis of American egalitarianism:

> I am of the opinion . . . that the manufacturing aristocracy which is growing up under our eyes is one of the harshest that ever existed . . . the friends of democracy should keep their eyes anxiously fixed in this direction; for if a permanent inequality of conditions and aristocracy . . . penetrates into [America] it may be predicted that this is the gate by which they will enter.[8]

[5]Jeffrey G. Williamson and Peter H. Lindert, *American Inequality: A Macroeconomic History* (New York: Academic, 1980), pp. 21–31.
[6]Williamson and Lindert, p. 36.
[7]Williamson and Lindert, p. 46.
[8]As quoted by Williamson and Lindert, pp. 37–38.

The Antebellum South   Although the average income of free people in the South before the Civil War was as high as or higher than that of those in most other regions of the country, there was probably greater inequality in income and wealth distribution there than in other sections of the country. One of the main reasons for this great inequality was the large number of slaves in the southern economy. More than one half of the average slave's income went to the owner rather than to the slave. But there were great disparities of income even among free southerners.

In the period just before the Civil War, almost half of southern personal income went to just 1,000 families. There were some egregious examples of concentrated wealth. The Hairstons had 1,700 slaves on all of their plantations. In Georgia, a Mr. Howell Cobb had over 1,000 slaves on his lands. In rural Louisiana 10 percent of the families held 96 percent of all wealth!

Income Distribution in the Late Nineteenth Century

The period from 1860 to 1920 contrasts sharply with the first half of the nineteenth century, when the concentration of wealth and income grew dramatically. Although there were regional variations, the high degree of income inequality reached on the eve of the Civil War continued throughout the remainder of the century and up to World War I, but the levels of concentration did not grow higher.[9] An uneven plateau prevailed generally, but the levels were higher at the end of the 1860s and early 1870s and also just before World War I. That overall plateau recorded levels of concentration that were far higher than those of today and peaks that may have been the highest income equalities in American history.[10]

Despite this absence of change generally in the distribution of income for 1860–1920, sharp alterations occurred in the South, where ex-slaves gained a dramatic redistribution of income in their favor. This resulted from emancipation, a decline in exploitation, and the right of laboring blacks to a greater reward for their labor. By comparison, southern whites, most notably, of course, slave owners, lost relatively (and absolutely), although whites in the Deep South still maintained incomes that were probably twice those of blacks in the 1870s.

Trends in Twentieth Century Income Distribution

We can see from Table 12.5 that there were notable changes toward greater equality during the years of the Great Depression and again during World War II. Individuals with the highest incomes (the top 5 percent) had their share drop from 30 percent to slightly less than 20 percent between 1929 and 1962, while the poorest fifth of the population gained from 3.5 percent to 4.6 percent of total income over the period from 1929 to 1962. However, it is important to note that the relative gains to the poorest fifth came in two bursts—in the early 1930s and

[9]Williamson and Lindert, pp. 75–82.
[10]Williamson and Lindert, p. 75.

Table 12.5 PREWAR AND POSTWAR INCOME DISTRIBUTIONS

Year	Lowest Fifth	Second Fifth	Middle Fifth	Fourth Fifth	Highest Fifth	Top 5%
			Percentage Share			
1929	3.5	9.0	13.8	19.3	54.4	30.0
1935–1936	4.1	9.2	14.1	20.9	51.7	26.5
1941	4.1	9.5	15.3	22.3	48.8	24.0
1947	5.0	11.0	16.0	22.0	46.0	20.9
1962	4.6	10.9	16.3	22.7	45.5	19.6

Source: Edward C. Budd, *Inequality and Poverty* (New York: Norton, 1967), Table 1, p. 13.

again in the early 1940s. The gains to the second- and third-poorest segments grew more steadily between 1929 and 1947, and the only segments to gain in the postwar period up to 1962 were the middle and second-richest fifth. Consequently then, the shift toward greater income equality, as revealed in Table 12.5, came primarily before 1947. Although alterations occurred after 1947, these were minor and there was no significant change overall. While the middle and second-richest fifth gained slightly between 1947 and 1962, the richest and two poorest fifths had their shares slightly reduced.

Today, the distribution of income in the United States remains unequal. While the richest 20 percent of the population receives more than 39 percent of money income, the poorest 20 percent receives less than 6 percent of money income.[11] Because the distribution has remained fairly stable (in the long run) over the last century, the path to personal enrichment has been primarily, although not exclusively, by way of national economic growth.

DEFINITIONS OF NEW TERMS

TRANSFERS   Transfers are government payments to the poor; that is, income is in effect "transferred" from taxpayers to the recipients of government aid. Transfers may be in cash or in kind, that is, in subsidies earmarked for goods and services.

WELFARE PROGRAMS   Welfare programs, programs of government cash payments, are one means of providing purchasing power to the poor.

NEGATIVE INCOME TAX   A negative income tax is a kind of income transfer. Individuals who earn less than a certain level of income are taxed negatively—that is, paid money by the government.

WORK DISINCENTIVE EFFECT   A work disincentive effect results from any program that tends to make people who could work decide not to.

HEAD-RIGHT SYSTEM   A plan called the head-right system granted 50 acres of land to anyone paying for his or her ocean passage to Virginia, with a provision that another 50 acres could be obtained if the person paid the way for someone else.

[11]Recall that this bottom share almost doubles if transfers in kind, such as food stamps and rent subsidies, are added to money income.

The Consummate Businessman

HENRY FORD II
(1917–)

Industrialist

Henry Ford II is a businessman who can do exactly as he pleases because, as he says, "my name is over the door." And he has done just that—from giving $50,000 to a Detroit ghetto recreation center to promoting change in his company, his city, and the country's business community. He had the privilege of being descended from one of America's wealthiest industrial families, but he also had to face the task of turning a money-losing organization into a major industrial power.

Between 1929 and 1941, the Ford Motor Company was on the brink of financial collapse. Edsel Ford, Henry Ford II's father and titular president of the company, was only a figurehead, and the senile Henry Ford was actually steering the sinking ship. The company was foundering because of mismanagement, poor cost control, and antiquated production methods. In 1945, Henry Ford agreed to make his grandson president of the company. Although the younger Ford had little formal training, he knew the advantages of strong, trustworthy counsel. He brought in the "Whiz Kids," a group of sharp, ambitious men who were willing to apply modern technological and managerial techniques to the problems of the company. "I knew it could be turned around; it never occurred to me I couldn't do the job," said Ford at the time. He fired hundreds of top management personnel and brought in former General Motors men who decentralized and reorganized the company along the lines GM had perfected over the preceding decade.

One of Ford's major problems has been with the United Auto Workers (UAW). He has generally succeeded in his determined efforts to improve relations with the union, but the Ford Motor Company remains a particularly tempting target for UAW strike action. Nonetheless, Ford has actively defended his company's interests in labor negotiations. He charged that the 1964 UAW job-security demands amounted to featherbedding and an undermining of the efficiency of the industry.

During his first eight years in the presidency, Ford made capital investments totaling an extraordinary $1 billion. In 1961 the company acquired Philco Corporation, which turned out to be a profitable move toward electronics and defense contracting. Ford's high and low points have been associated with auto models. The Edsel, introduced in 1957, became one of the major disasters in the history of the industry, selling only 110,000 units in three years and incurring a loss of $250 million for the company. The Maverick and Mustang, though, have had substantial success on the market.

Because of his interest in urban renewal of the depressed sections of Detroit, his backing of the Ford Foundation, and his position (by default) as the most "concerned" of America's big automakers, Ford is considered a model of enlightened corporate management. According to Ford, we are in "the worst domestic crisis since the Civil War," and we must "make some basic changes in our schools, our housing, our welfare system. We also need to make basic changes in our employment practices—in whom we hire, how we hire, and what we do with people and for people after they are hired." As early as the 1940s, Ford ordered his managers to hire blacks and members of other minorities. After the Detroit riots of 1967, Ford opened two hiring centers in the ghetto, recruiting the hard-core unemployed—those who had never worked and who were often illiterate and ex-cons. Ford gave them bus fare and lunch money until they received their first paycheck. Most started at $3.25–$3.80 per hour as sweepers, stockboys, assemblers, or press operators. Now about half of the work force at the River Rouge plant are blacks.

But many have discovered the limits of this image. Ford refuses to read Ralph Nader's *Unsafe at Any Speed,* a book that strongly attacks the design failings of auto manufacturers. In response to the proposed "safety cars," Ford said, "If you want to ride around in a tank, you won't get hurt. You won't be able to afford one though. . . ." He also balks at safety legislation, maintaining that "if you start by law to fool around with model changes, to tell the industry it must do this, that or the other thing within a period of time in which it cannot be done . . . you upset the whole cycle of this industry."

Areas such as safety and antipollution programs have, however, become more important in Ford's budget. In 1972 there were 6,600 people employed in these endeavors. From 1967 to 1972 over 0.5 billion dollars went to safety and pollution research and engineering. In spite of these outlays, which have continued to grow, the company has remained profitable, ranking fourth in sales and sixth in assets among the top industrial corporations in the United States in 1980.

Index